# The Art of **JAMA** II

Covers and Essays From

*The Journal of the*
*American Medical Association*

# WINGS

*We have*
*a microscopic anatomy*
*of the whale*
*this*
*gives*
*Man*
*assurance*

*William Carlos Williams*

*We have*
*a map of the universe*
*for microbes,*
*we have*
*a map of a microbe*
*for the universe.*

*We have*
*a Grand Master of chess*
*made of electronic circuits.*

*But above all*
*we have*
*the ability*
*to sort peas,*
*to cup water in our hands,*
*to seek*
*the right screw*
*under the sofa*
*for hours.*

*This*
*gives us*
*wings.*
          *— Miroslav Holub*

*Selected Poems: Miroslav Holub.*
Translated by Ian Milner and George Theiner
(Baltimore, Maryland: Penguin Books; 1967:22).
©1967, Miroslav Holub. Translation ©1967,
Penguin Books Ltd.
Reproduced by permission of Penguin Books Ltd.

# The Art of JAMA II

Covers and Essays From

## The Journal of the American Medical Association

M. Therese Southgate, MD

Senior Contributing Editor

The Journal of the American Medical Association

Chicago, Illinois

with 102 full-color illustrations

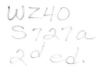

AMA Press

| | |
|---|---|
| *Vice President, Business Products* | Anthony J. Frankos |
| *Editorial Director* | Mary Lou White |
| *Senior Acquisitions Editor* | Barry Bowlus |
| *Director, Production & Manufacturing* | Jean Roberts |
| *Print Coordinator* | Ronnie Summers |
| *Director, Marketing* | J. D. Kinney |
| *Marketing Manager* | Reg Schmidt |
| *Graphics Manager* | Charl M. Richey |
| *Imaging Specialist* | Chris J. J. Meyer |
| *Copy Editor* | Laura King |

JAMA Staff

| | |
|---|---|
| *Editor* | Roxanne K. Young |
| *Assistant Editor* | Juliana M. Walker |
| *JAMA Book Liaison* | Annette Flanagin |

Additional copies of this book may be ordered by calling 800 621-8355.
Mention product number OP080001.

ISBN 1-57947-159-5

BQ71:0020-00:5/01

**To Joan Preising, OSF, PhD**

*For four years Sister Joan taught me chemistry.*

*For the past fifty she has been teaching me everything else.*

# FOREWORD

## James D. Burke, PhD

Director Emeritus, Saint Louis Art Museum
E. Desmond Lee Scholar-in-Residence, Washington University
Scholar-in-Residence, The Mercantile Library, University of Missouri, St Louis

Appearing every week, an international scholarly publication provides a one-page essay that sets forth a continuing commentary on the relationship among art, art history, the humanities at large, and the communities of science and medicine. Most are written by one of the most fluent, touching, and humane writers of our time, M. Therese Southgate, MD. For each week, for over three decades, *The Journal of the American Medical Association*, unique among the scholarly journals of science and medicine, had a work of art on its cover. And each week, there, for more than twenty-five years, has been an essay accompanying the image that brings its readers into contact with ideas of art and culture expressed in the broadest terms. In effect, it is not only a long-running curriculum of art appreciation and art history, but also an immense road map of civilization, delivered in small bites. Few, if any, journals devoted to art—much less medicine—have so remarkable a record of producing such an ongoing review of the human record in visual form.

Whatever could have possessed the editors of this renowned journal to embark on this program, starting thirty-seven years ago? Why have the successive editors continued this so effectively?

The larger answer lies in that informal curriculum. There, as Dr Southgate has remarked, is the concept "to show that everything is related: art, medicine, life." The unity and interconnections of human thought are brought together, in essay after essay, week after week. It provides a continuing education in science and the humanities for each reader, in sum total the equal of undergraduate courses at many colleges.

Our journey, as *JAMA* readers, takes us through a broad view of Western art in this collection of essays. In the pages following, one will visit places as different as Christiania and Columbus; Paris, Pontoise, Prout's Neck, and Pasadena; Havana and Haarlem; Goa, Geneva, and Ghent; Nantucket, North Kingstown, New Orleans, New Hope, Newtown, Nuremberg, and Nice.

Here we will find ourselves looking at paintings and learning about the lives of the artists. Like Giorgio Vasari, the famed sixteenth-century biographer of artists, Dr Southgate loves to remind us of the vitae of these people and to set them in the midst of the ideas and ideals of their times. Like Vasari, she brings them to life for us as we read. Thus, the pages that follow bring us to artists who dealt firsthand with the Dust Bowl, the Franco-Prussian War, Hitler, or the Revolution of 1848. They earned the Croix de Guerre, followed the Golden Section of the ancient Greeks, were members of the Academy of Natural Sciences in Philadelphia, revolted against Impressionism, and were concerned with automobile safety, the place of women in society, and horticulture. In the course of one memorable set of four issues, the *JAMA* essays took us past Isabella Brant in Antwerp to Joe DiMaggio in New York to Martin Luther in Wittenberg to Marie Antoinette in Paris!

In the world of ideas these images represent, there are many voices here that urge us to recall our literary and historical favorites of the past. Petrarch, Voltaire and Proust, Lord Byron, Simone de Beauvoir, Walt Whitman, Somerset Maugham, St Matthew, William Osler, Andre Malraux, George Washington Carver, Émile Zola, and,

yes, Horatio Alger are all present. Each member of this vast cast of characters is linked to a work of art in some meaningful way.

As the history of art goes, these pages begin with the Renaissance in Italy and take us on a journey to the present. Here we will find the low life of the Paris cabarets in the paintings of Henri de Toulouse-Lautrec, the elegant life in Belle Époque salons and Julius L. Stewart, the rustic life and nostalgia for rural life in Jean François Millet, the quiet domestic life of Dutch households and Pieter de Hooch. There is abstraction painted by Marin, Mondrian, Gorky, and Kandinsky, and the high point of Impressionism seen in major works by Manet, Monet, Renoir, and Degas. There are landscapes and still lifes. There are great portraits painted by Dürer, Hals, Vermeer, Rembrandt, Fragonard, and Rogier van der Weyden. There are grand manner portraits by Van Dyck and Sargent, and the precious rural sentiments of American country life after the ghastly horrors of the Civil War as depicted by "J. G." Brown and Winslow Homer. This volume includes a selection of a fine group of folk art paintings, some from the famed Garbisch collection and others including important works by Ammi Phillips and Grandma Moses.

The usual histories of art give short shrift to children. Many artists simply couldn't portray them well, resulting in images of miniaturized adults. That is decidedly not the case here: we discover the pleasure of an exceptional selection of some of the most perfect and beautiful portraits of children in these pages. Dr Southgate's discerning eye has sought out rare images of children by Cranach (two), Holbein, Homer, Krohg, Liotard, Murillo, Potthast, and Renoir, among others.

The essays relate the art and the artists to medicine; after all *JAMA* is a medical journal and Dr Southgate was trained as a physician. She frequently sheds light on her artists by recalling for us their medical conditions, ground where most art historians fear to tread. Only a doctor of medicine would so readily acknowledge the alcoholism of Munch, Toulouse-Lautrec, Ensor, Hals, and Lawson or the deafness of Prendergast and Goya. As we pass by the images, we confront suicide and stroke, tuberculosis, blindness, bone disease, diabetes, plague, cholera, and more. As the physician-reader of *JAMA* knows in his or her daily practice, artists are humans suffering with the same conditions as their patients, coping for better or worse as they pursue their art. Here we learn of the great painters whose careers were cut short: George Bellows' death at age forty-two of a burst appendix, Hans Holbein's death at forty-six of plague, Grant Wood's death at fifty of liver cancer. And we find here the sad irony of famous painters with serious eye problems, afflicting Monet, Degas, and Eakins.

In the end, these superb essays help us look at art and know its many aspects. Dr Southgate relates not just the facts of the artists' careers, noting their medical and scientific, literary and historical relationships, she does more. Page after page, she gives an appreciation of the works of art in formal terms, gently pressing us to see the color, design, form, drawing, expression, and artistic emphasis. The art is her guide, so we are treated to her keen observations and personal warmth as we view the world she sees with affection and respect. This alone makes the *JAMA* essays worthwhile. In Dr Southgate we have a patient and warmhearted companion, who quite deeply cares for our souls. Implicit in her many years of writing is Juvenal's ideal of *Mens sana in corpore sano,* a sound mind in a sound body, an endless reminder that our minds and our health should achieve balance and ideal unison. Thus, *The Art of JAMA II* gives us not just the practice and science of medicine weekly, but also a constant reminder of the place of our human condition in the larger world. It is a noble undertaking.

# FOREWORD

## Edmund D. Pellegrino, MD

John Carroll Professor of Medicine and Medical Ethics
Center for Clinical Bioethics, Georgetown University
Washington, DC

In the 1960s, *The Journal of the American Medical Association* made a bold move for a professional journal: it replaced the customary Table of Contents, which had occupied its cover each week for some eighty years, with a reproduction of a work of fine art. In 1964, this became an established policy. Ever since, *JAMA* covers have greeted their readers with an aesthetic overture to THE JOURNAL's usual scientific content. Since then many other distinguished scientific journals have done the same, giving the lie to the canard that art and science should be strangers to each other.

Like its predecessor, *The Art of JAMA: One Hundred Covers and Essays From The Journal of the American Medical Association,* published in 1997, this second volume is a collection of splendid *JAMA* covers and their accompanying interpretative essays. Like the first collection, these covers range over a wide spectrum of visual and graphic art from many countries and cultures. Their aesthetic quality is consistently high. The choices are cosmopolitan, and the interpretative essays are gracefully written and informative. Any *JAMA* reader with the foresight to have perused these covers and essays attentively would have been the beneficiary of a genuine education in art history.

The works were chosen for their intrinsic merit as art. Some are directly related to medicine: physicians or patients. Others depict a less obvious and more subtle relationship. All, however, speak to an affinity between medicine and the visual arts, which is too often insufficiently appreciated. The essays skillfully link the art,

the artist, and the times to portray the social milieu within which physicians and artists practice their respective arts.

A work of such sustained high quality and creative imagination would be impossible without a guiding genius. *JAMA* was fortunate to have found one among its editors. M. Therese Southgate, MD, has carried the responsibility for the selections and for the interpretative essays for some twenty-five years. She has proven an ideal catalyst to awaken the dormant aesthetic sense in many of her fellow physicians, a sense that had become stultified by the exigencies of medical training and practice. Only of late have medical educators sought to remedy this stifling of a source of awareness and delight in the lives of physicians by introducing courses in the humanities and visual arts into the medical curriculum.

The reproductions in both volumes attest to the fact that medicine is not only a natural and a social science, but it is also an art. To comprehend fully the complexities of the human predicament of illness, the intellect, the imagination, and the emotions of the practitioner must be engaged simultaneously. To be sure, no physician can grasp all three dimensions fully. A medical education should reveal the possible connections among them and thus help to make for a better, more humane practitioner.

Certainly, there have always been physicians seriously attracted to the visual arts as collectors, amateurs, or aficionados. Historically, the central place of illustration in the teaching of anatomy dates back to Aristotle and the Alexandrian anatomists.

More personally, every physician will remember gratefully the meticulous draftsmanship of the dissection manuals that helped all of us make sense of our own muddled and often inept cadaver dissections.

The Renaissance artists and physicians clearly recognized the connections between their respective arts. Each in his way sought to comprehend the intricacies of the human body, the one to paint with more conviction, the other to diagnose with more precision. To this end, artists as well as physicians shared a common enthusiasm for the public dissections of their day. More recently, we have learned how the clinician's eye, scrutinizing the realistic depictions of the great painters of past and present, can contribute to the history of disease. Even a casual glance at Daumier's disturbingly frank depictions of doctors and patients will convince even the vainest physician of the need for humility.

These are, however, instrumental connections in which medicine and art may serve each other's purposes. But the affinities between them are deeper than that, as Dr Southgate points out in her preface to the first volume of this collection of covers. They lie at the phenomenological level. There is an underlying similarity in certain aspects of the world lived by the painter and the physician. At this level both combine detachment and engagement in their relationship to their patients or their subjects. Both need the capacity simultaneously to isolate the self and to engage that self in the lived world of the other human beings they encounter clinically or pictorially.

In *Intoxicated by My Illness,* a moving account of his own grave illness, Anatole Broyard, the late brilliant critic for *The New York Times*, said this of his doctor: "He should be able to imagine the aloneness of the critically ill, a solitude as haunting as a Chirico painting." Few patients could express this longing as eloquently as Broyard, and few physicians would recognize what they do daily in such evocative artistic terms. But Broyard recognized the way both painting and medicine must enter and reflect the predicament of suffering humanity. In the late nineteenth century Sarah Orne Jewett, reflecting in her novel on the country doctor, said, "Nobody sees people as they are and finds the chance to help poor humanity as the doctor does. The decorations, the deceptions of character, must fall away before the great realities of pain and death."

The 1975 Nobel laureate poet Eugenio Montale puts it another way: "Can the maximum of isolation and the maximum of engagement . . . coincide in the artist . . . ?"

For the physician, Montale's question comes to this: Can the physician experience optimum engagement in the world of the patient so as to be truly compassionate while still preserving the distance and objectivity scientific and rational medicine demand?

Montale warned against the wrong kind of engagement—for the writer, political or polemical engagement. For the physician, the danger is in the extremes of overisolation or overengagement, destroying that balance between feeling something of the patient's predicament and yet being able to stand back and observe, weigh, feel, touch, and smell. The painter similarly destroys her art when she becomes didactic or when she loses herself in her subject.

The polemical and political art of the Soviet Union gives ample testimony to the dangers of—whether political or ideological—overengagement. The physician whose compassion submerges his objectivity risks the loss of competence. When the physician, the painter, the writer, or the artist fuse detachment with compassion,

isolation with engagement, they optimize the potentialities of their respective arts. It is then that they fulfill the ancient definition of art— a technique that aims to do a thing well and to recognize when it is well done. It is in this association of their perspectives in their ways of knowing the world that gives to medicine and the artist their special affinity for each other.

In her quarter-of-a-century dedication to the relationship of art and medicine, Dr Southgate has quietly cultivated this affinity. Her selections and her perceptive essays are more than didactic exercises. They provide moments of delectation; they open up the world of imagination to the physicians and, in the subtlest of ways, enrich their lives. In her quiet, entrancing, and subtly instructive way, Dr Southgate invites physicians to know themselves and their world better. In her own way, Dr Southgate has been an educator who through the pages of *JAMA* has had a wide influence on physicians in every branch of medicine, a privilege even the most dedicated and experienced teachers of medicine rarely enjoy.

# PREFACE

For more than eighty years, from the time of its founding in 1883 under the editorship of Nathan Davis, *The Journal of the American Medical Association* carried the traditional table of contents on its cover. In 1964, its tenth editor-in-chief, John H. Talbott, MD, began reproducing a work of fine art on the cover, eventually replacing the table of contents altogether with the artwork. What was once heresy has now become its own tradition. Nearly two generations later—some forty years—most *JAMA* readers cannot remember an issue that did not have a work of fine art on its cover. Give or take a few, more than 1,700 works of art have been reproduced on the weekly *JAMA* covers since 1964.

Beginning in 1974, it was my privilege to begin selecting the *JAMA* covers each week; occasionally, I wrote an essay to accompany one or another. Gradually, I began writing more often, until, since 1988, I have written almost weekly—a total of some seven hundred essays. Readers were generous; a steady stream of letters suggested that these essays be collected and published as a book. Accordingly, *The Art of JAMA*, which comprised one hundred of the cover reproductions and essays published in *JAMA* between 1974 and the end of 1987, appeared early in 1997. Its reception has prompted the publication of a second volume, this one comprising 102 reproductions and essays that appeared in *JAMA* between 1988 and 1990. They are arranged chronologically. Like the first volume, *The Art of JAMA II* has kept the coffee-table format, with essays and reproductions on facing pages. Depending on the response to this collection, other volumes will follow at appropriate times.

In spite of the forty-year tradition, the question remains: "Why art on the cover of a medical journal?" especially when the subject of the work is not overtly medical. Indeed, what do the fine arts—except where the painting depicts a medical subject, perhaps—have to do with medicine at all? As I stated in my Preface to the first volume of *The Art of JAMA*, the answer is both elusive and obvious. To put it into words is difficult, yet when one looks at the paintings, one knows, intuitively perhaps, that the visual arts have everything to do with medicine. In a sense it is medicine that unites art and science. Art and medicine exist in a relationship as intimate and as necessary as that between the human body and spirit. They have an affinity for one another at the deepest levels of human existence.

Aristotle described art as trying to complete what nature could not, as the ideal humans strive for, all the while knowing that whereas one can envision the ideal, in reality one can only approach it, not reach it. The goal of medicine would seem to be much the same. Disease and illness cannot be abolished, but the ideal state of the human organism can be approached. If art reminds us of our human condition, even more so does the practice of medicine, in which we recognize that all—patient as well as caregiver—are afflicted beings. But not without hope, and that is where the visual arts play such an important role in medicine. The very act of painting a picture signifies hope, as does the act of treating a patient. That is why painters paint and physicians practice medicine.

Both artists and physicians bring to their work a special quality of attention that enables them to be creative in the deepest sense of the word. As I noted in the earlier Preface, both medicine and art are about seeing, first with the eyes of the body, but if one is attentive enough, then with the eyes of the mind and of the heart. That is when the physician truly, as we say, "attends" the patient. In a wordless way, the physician passes from seeing only a disease to seeing the person who is afflicted with the disease. That is the moment when healing begins, when the journey toward the ideal commences. Paradoxically, the healer is healed as well. That is perhaps what is meant when we speak of "the art of medicine."

Preparing a collection of previously published essays is, I imagine, a lesson in humility for any writer. Certainly that was the case for this writer. Reading and rereading thousands of one's words published a decade ago—written then in the flush of inspiration and the warm glow of discovery, read now in the dispassionate light of experience that one hopes has translated to maturity and even wisdom—helps ensure that result. The paintings still awaken this spirit and rouse these emotions, but in the accompanying text I find many a sentence I would not today style in quite the same way. I find things I wish I had said and did not. I find other things I wish I had omitted and did not. Thus, I availed myself of my blue-pencil prerogative and have wielded it rather vigorously in the cases that were particularly bothersome to me. Where I discovered errors, I corrected them, although time may discover more. One error, in particular, discovered not by me but by my readers, still brings a blush of embarrassment to my cheeks. For the most part, though, I have left the stories alone, believing, hoping, that wisdom has taught me to prefer humility over any infelicity that may remain. If the creative act should tempt the artist or writer or physician to liken himself or herself to the gods at times, the outcome reminds them that they are not. This writer is fortunate in having a true work of art accompany each essay: if the essays should be wanting, the paintings are not. With time they have only mellowed and grown greater. They have gained depth and wisdom at exactly the same rate and in the same degree as the viewers who look at them again and again, either in the museums or in the many fine reproductions that technology has made possible.

One of the bonuses of writing the weekly cover essays for *JAMA*—and one of the chief sources of enrichment in my task—has been letters from readers. They have told me their likes and dislikes—sometimes quite emphatically—but most often they have shared their own thoughts and insights. It has been borne home to me time after time that there is no "right" way or "wrong" way to interpret a painting. There are even more ways of looking at a painting than there are of looking at a blackbird, as many ways as there are viewers. And all of them are valid.

Some letters called errors to my attention and some of the changes in this volume have been the result of those letters. One of the most egregious errors, the one for which still I blush, appeared in the story for John George ("J. G.") Brown's *The Cider Mill.* My eyes played tricks on me: I misinterpreted the tongue of the wagon as a crutch against which one of the little girls was leaning. Some fifty readers called this error to my attention—kindly, I must add. I am pleased to say that in this volume the little girl has been "cured." Thank you!

A note on the titles of the paintings: In many cases the title used in the original story does not agree with the title now given in the current story. This is because titles of paintings are notoriously fickle: they change with time and with new perceptions, they

often change when ownership changes, and they change as the result of new scholarship, when research discloses additional facts about the artist or the work. Thus, Walter Page's *The Eve of Life* has become *The Grandmother*, and Manet's *Gare Saint-Lazare* is now *The Railway*. In many cases I have preferred the "old" title, as that is how the painting was identified in the sources I consulted; indeed, sometimes the story of the painting was built around the title and it was essential to readers' understanding that it be kept. Where appropriate, the original titles have been given in parentheses. In the credit lines, however, the "new" titles have been used and they should be considered the official titles—for now.

Writing the author's preface is both a joy and a sweet sorrow. Although it appears first, the preface is usually written last, just before the book goes to press. If the preparation of a book can be likened to the lengthy human gestation process from conception to delivery, the preface is the final stage of labor. What was earlier conceived is now separated from its author and must make its own way in the world. On the other hand, acknowledging all those persons who contributed to *The Art of JAMA* collections, both in the original publication of the cover stories a decade and more ago and also more immediately, in preparing this particular volume is an unalloyed joy. At grave peril of omitting someone, I nevertheless wish to list the following persons who have contributed to this work, either early on or more recently.

First, my gratitude goes to all my colleagues at *JAMA*, now as in the past, whose daily interchange is always a source of inspiration. I wish to thank the three editors-in-chief under whose aegis these original covers were produced: Robert H. Moser, MD, William R. Barclay, MD, and George D. Lundberg, MD. I wish also to thank John H. Talbott, MD, who instituted the fine-art covers, and *JAMA*'s current editor-in-chief, Catherine D. DeAngelis, MD, whose enthusiastic support provides the environment in which creativity can

flourish. The assistance of managing senior editor Annette Flanagin, also *JAMA* Book Liaison, was invaluable. Among the many *JAMA* staff members who have assisted in the preparation of these stories over the years, I wish to note Charlene Breedlove, Fanny Brown, Lori Burnette, Celina Canchola, Mary Cannon, Helga Fritz, Lenette Gardner-Gullens, Dan Halibey, Dan Reyes, Jennifer Sperry, and Bonnie Van Cleven.

Among AMA staff I extend thanks to the many staff librarians who have assisted me, among them in particular Ann White and Lorri Zipperer, as well as Sandra Schefris and Yolanda Ellis. AMA Press staff include senior acquisitions editor Barry Bowlus and director of production Jean Roberts, as well as editorial director Mary Lou White. A special note of thanks goes to Charl Richey and Chris Meyer, who were responsible for this volume's color reproductions and layout, and to Laura King, who copyedited the text.

All of the museums have been most cooperative, but I wish to note the National Gallery of Art in Washington, DC, in particular Ira Bartfield, Deborah Chotner, Anke A. van Wagenberg-ter Hoeven, Sarah McStravick, and Arthur Wheelock; and the Kimbell Museum in Fort Worth, Texas, in particular, Anne Adams, Registrar. Jefferson C. Harrison, Jr, The Chrysler Museum, and Michael Quick, The Los Angeles County Museum of Art, supplied me with material concerning works in their collections that was not otherwise available. Cecelia Chin at the National Portrait Gallery has been an invaluable source for American art. I am especially grateful to the private owners who gave permission for their works to be reproduced. As in the first volume of *The Art of JAMA,* Ben and Jess Shenson, MD, have once again given generous access to the works of Theodore Wores. Here, in *JAMA*'s home city, the Art Institute of Chicago's Ryerson Library is a particular source of gratitude. Not only does its environment invite scholarly research, but its reference librarians over the years have never failed me.

Special mention must again be made of Thomas Handrigan, publishing operations color graphics manager and an artist with an eye. Tom worked with me on every cover from 1974 until his retirement in 1994, prior to the publication of the first volume of *The Art of JAMA*. Even so, he served as my consultant on that book. Tom died, suddenly, on June 16, 1997, shortly after publication of that volume. His presence still remains on every page of volume II. Often we discussed artistic or technical aspects of a painting, and these thoughts helped generate my version of the final story. So vivid are these memories that for certain paintings, even after more than ten years, I can almost reconstruct the ambiance of the day on which we talked.

To *JAMA* colleagues Juliana M. Walker and Roxanne K. Young, assistant editor and associate editor in the Department of Medical Humanities, I can say truly that without their help, encouragement, and perseverance over the long process of preparing this volume for publication, it would not have been completed; nor would it be in such fine shape. Juliana, who over two years has been in constant contact with all the museums represented, tracked down and contacted current owners of the paintings reproduced, checked and double-checked titles, obtained all necessary permissions, rechecked vital data concerning the artists, shepherded all the contracts through the proper channels, saw that the bills were paid, and in general handled all the other administrative and editorial tasks that—often unnoticed—go into publishing a book. To Roxanne, who is also director of the Department of Medical Humanities, I am indebted as colleague, editor, and friend. Her critical eye never fails to improve what it sees. Even while she was simultaneously seeing her own book through the publication process, she found the time and energy to serve as my arbiter on matters that ranged anywhere from grammatical incorrectness (my eye is often blind to dangling participles and misplaced modifiers, among other things) to questions of taste. Her unfailing eye for color has scrutinized everything from the advertising copy to the proofs of the reproductions and the book jacket. And her unfailing "blue pencil" has been ready with whatever advice was needed. Perhaps it is best to describe her contribution by saying that had it not been there, it would have been obvious to all. What inadequacies there may be are entirely the responsibility of the author, not the editor.

Finally, I must thank my readers, in particular Therese Fellbaum, who has for many years faithfully read each story as it is published, and who read every word of and commented on every story in the present volume when it was still in typescript. I also thank all of the many other readers who have written over the years. Just as studying each painting in preparation for its essay has enriched my life, so too have your comments been doubly enriching, and I say thanks. Without readers, a book is only a book. Once it is opened, however, it becomes a dialogue that continues as long as there are readers. May this volume become a happy addition to your library.

*M. Therese Southgate, MD*
Chicago, February 5, 2001

# THE ART OF JAMA II ❧

# The Art of **JAMA** II

## Covers and Essays From

*The Journal of the*
*American Medical Association*

# GEORGE WESLEY BELLOWS ❧

## New York

In the autumn of 1904, the talk of New York was its new subway system, inaugurated by Mayor McClellan on October 27 with a fanfare of whistles and a salute of guns. The mayor himself drove the first train, from Broadway to 145th, and brought it in on time. Passengers marveled at the clean white stations and the silence of the olive-green cars. Aboveground, others congregated to watch the riders emerge from the tunnel. All celebrated their emancipation from street congestion and their deliverance from the whims of the weather.

One of those who celebrated was a tall (six-foot, two-inch), young (twenty-two-year-old) man newly arrived from Columbus, Ohio. Only a few weeks earlier, he had said good-bye to his staunch Republican father, who had designed many of Columbus' buildings, including the courthouse and the high school his son had attended, and who wanted him to be a banker, to his devout Methodist mother, who wanted him to be a bishop, and to an uncompleted degree at Ohio State University, because he had refused to take the final exams. He had also said good-bye to the OSU glee club, where he was a baritone, to the band, where he played drums, and to the yearbook, for which he supplied cartoons. And to the OSU basketball team, the OSU baseball team, and an offer to play shortstop for the Cincinnati Reds. But most of all, he had said good-bye to Columbus, which up until then had been the whole of his life. He had set his will on becoming an artist, and it was Manhattan, not the Midwest, that was his mecca.

George Wesley Bellows (1882-1925) characteristically lost no time once he arrived in New York. He moved into the YMCA, which not only was within walking distance of the New York School of Art, a bonus for one on a severely curtailed budget, but which also had basketball and baseball teams, a necessity for a young athlete. And it allayed his parents' fears about their only child, living on his own for the first time. At the New York School of Art, Bellows studied in Robert Henri's class, a class that included Edward Hopper, Rockwell Kent, and one Emma Louise Story, among others. Bellows took to Henri's classes and to New York like

> *. . . to him everything that existed was beautiful simply because it existed . . .*

they were the eternal answer to a question he had never known how to ask. With his canvas he embraced the city and its life; with his colors he pried out its moods and its secrets. Every sight of daily life in the streets of New York was recorded in his mind; later, from his remarkable visual memory, coupled with his superb hand-eye coordination, they were given a shape and a color and an order. They became a cross-eyed urchin, a geezer with his dog, a tugboat on the icy Hudson, a summer night on Riverside Drive, forty-two kids on an East River pier, a ringside spectator at Sharkey's boxing club, a ghostly excavation site, lonely tenements, teeming tenements, steaming streets, a choked intersection, a bridge, the unemployed, the newly arrived, immigrants—Bellows preserved them all. Because he painted what he saw as he saw it and because what he saw was usually in the streets, among the refuse, academicians and critics dubbed him a

member of the Ashcan school of painting. To Bellows it did not matter: to him everything that existed was beautiful simply because it existed; that alone made it a proper subject for art. And he was successful. Within five years after his arrival in New York City, Bellows had exhibited at the National Academy of Design, had made his first sale to a museum (Pennsylvania Academy of the Fine Arts), and had been elected an associate member of the National Academy of Design, at age twenty-six the youngest member in its history. The following year, 1910, he established his permanent studio at 146 East Nineteenth Street and married his one-time classmate, Emma Louise Story of Upper Montclair, New Jersey. George Wesley Bellows of Columbus, Ohio, had met New York and New York was his.

*New York* belongs to the first year of George and Emma's marriage, when the couple were expecting their first child, Anne. For his motif, Bellows has chosen one of the most common scenes of life in a large city and also one of its most frustrating: a traffic jam. According to Bellows' principal biographer, Charles Morgan, the painting is a "remembered synthesis" of a midsummer traffic jam in the Madison Square area of Manhattan. To this sweltering summer memory Bellows has added snow, wind, and cold and placed it smack in the middle of winter, when time itself seems to have become as completely stopped as the traffic in the square; 1911 is gridlocked at February.

At first glance, the painting looks simply like chaos with some color added—a confusion of people, horses, carts, trolleys, drays, hansoms, automobiles, and elevated trains. Then specifics step forward: Pedestrians from all walks of life hurry

*Continued on p 206*

# JAMA®

The Journal of the American Medical Association

February 5, 1988

# ÉDOUARD MANET

## The Railway

Debonair, dapper, haute bourgeois; sophisticated, self-possessed; arrogant sometimes, aloof often, witty always; master of the perfect, though often hurtful, mot; a true boulevardier, a frequenter of cafés; happily married but remaining a ladies' man—this was Édouard Manet (1832-1883), at age forty the consummate Parisian and center of a coterie that included, besides many other painters, such literary lights as the novelist and critic Émile Zola and the poet Stéphane Mallarmé. Yet, according to colleagues, he could look utterly lost when faced with a blank canvas. And once the painting was completed and hung at the Salon, he would wander about before the opening, fretting to his friends, nervous and uncertain about the response he would receive. Well might he be.

In 1863, his now famous *Le déjeuner sur l'herbe* won him public recognition—in the form of outrage over a scene the viewers considered scandalous. The even more provocative *Olympia*, which followed in 1865, brought even more outrage and public ridicule. Before he was thirty-five, the name M Manet was indeed well known on the boulevards and in the cafés, but it was not the type of recognition Manet wanted. What he coveted, even lusted after, was the official recognition of the Salon in the form of prizes and awards and the approval of the public in the form of praise. Finally, at age forty-one, after a visit to Holland where he admired the work of Frans Hals, Manet submitted a painting of a good-natured burgher enjoying a pipe and a beer to the Salon of 1873 and won its approval. The subject was one a good Parisian could understand. It was with renewed hope, then, that Manet submitted three paintings to the next Salon, in 1874. Only one, *Gare Saint-Lazare* (also known as *The Railway*), was

accepted. To Manet's bewilderment, the critics reverted to ridicule and the public once again laughed. Cartoonists had a field day with the heavy iron fence, changing its bars into those of a jail or, even worse, making them the grille of an insane asylum that prevents its two occupants from escaping from Manet as they would have

> " *. . . a lesson that one must risk oneself entire and anew each time . . .* "

wished. And why, asked the columnists, is this called a railway? Where is the train? Why are the woman and girl just sitting or standing there? What are they doing? Where's the story?

More than a century years after his premature death, viewers still puzzle over Manet's paintings. The ground is rich and the possibilities for speculation as inexhaustible as the viewers who come to see. For example, in a monograph devoted exclusively to this single Manet painting, Harry Rand, curator of painting and sculpture at the National Museum of American Art, notes that whereas seventeenth-century painters were concerned with expressing their ideas in accord with the new science of optics, the late nineteenth-century painters concerned themselves with the fledgling science of psychology. Thus, says Rand, *Gare Saint-Lazare*, which always remained one of Manet's favorites, can be read as an essay on the theme of consciousness. Each of the living principals—the woman, the girl, the dog—is engaged at a different level of consciousness: the child

forms images out of the steam of a locomotive that has just passed, the woman meditates over a book of poetry she has been reading, and the sleeping puppy dreams in his mistress' lap. Each demonstrates a different level and type of the conscious life.

Bothersome, however, is a curious contradiction in the attire and attributes of the girl and the woman. The woman, for example, is swaddled, neck to ankles, in a dark blue dress of heavy, autumn-weight fabric. She holds a book in which her fingers are interleaved, while a pied puppy whose eye patch matches her own hair sleeps in her lap. Just behind the puppy is a closed red fan. In contrast, the child is dressed for a spring day in a blue-white, sleeveless, low-cut dress of diaphanous material, its skirt billowing about her like the blue-white steam she makes dreams of. Close to her, at her right on the ledge, is a bunch of grapes, at first almost unnoticed by the viewer. Seemingly unrelated to anything else, they may be, however, together with the railway, the painting's unifying symbol. Perhaps Manet's "illogic" in the costumes is not illogic at all, but rather the peculiar logic of dreams, a portrayal of different aspects of the same thing under several guises.

For example, the grapes, which the child presumably is eating because Manet has placed them so close to her right hand, are most obviously a symbol for autumn, for harvest time. But when grapes are processed they become wine, which, in the Christian iconography Manet was familiar with, is a sacramental symbol for life-giving blood. Again, a railway terminal, such as the Gare Saint-Lazare, marks the end of a journey, but it may also mark the beginning of a journey or any of the stopping places along

*Continued on p 206*

# JAMA®

The Journal of the American Medical Association

May 20, 1988

# EDVARD MUNCH

## Self-portrait With Bottle of Wine

From the time he was eighteen and a student at the School of Design in Christiania (Oslo) until he died at his home in Norway at the age of eighty, Edvard Munch (1863-1944) made scores of self-portraits, so many in fact that he is rivaled in this genre only by the French painter Élisabeth Vigée-Lebrun and the Dutch master Rembrandt. His first self-portrait, in three-quarter view, shows a proud, stern, even arrogant youth, one who could be kin to the Florentine youths of some four centuries earlier. One of the last self-portraits, made as he was approaching his eighties, shows a tall man, full face, beside a window; the slightly drooping shoulders are squared, the head held high, the chin set, the mouth curved downward, the eyes alert but askance, like those of prey being stalked. Outside the window winter is painted in tones of apocalyptic green. In the sixty-odd years between the two portraits, Munch portrayed himself in innumerable settings and poses, from those as common as a man with a cigarette, as bizarre as himself as the murdered Marat, and as macabre as a man with the arm of a skeleton.

*Self-portrait With Bottle of Wine* shows Munch at age forty-two when he was in Weimar at the time of his presentation to the royal court. Already he had a severe drinking problem and it was steadily worsening. In fact, as early as his mid thirties, Munch had noted in his diary that he began drinking as soon as he awakened in the morning and drank all day. Shortly thereafter, in attempting to extricate himself from a romantic entanglement with Tulla Larsen, the thirtyish, unmarried daughter of Norway's largest wine merchant, Munch shot off one of the fingers of his left hand and permanently injured another. Over the next decade or so, he was engaged in a number of public brawls that the press reported both in Norway and abroad. Toward the end of this period, Munch sought treatment at a number of watering places in Europe, but nothing was successful. He began charging that friends and strangers alike, as well as the police, were persecuting him. In the meantime, the color contrasts in his paintings became harsher and his stroke more violent; sometimes he even squeezed pure color directly from the tube onto the

> *. . . he sees not with his anatomic eye, but rather with his mind's eye.*

canvas. Finally, in 1908, after a period of intense hallucinations and accusations of persecution, Munch entered a clinic in Copenhagen, where he stayed for eight months. From then until he died, some thirty-eight years later, he never again used alcohol.

When he painted *Self-portrait With Bottle of Wine* in 1906, Munch was in the depths of his illness. His mood is one of alienation and despair, of hopelessness. He sits alone in a near-empty restaurant, his back to the room. His shoulders are slumped, his hands limp in his lap. Both his face and his hands are suffused with red. His gaze is inward, and his eyes are widened in terror at what they see. Before him, ignored, is a bottle, a glass, and an empty plate. There are no eating utensils. Behind him, back to back and ramrod straight, are two waiters looking in opposite directions. In the corner is the vague shape of a faceless woman. Except for the expanse of the snowy tables, the colors

are harsh contrasts of red, green, and orange, the red surrounding Munch's head, the green surrounding the woman. One waiter is outlined in red and green, the other in orange and green. Thrusting upward into the picture, the aggressive diagonals of the tables tip the room toward the viewer, obliterate the ceiling, and increase the oppressive, trapped feeling of the painting. It is these diagonals, which are so insistent, that are perhaps the way into the painting. When extended, they intersect at Munch's forehead, just above his right eye. Thus, what Munch places behind the seated man—the red, the green, the orange, the waiters, the woman, and the sinuous line of the amoeba-shaped orange—he sees not with his anatomic eye, but rather with his mind's eye. They are symbols for his thoughts, his mood, and his feelings as he experienced them in Weimar.

In Munch's vocabulary, red was the color of the mature, passionate woman. It was also the color of blood spilled by the murdering woman, a theme that Munch increasingly returned to after the shooting episode with Tulla Larsen. Green, on the other hand, was the "sickly green" of death, a symbol as old as the green horse of the Apocalypse. It, too, was associated with woman, recalling the loss of the two women he had loved best in his life, his mother and his sister Sophie, one year older than himself. By the time Munch was fifteen, both had succumbed to tuberculosis. But even before adolescence, death had been always present to Munch, and she was a woman, waiting for him. The exact time of her coming and the guise she would wear remained unknown, but she was always present in what he did. She sits now, as always, featureless in the corner, huddled in her shroud, watching him. The two waiters,

*Continued on p 206*

# JAMA®

The Journal of the American Medical Association

May 27, 1988

# CHRISTIAN KROHG ⤳

## *Sovende barn (Sleeping Child)*

Outside Norway, Christian Krohg (1852-1925), painter, novelist, and journalist, is today remembered chiefly for his association with his compatriot Edvard Munch. Eleven years Munch's senior, he supervised and corrected the work of Munch and a group of other young artists as they were setting up in Christiania (Oslo) in the early 1880s.

Krohg was born in Vestre Aker, near Christiania, the son of the judge and literary man Georg Krohg and Sophie Amalia Holst. Like Munch, Krohg lost his mother and his sister to tuberculosis during his childhood and, again like Munch, was cared for by his father's sister. He himself was a sickly child. He finished law studies in keeping with his father's wishes, but in 1873 he went to Karlsruhe and Munich, where he studied painting with Hans Gude and Karl Gussow. When Gussow moved to Berlin in 1875, Krohg followed and remained there for four decisive years. It was in his experience of the large industrial city that he developed both his philosophy of life and his social conscience and also his realist theories of painting. The Danish critic Georg Brandes, whose portrait Krohg did in Berlin, said of him and his comrades, "[They are] enthusiastic nihilists, socialists, atheists, naturalists, materialists, and egoists. They put the most horrible ideas into one another's mouths as far as social order and one's neighbors go." And indeed, Krohg and the poet Hans Jaeger were to become the leaders of the notorious Christiania bohemians, a group of intellectuals in social and artistic revolt against established values and standards, not only in painting and in literature, but in social mores and personal behavior as well. Krohg would later be ostracized in Christiania because of the scandal caused when he published his novel *Albertine*, an exposé of police corruption and prostitution in that city. When the book was banned, Krohg painted what has become one of his best-known paintings, *Albertine in the Police Doctor's Waiting Room*; it shows a young woman accused of prostitution being admitted to an inner office, where she will be subjected to a degrading physical examination by a police doctor.

But Krohg had not always resorted to such sensational topics. After his years of upheaval in Berlin, he had returned to Norway, and in the summer of 1879 he made his first visit to Skagen, an artists' colony in a Danish fishing

> *. . . it is the shoes . . .*
> *that tell the story . . .*

village on the North Sea. Here, amid a simple life and humble surroundings, he developed his naturalistic style and his philosophy of realism. These ideas were reinforced two years later when, in 1881, he made his first trip to Paris. There he saw the works of Courbet, Bastien-Lepage, Manet, and the Impressionists and discussed the ideas of the realist novelist Émile Zola. During the summers from 1882 to 1884, Krohg returned to Skagen and tested his ideas in a series of paintings of members of one of the local fisher families as they went about their various humble chores or, exhausted, dropped off to sleep in the middle of a task. Krohg was particularly sensitive to the activities of the women and children and the elderly.

The simple but charming *Sovende barn (Sleeping Child)* dates from one of these summers. Here Krohg chooses a child to symbolize not only lowliness, but also the helplessness and dependency that characterize childhood. He shows the child at its most vulnerable, when it is asleep. At the same time, the child assumes an attitude of complete trust as it flings out its arm and abandons itself to its sleep. An unseen person's concern for the child is visible in the chair, which has been pushed up against the bed to guard against the child's falling. It is perhaps the same chair where the mother sat as she took off the child's shoes and watched until the child slept.

The clean, clear lines of the painting and its brilliant, jewel-like colors reflect the clear-cut struggles of rural life as they appeared to Krohg after life among the poor of industrial Berlin and the intellectuals of Christiania bohemia. The innocence and simplicity of the scene are the innocence and simplicity of the child. Only in the contrasts of the green chair and the red bed, which are contrasts in line as well as in color, do we have a hint of the harshness of that existence. But it is the shoes, which Krohg has carefully arranged in full light, that tell the story. At a time when infectious disease in Norway, especially tuberculosis, decimated families, including Krohg's own, the scuffed-up, well-worn shoes, casually dropped, ready to be put back on, are Krohg's assurance to his viewers that the flushed child is not ill, but only napping, exhausted from active play.

Krohg made one final visit to Skagen, in 1888. After that, he continued to paint and to teach in Copenhagen, Paris, Berlin, and Spain, as well as in Christiania. Krohg also turned to journalism in addition to fiction writing. For more than twenty years, beginning in 1889, he wrote a column for Christiania newspapers. In 1909 he became the first director of the Christiania Academy of Fine Arts, where he remained until his death in 1925. Krohg was married to Othilia

*Continued on p 207*

# JAMA®

The Journal of the American Medical Association

June 3, 1988

# AUGUSTE RENOIR ❧

## A Girl With a Watering Can

Few painters have been able to portray the child and its world as exquisitely as has Auguste Renoir (1841-1919). Among his contemporaries in nineteenth-century Paris, others, such as Mary Cassatt and Edgar Degas, frequently painted children, but Cassatt usually concentrated on the mother-child relationship by showing the two together, whereas Degas' children most often appear as objects being used for adult ends, as in his paintings of young ballet dancers. Only Renoir could catch the poetry of the child in its paradox of fragility and strength, in its quiet sense of its own autonomy in the world it inhabits.

Renoir completed *A Girl With a Watering Can* in 1876, when Impressionism was at the height of its development (although the Impressionists themselves had thus far gained only notoriety for their efforts). The painting is, like Renoir's lifelong disposition, a happy scene, a painting of a sparkling summer day, a garden full of blooming flowers, and a healthy child to enjoy them. In her blue velvet dress, lavishly bordered with lace, her high-button shoes, her prim pantalets, and her perky red bow, she stands, queen of all she surveys. Ready with watering can in one hand and some daisies in the other, she accepts the obeisance of her subjects and prepares to bestow on them her largess. The garden is her secret kingdom and one who is not a child may not pass except by invitation. Clearly, Renoir is welcome.

*A Girl With a Watering Can* is Impressionism in Renoir's fullest statement.

Though he embraced the principles of the style—short brush strokes, softened outlines, bright palette, virtual absence of black, and juxtaposition of strokes on the canvas to give the effect of shimmering light—Renoir yet maintained a certain reserve toward the new style. While others, such as Monet, Sisley, and Pissarro, concentrated on landscapes to best show these effects, Renoir never abandoned his classic sense of the human figure. Most often this, rather than landscape, was Renoir's chosen subject. He also remained devoted to the masters,

> *. . . its paradox of*
> *fragility and strength,*
> *its quiet sense*
> *of its own autonomy . . .*

especially to Raphael, Rubens, and Velázquez among non-French painters. Like Rubens, he admired the undraped figure; the skin of his female nudes is a delicious concoction of color, sensuous and warm, yet delicate as a rose petal. Some of this delicate rose-petal texture and color may be seen in *A Girl With a Watering Can*, where her complexion reflects the roses beside her.

Renoir also retains some of the classic principles of composition in the various pairings and echoes in the painting, both of shape and of color. For example, the prominent buttons that march up the coat are white on deep blue and have dark centers; the eyes, to which they lead us, are reversed to deep blue on white, with dark centers. Again, the hair bow, which is "Renoir red," a red he wished to be "sonorous, to sound, like a bell," is repeated, slightly muted, by the child's lips with their slightly upturned corners. At the same time, the child's hair disappears into the sunshine, while the shimmering atmospheric effects surrounding her are conveyed by the short, choppy strokes and dabs of the flowering shrubbery, the grass, and the white gravel path, here, like light, containing all the colors of the painting.

*A Girl With a Watering Can* is perhaps the best-loved painting at the National Gallery of Art. Certainly, it is among the top ten of those most often visited, and postcards and other reproductions of this painting are among the most often requested. Who the little girl is who has charmed millions is not recorded. But, named or not, she has warmed us from the end of the nineteenth century to the end of the twentieth century. One hopes that the twenty-first century will also be pleased to become one of her loyal subjects.

*A Girl With a Watering Can*, 1876, French. Oil on canvas. 100.3 × 73.2 cm. Courtesy of the National Gallery of Art, Washington, DC; Chester Dale Collection.

# JAMA

The Journal of the American Medical Association

June 10, 1988

# JEAN-LOUIS FORAIN

## The Artist's Wife Fishing

Today, Jean-Louis Forain (1852-1931) is most often remembered as one of the fifty-five or so painters who participated in the various Impressionist group exhibitions between 1874 and 1886. At the invitation of his friend and mentor, Edgar Degas, Forain showed works at four of the eight exhibitions, those of 1879, 1880, 1881, and 1886, after which the group disbanded. Impressionism had run its course. Forain, on the other hand, at age thirty-four, had only just begun.

Born in Reims, Forain studied at the École des Beaux-Arts in Paris, where he was interested primarily in the works of Goya and Rembrandt. Among his French contemporaries, he was, besides Degas, influenced by Manet, but it was the political and social satiric drawings of Daumier that determined his course. By age twenty-four, Forain, like Daumier before him, was contributing caricatures and cartoons to Paris newspapers and journals. With his nimble wit and biting humor, all aspects of Paris life were subjected to his brush, from café life, the theater, and the streets to political scandals, the law courts, and the misery of the poor. Eventually, his work would appear in all the major newspapers and magazines of his time. The illustrations were acclaimed by critics and public alike, though the appreciation was probably more for their sharp-tongued message than for their skill. Nevertheless, Daumier had a worthy successor. Indeed, one critic places Forain in the grand tradition of Rabelais and Molière.

In spite of his reputation, however, Forain was not all bristles and barbs. Intensely religious at a time of intellectual pessimism, when all beliefs and values were under the

*. . . sunset, the melancholy moment of the Angelus hour when day and night embrace . . .*

closest scrutiny and even attack among the intellectual and artistic circles of Paris, Forain was himself committed to the traditional middle-class values of work, marriage, home, and family. At the same time, however, he could abandon the traditional academic style of painting he learned at the École des Beaux-Arts to follow the avant-garde Impressionist style in portraying idyllic domestic scenes from his own life.

*The Artist's Wife Fishing*, completed when Forain was in his mid forties, is one such scene of domestic bliss. Madame Forain, elegant and corseted, fishes in the stream; behind her the obviously uncorseted nurse holds the child. A poodle romps in the background, chattering birds return to their nests, and a fish makes off with the bait. The time is sunset, the melancholy moment of the Angelus hour when day and night embrace in a moment of stillness before they go their separate ways to past and future. Above, purple clouds trail like banners announcing the coming night. Below, dividing husband and wife, the stream flows on like time, even while it tries to hold on to the colors of day. *The Artist's Wife Fishing* is a simple evensong that Forain raises to a rhapsody in rose.

In later life, Forain turned more and more to scenes of social injustice, especially to the denial of justice to the poor. He also turned to scenes of World War I and to illustrations for the New Testament. Several collections of his graphic work were published. Forain died in Paris in 1931, aged seventy-nine.

*The Artist's Wife Fishing*, 1896, French. Oil on canvas. 95.2 × 101.3 cm. Courtesy of the National Gallery of Art, Washington, DC; collection of Mr and Mrs Paul Mellon. ©2001 Artists Rights Society (ARS), New York, New York/ADAGP, Paris, France.

# JAMA®

June 17, 1988

The Journal of the American Medical Association

# DOMENICO VENEZIANO

## A Miracle of St Zenobius

Though there is general agreement that Domenico Veneziano (c 1410-1461) is one of the great masters of the early Italian Renaissance, perhaps second only to Masaccio, little is known about the events of his life or about his personal characteristics. If his letters are a judge, however, one could be justified in concluding that he was a clever man who not only could read the signs of the times accurately but also knew how to approach the tricky world of Florentine politics with the least risk to himself. Moreover, he was not shy in marketing his talent.

On the first of April in 1438, less than five years after Cosimo had founded the de'Medici dynasty in Florence, Domenico wrote from his home in Perugia to Cosimo's son and heir, Piero (the Gouty), asking for a job. First he inquired after Piero's health, then he noted his own unworthy status and swore to his love for the nobility and the people of Florence. Finally he came to the point: He had heard it said that Cosimo wanted a magnificent altarpiece, "which pleases me very much . . . it would please me more if . . . I could paint it. I am in hopes with God's help to do marvelous things . . . I long to do some famous work . . . I promise you my work will bring you honor." What, if anything, Piero replied is not known, but Domenico was in Florence the following year, 1439, working on frescoes for the chapel of Sant'Egidio in the hospital of Sta Maria Nuova. Except for a few fragments, the frescoes have been lost, as has most of Domenico's work. Between 1442 and 1448, however, Domenico executed a signed work in Florence that has survived, an altarpiece for the church of Sta Lucia dei Magnoli. Originally consisting of a main panel with five smaller panels, the *predelle*, the

altarpiece was dismantled and its panels dispersed to Berlin, Cambridge (England), and Washington, DC. The central panel is at the Uffizi in Florence. Now judged to be one of the most important works of the mid fifteenth century, the St Lucy altarpiece is witness to Domenico's own assessment of his talent.

*A Miracle of St Zenobius* is one of the *predelle* from the St Lucy altarpiece. Zenobius, the principal patron of Florence and a pop-ular subject for its painters, was a member of the famous Geronimo family of Florence and became bishop of that city in

*. . . powerful screams intended literally to call her son back from the dead.*

the fourth century. According to legend, at various times he resuscitated no fewer than five persons from the dead, including a child who had been killed in front of the cathedral. Here, he restores to life a widow's son, killed by an oxcart. According to catalog notes, this painting shows the Borzo Albizzi, where the miracle reportedly took place, with the church of S Pietro Maggiore, since destroyed, in the background.

Domenico was a true Renaissance man, many sided, as much scientist as artist. He was an innovator in color, so much so that the sixteenth-century biographer Giorgio Vasari insisted that he had painted in oil. He also set himself to solve the problem of the logical ordering of space by adopting the newly discovered Florentine concept of perspective. But, technical matters aside,

Domenico was an artist as well. His colors glow beyond anything the Florentines had yet seen, his figures are individualized and express emotion, and his structures move across the surface with the cleanness of plainchant on parchment. Most important, he was very much a man of his time. Trained in Venice, as his name implies, he was probably familiar with the spirituality expressed in the Gothic style of northern Europe. At the same time, working in Florence, he is a humanist who is not afraid to open a dialogue between faith and reason. He has, in fact, been called "the first great link between the Gothic and the Renaissance."

Had Domenico worked a century and a half earlier, his *A Miracle of St Zenobius* would have been a classic lamentation scene, such as Giotto painted in the Arena Chapel in Padua, and his figures would have sported halos. Whereas Giotto portrayed the Virgin mourning over the prostrate body of the dead Christ, with the faithful women arrayed on the left and the confused disciples on the right, Domenico straddles the divide between the religious and the profane and humanizes the scene into a bit of each. Now it is a contemporary woman, a Florentine, a widow in black, who mourns over the body of her dead son, and she mourns not in silent, dignified grief, but in powerful screams intended literally to call her son back from the dead. As in the Giotto lamentation, the women are on the left, but the Magdalen now becomes an aristocratic woman in red. In the place of the disciples, Florentine monks bow their heads in prayer, while the Romans become physicians who, consulting among themselves, conclude the case is hopeless. Zenobius, meanwhile, raises his hands to heaven.

*Continued on p 207*

# JAMA®

### The Journal of the American Medical Association

June 24, 1988

# WINSLOW HOMER ⌁

## Snap the Whip

The last third of the nineteenth century is remarkable for parallel revolutions that were taking place on either side of the Atlantic. While Manet and the Impressionists were doing battle with the critics and the academicians in Paris, the American painter Winslow Homer (1836-1910) was working in New York City as an illustrator and Civil War correspondent for the popular *Harper's Weekly*. In his free time, he roamed up and down the northeastern seaboard doing sketches and oils. Except for some boyhood training in watercolor from his mother, an exceptionally fine botanical painter, Homer was self-taught; slowly he worked out his own theories of light and color. For technical data, he relied on the French chemist Chevreul's book on color ("It's my bible," he said), but for the rest he relied on his own eye. Although Homer's theories were remarkably similar to those of the Impressionists, they were nevertheless arrived at quite independently; both stressed the variability in color seen at different times of the day and on the necessity, therefore, that outdoor subjects be painted outdoors. Moreover, Homer's theories were developed from quite different subject matter, the American countryside and coast, the American farmer and fisherman, and American light. Homer's would become a uniquely American art. It was criticized, sometimes, for being less finished and more homespun than that of his more sophisticated Philadelphia contemporary, Thomas Eakins. Nevertheless, his work reflected the mood of the people of this still largely rural country struggling to heal itself after its war. What humorist Samuel Langhorne Clemens was at that moment doing for the Mississippi with words, this self-taught, fiercely independent Yankee painter was doing for New England in color and line.

*Snap the Whip* is one of two variations Homer did in oil on this familiar childhood game. (The other is at the Metropolitan Museum of Art and has fewer boys, a different sky, and a different background.) Released from school and free at last, the boys celebrate their strength and prowess in a rough-and-tumble competition. At the left, two girls with a hoop watch. In front of a tiny, distant cabin, people are waving; to the right of them is a tiny couple with a baby. The entire scene is anchored firmly to the base of the mountain by a little red

> *. . . as American as the McGuffey reader . . . the one-room schoolhouse and the spinster teacher who boarded nearby.*

schoolhouse, stable as a rock in a landscape. Homer, like the good journalist he is, does not miss the telling detail: the bandaged toe on the biggest boy, the feather in the cap of another, the loose suspender, the missing trouser button. The scene is as American as the McGuffey reader. It conjures up the one-room schoolhouse and the spinster teacher who boarded nearby. It is a memory of what it was like to run free under the sun, shoeless, schoolless, and choreless—until the cows came home. It is an instant of action, the click of a Kodak, a frame of time that will not come again but that lives forever.

The American critics were less unkind to Homer than the French critics were to Manet, probably because Homer's choice of subject never offended even the most tightly laced sense of Yankee decorum. On the other hand, the American novelist Henry James, before he departed the United States—forever—to live in Europe, wrote that he found Homer's work "damnably ugly" (as he did almost everything else in the United States). He detested Homer's subjects—his fences, his skies, his meadows, his "freckled straight-haired Yankee urchins," his maidens like "a dish of rural doughnuts and pie." Still, he conceded, there was something about Homer that he liked (though he did not say what). George Sheldon, one of Homer's early biographers, referring to the unfinished quality of Homer's work as well as to the fact that he was self-taught, put his criticism more felicitously: Homer's paintings have, he wrote, "an abundance of free touches made in inspired unconsciousness of rules."

Homer was in his mid thirties when he painted *Snap the Whip*. He would go on for nearly another four decades before he died at his home in Prout's Neck, Maine, at age seventy-four. His subjects changed greatly: from scenes of Americana to scenes of the sea. He showed its many moods and the awesome price it exacts from those who choose to defy it. Though he lived in seclusion for many years and had a reputation for being crusty, Homer was loved by the fisherfolk who were his neighbors. At his death, the press duly mourned him as a painter of the "American archetype." Perhaps the most telling tribute, however, came from a neighbor, the village postmaster: "He was a good man and a good citizen. If any man had a setback he was the first to help him. He was good to the poor. We shall miss him for a long time to come."

*Snap the Whip*, 1872, American. Oil on canvas. 55.9 × 92.7 cm. Courtesy of The Butler Institute of American Art, Youngstown, Ohio.

# JAMA®

## The Journal of the American Medical Association

July 1, 1988

# PAUL GAUGUIN

## Breton Girls Dancing, Pont-Aven

To all appearances, the young stock-broker at the banking firm of Bertin in Paris had everything going for him. Son of a liberal French journalist and a mother descended from the Peruvian nobility, he had just completed six years as a seaman, three on merchant ships working between Le Havre, Rio de Janeiro, and Scandinavian ports and three on a French naval cruiser. Now, at age twenty-five and established in his banking career for two years, he married a young woman from Copenhagen, Mette-Sophie Gad, and the couple settled, apparently for good, in Paris to raise their family. Paul Gauguin(1848-1903) seemed cured of the wanderlust and yearning for exotic places that had for so long afflicted him.

Occasionally, he painted, and in 1876 the Salon accepted one of his landscapes. At only age twenty-seven, he had won the approval of the same jury that had rejected (again) paintings by professionals such as Manet and Cézanne. Most remarkable, however, was this young stockbroker's keen eye for what was good among the newer painters. As a collector, he invested a considerable sum in paintings not only by Manet and Cézanne, but also by Pissarro, Renoir, Monet, Sisley, Guillaumin, Jongkind, Daumier, Degas, and Cassatt. And as he collected, he turned increasingly to painting his own works and also to sculpting. He was even represented in several exhibitions, though without critical success. In 1881, he spent his summer holiday painting in Pontoise with Pissarro and Cézanne. Then, in 1883, just after the birth of the couple's fifth child, a general economic crisis throughout France brought disaster. He lost his job in the bank. For a time, the family lived with Pissarro in Rouen while both men painted, but in 1884 the family had to return to the wife's home in Copenhagen.

In Copenhagen, he attempted to reestablish himself with a commercial firm, but his efforts were unsuccessful, as was an exhibit of his paintings and sculpture. Indeed, the exhibit was ordered closed by the Danish Academy. Nevertheless, in his own words, "penniless, up to the neck in squalor," with himself and his wife reduced to giving French lessons, he became ever more firmly committed to art and, moreover, to developing an entirely new type

*. . . they move gracefully, gravely, solemn as postulants in procession . . .*

of painting. Writing from Copenhagen in early 1885 to a former banking associate in Paris, he said, "As for myself, it seems to me at the moment that I am mad, and yet the more I brood at night in bed, the more I think I am right. . . . The farther I go into this question—the translation of thought into a medium other than literature—the more I am convinced of my theory—we shall see who is right. . . . Here I am tormented more than ever by art, and neither my money worries nor my quest for business can turn me aside from it." The words proved to be accurate: six months later, Gauguin, no longer a young man, gave up any further attempts at a business career. He left his wife and five children in Copenhagen and returned to Paris to devote himself henceforth to painting and sculpting exclusively.

Rejecting the Impressionist's notion that reality could be most accurately represented by reproducing exactly every nuance of color and every shimmer of light as they were presented to the eye, Gauguin worked instead for the broader transformation of thoughts, moods, and sensations into color and line. Originating in a literary movement, this concept became known as Symbolism, Synthetism, or Cloisonnisme. In its broadest interpretation, Symbolism included, in France, such painters as Moreau, Puvis de Chavannes, Redon, van Gogh, Bernard (who, with Gauguin, may be considered the founder), Denis, Sérusier, Vuillard, Bonnard, and Toulouse-Lautrec; in Belgium, it included Ensor; in Norway, Munch; in Switzerland, Hodler; in Russia, Vrubel; in Spain, Picasso; and in England, Burne-Jones, Beardsley, and Augustus John. Each artist devised a personal vocabulary of color and line to present his thought and emotions. Often the vocabulary is obscure; sometimes it is so personal as to make meaning almost inaccessible; always, however, the search is rewarding.

*Breton Girls Dancing, Pont-Aven* is one of Gauguin's earlier works in his new manner; it was completed in the summer of 1888 during his second stay on the Brittany coast. (Later that same year, during what turned out to be his tragic visit with van Gogh in Arles, Gauguin retouched the right hand of the girl on the left to satisfy a prospective buyer, who felt the hand had been given an importance it did not deserve.) In keeping with his belief in the near-mystical powers of certain lines and numbers—"noble lines" and "false lines," lines that "reach to infinity" and lines that "limit creation," "perfect triangles" and "elegant triangles," and the "figures 3 and 7"—Gauguin shows three Pont-Aven girls dancing on a hillside covered with the first cuttings of the hay. Arranged in a broken circle, they move

*Continued on p 207*

# JAMA®

The Journal of the American Medical Association

July 8, 1988

# DAVID TENIERS THE YOUNGER ✦

## The Surgeon

What the Italian astronomer Galileo saw in the skies of the seventeenth century, the Dutch naturalist Anton van Leeuwenhoek saw in a drop of water: a universe never before seen by the human eye—in the one case, a universe that was vast, majestic, and overpowering, in the other, a universe that was tiny, fragile, and fleeting. Each saw the same world, but from different perspectives, one through a telescope, the other through a microscope.

The Flemish painters of the seventeenth century also had widely separated perspectives. Some, like Rubens, saw everything on the grand scale: life was an epic, made up of heroes, robust gods and goddesses, decisive historical events, royalty in full dress. Others, like David Teniers the Younger (1610-1690), saw life in a smaller frame, in more intimate glimpses of what the common folk did every day, in their work, their eating and drinking, their fighting, their ailments, their loving. Some, like Rubens, trained their eye heavenward and saw the stars; others, like Teniers, looked inward and saw the significance of the insignificant things of a daily life that was as ordinary as a drop of water.

Teniers the Younger, so called because his father was also David and a painter, was born in Antwerp and received his training from his father. He became a master at the age of twenty-two and by age thirty-five was dean of the Academy of St Luke in Antwerp. He was a friend of Rubens and married the daughter of another well-known painter, Jan Brueghel. In 1651 Teniers moved to Brussels, where he entered the service of the archduke Leopold Wilhelm, regent of the Netherlands, as court painter and curator of the archduke's extensive art collection. In this latter capacity, he not only documented the pieces of the collection by making a

small copy of each, some 244 in all, but he also made paintings of the galleries showing how the pictures were hung, a feat of some historical interest today. Teniers was widowed in 1656 and married the daughter of the secretary of the Council of Brabant. In 1665 he helped found the Academy of Fine

> *. . . a daily life that was as ordinary as a drop of water.*

Arts in Antwerp, and in 1680, when he had reached the biblical quota of three score and ten years, he was granted the title of nobility he had so long sought.

More prolific than original (he is said to have produced some 2,000 paintings during his eighty-year life span), Teniers was exceedingly popular during his lifetime and his popularity continued throughout the following century. Today, he is best remembered for his genre paintings, small, extraordinary portrayals of the ordinary activities of daily life, activities that are mostly taken for granted and go unnoticed until an artist puts an eye on them. In this, Teniers is indebted to his Flemish contemporary, Adriaen Brouwer, who had trained his eye on the lusty, bawdy, lowbrow life of Flemish taverns. Teniers, on the other hand, had his eye on the market as well as on everyday life and refined these scenes into something that would be more acceptable to the Spanish aristocracy of the Netherlands.

*The Surgeon* is similar to a Brouwer painting entitled *The Village Quack*, in which Brouwer is very explicit in his opinion of the surgeon. Teniers has added several figures to the original group of three and has taken

out Brouwer's bitterness and sarcasm. What we have now is a quite respectable painting of the milieu of a barber-surgeon in the seventeenth-century Spanish Netherlands, from the master, who is opening a boil, to the journeyman, who prepares a patient for bloodletting, to the apprentice, who holds a dressing in readiness for the master. Scattered throughout the painting, like objects in a still life, are the trappings of the barber-surgeon's trade: various jars, bottles, flasks, and a barber bowl.

In the tradition of the time, moral commentary is furnished by the use of commonly understood symbols. The monkey chained to the ball and holding the apple, for instance, was used in Gothic art as a symbol for the fall of man and his imprisonment in ignorance. In Renaissance art, the apple was an attribute of the five senses, specifically taste, but when held by a monkey it signified an ungovernable appetite for any vice. In seventeenth-century Flemish painting, the monkey came to illustrate a popular saying, "Art is the ape of nature." In *The Surgeon*, the monkey apes the apprentice, who is still chained to his ignorance. The hourglass just above the monkey alludes to the passing of time, the human skull on the shelf to the fact that all will die, the master's purse and key to the power and possessions that death will take away, the globe to the world, and the fish (recalling Jonah's sojourn in the belly of the whale) to death and resurrection. More subtle is the draped curtain in the upper right corner; it suggests, perhaps, that "All the world's a stage and all the men and women, merely players," an idea that is reinforced by the drawing on the wall, which shows what appear to be characters acting on a stage. Finally, the man peering out of the window at the top often appeared

*Continued on p 207*

# JAMA®

## The Journal of the American Medical Association

July 15, 1988

# WALTER GILMAN PAGE

## *The Grandmother*

In the nineteenth century, especially in Scandinavia and France, but in other countries as well, a genre of painting emerged that concerned sickness, convalescence, invalidism, and death. It was in this tradition that the Boston-born Walter Gilman Page (1862-1934) painted *The Eve of Life* (also known as *The Grandmother*). Generally regarded as his masterpiece, it was painted at the end of his studies in Paris and was probably shown at the Salon of 1889. Theodore Child, a critic reviewing the Paris Salon of that year, complained of the great number of "funeral, dolorous, or elegiac" paintings in that exhibition, possibly including Page's among them. Another critic called attention to the "strongly drawn and expressive figure"; it reflected Page's academic training with Gustave Boulanger and Jules Lefebvre at the Académie Julian in Paris and his earlier study with Otto Grundmann at the Boston Museum School. On the other hand, Page's unromantic treatment of his subject harked back to the realism of Courbet (and looks forward to the new American realism to come after the turn of the century).

The pose of the woman in *The Grandmother* recalls Munch's powerful painting of only some three years earlier (could Page have seen it?) in which he shows his dying sister propped up in a chair, her face profiled against a white pillow, a table and a glass at the right. Munch's portrayal was an almost microscopic dissection of pain, a personal apocalypse of his own grief and guilt as well as of the anguish of his sister and his aunt. Page's view is more removed. It invites the viewer not so much to "feel" what it is to be old and sick but to reflect philosophically—at a certain distance—on old age and death in general. For example, the title is itself a triple pun: *The Eve of Life* can mean, most obviously, dying, the end of life, its twilight. Or, it can refer to a mother, or grandmother, or Eve, the grand Mother of Life. Or, finally, reflecting the society in which Page lived, it can be taken in a religious sense, signifying the brink of a new life, an afterlife.

The cheerless, drab color scheme of the painting, the heavy, square table and chair, and the coarse dress and shawl all attest to

> *Like violets, which put down roots in a harsh winter earth and survive to bloom all summer . . .*

the harsh environment in which the woman lives. Her heavily veined hands with their too-large widow's ring are witness to a life of hard work and now sickness. The tired eyes, which have seen her children and her children's children, and probably too much more besides, look at something unknown, weary still, but with some degree of interest. Whatever shape this unknown has we cannot see, but we sense that it belongs to her alone, and to no one else, and that it is even perhaps not entirely unwelcome. Intuitively, we know that she has a terminal illness; perhaps it involves the reproductive system. Like violets, which put down roots in a harsh winter earth and survive to bloom all summer, she also has survived a great deal and has bloomed. Now, she is like the violets in the glass beside her or the one in her hand, cut from their roots.

After his Paris studies, Page returned to the United States, where he worked and showed primarily in the Boston area. Very successful in portraiture, which included paintings of many well-known public figures in New England, he also did some history painting of the American past. He was active in civic affairs, serving in such capacities as member of the Boston School Board and the Boston Commission on Historic Sites and as chairman, in 1929, of the Massachusetts State Art Commission. One of the difficulties with his work, Page told a Chicago newspaper reporter in 1897, "is that I scarcely ever have anything to exhibit. Most of my works are orders, and once they are out of my hand I am at a loss for the wherewithal to make an exhibition." Thus, Page is not as widely known today as some of his American contemporaries, since much of his work remains in private collections and has yet to be distributed among public museums.

Page died in Nantucket, Massachusetts, on March 24, 1934, aged seventy-one.

*The Grandmother*, 1889, American. Oil on canvas. 92.4 × 73.3 cm. Courtesy of the Los Angeles County Museum of Art, Los Angeles, California; gift of Mrs Barney Kully.

# JAMA®

The Journal of the American Medical Association

August 12, 1988

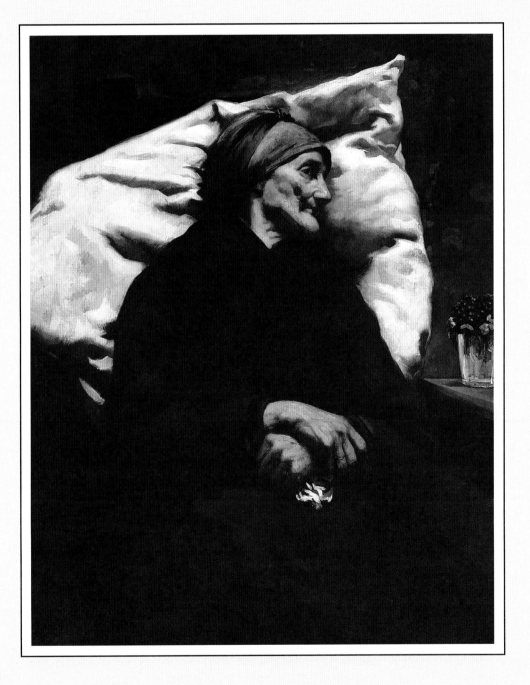

# CLAUDE MONET

## Woman With a Parasol—Madame Monet and Her Son

As a teenager in Le Havre, Claude Monet (1840-1926) had earned money for caricatures of local people, as well as a certain amount of fame. Now, twenty years later and a committed painter, he was also the father of a seven-year-old boy, the husband of Camille (née Doncieux), his twenty-eight-year-old model and former mistress, and the acknowledged leader of a group of painters derisively called Impressionists by the Paris critics. In constant flight from landlords and other creditors, Monet often begged his friends for sums as small as twenty francs in exchange for one of his landscapes—ironically, the same amount he had received for the caricatures of his teens. The couple's plight had been eased somewhat two years earlier when Camille's father had died, leaving her an inheritance, but that money had dwindled rapidly, and once again, in Argenteuil in the summer of 1875, the couple was in desperate financial straits. Nonetheless, Monet's inspiration continued unabated, and Camille, now often with their son Jean, continued as his model while he tested and retested his theories of light. Again and again, he shattered light into a thousand shards of color and then refitted them into the new version of reality he had seen. *Woman With a Parasol—Madame Monet and Her Son* belongs to this summer in Argenteuil.

With her parasol pointed at the sun, Camille stands atop a windy knoll while Jean stands a little apart, watching his father paint. Monet's low perspective silhouettes Camille's figure against the sky, like that of a goddess on a pedestal. Its pyramidal shape, in fact, recalls the shape the ancients gave to the sacred. The parasol, whose left edge bisects the figure of Jean and whose upper edge repeats the peplum of Camille's costume, serves to unite the figures of the mother and son. But the parasol serves another purpose as well. More important than its shape is its color. Blue on the top and green underneath, the parasol demonstrates Monet's theories of reflected light in shadows and unifies the scene as the parasol takes on the green of the grass beneath and the blue of the sky above. Moreover, the grass-colored shadow of the underside is then reflected downward over Camille's face, muting her flesh tones. Similarly, the yellow flowers not only add an accent to the grass but also introduce a note of complexity to the colors of Camille's

> *. . . he shattered light into a thousand shards of color . . .*

costume. In contrast, Jean's face, which is shaded only by the straw-colored brim of his hat and which is nearer the yellow flowers, is much rosier. Finally, Camille's figure, patterned against the sky as it is and softly contoured in the colors of the sky with just a touch of the color of the flowers at her feet, has an ethereal, translucent quality to it, both taking on the colors of her surroundings and dissolving into them. It is as though Monet is able to take air and to make it visible for a few seconds before it vanishes and reappears in a new form.

Thus, to the casual viewer, the painting is a pleasing composition of a woman with a parasol standing on a hill on a windy summer day, the parasol providing the painter with a clever method for demonstrating his theories of color. To Monet, however, Camille on a hillock in an Argenteuil summer was more: she was nothing less than the goddess of light on a mountain or, more simply, his sun. Tragically, the shadow across Camille's face in this otherwise tranquil scene is a shadow across Monet's sun as well. Little more than four years later, just months after the birth of the couple's second child, Camille would be dead. Her illness had begun that summer in Argenteuil. But even as she died, she was Monet's light. Seated at her deathbed, Monet made one last painting as the dawn light broke across her features, a haunting, spectral portrait in shifting tones of blues, yellows, and grays.

Like the molecular scientist who can break up DNA and shift its segments about, Monet could break up light into fragments of reality—in his case the glance of light off a leaf, the shimmer on a blade of grass—and reassemble them into a new reality, one that, astonishingly, turns out to be greater than the sum of its parts. Cézanne's oft-quoted remark that Monet was "only an eye, but what an eye!" may well be truthful, simply because, for Monet, to see was to paint. For us, to look at Monet is to see.

*Woman With a Parasol—Madame Monet and Her Son*, 1875, French. Oil on canvas. 100 × 81 cm. Courtesy of the National Gallery of Art, Washington, DC; collection of Mr and Mrs Paul Mellon.

# JAMA®

The Journal of the American Medical Association

August 19, 1988

# AUGUSTE RENOIR

## Claude Monet

The future Impressionist painters Auguste Renoir (1841-1919) and Claude Monet first met as students in 1862 in Paris when each was beginning his formal art training at the studio of Gleyre. Renoir was twenty-one, Monet twenty-two. Ten years later (the same year Monet would complete *Impression Sunrise*, surely the most famous title ever given a painting), Renoir and Monet were fast friends and working companions. United in their common pursuit of light—catching it in its various mutations from color to color and fixing it to the canvas—they would often set up their easels in front of the same motif, side by side, and proceed with the dots and comma strokes they had evolved in common. (Sometimes the finished paintings looked so much alike that, according to one story, when one of these "twin paintings" came to market fifty years later, neither Monet nor Renoir was at first able to identify who had done it.) In 1872, they were working together in Argenteuil, where Monet and his wife, Camille, had a small house. Monet stayed mostly with landscapes, painting figures more or less as an accompaniment to them, but Renoir was interested in painting the human figure in its own right. On several occasions he used Monet as his model, as well as Camille and the couple's son, Jean. Especially fascinating to Renoir in his portrait work was the challenge of catching the many lights reflected from human skin, whether it be the clear skin of a child, the dappled skin of a nude beneath a leafy tree, or the ruddy, outdoor complexion of a bearded man beside the fire in his home. *Claude Monet*, a portrait of his friend in a quiet, meditative mood, is Renoir's acceptance of this challenge.

In *Claude Monet*, Renoir demonstrates all he had learned in the previous ten years, not only during his brief study at Gleyre's and his several years of copying at the Louvre, but, most of all, from his intensive studies in the open air, before nature and the living model. Just as in the education of the physician, only so much can be learned from books and after that the student must go to

*. . . both the practice of painting and the practice of medicine are "the art of learning to see."*

the bedside and look at the patient and talk to the patient, the Impressionists knew intuitively that only so much could be learned from the masters; after that they had to go directly to nature herself if they were to learn her secrets. Line might be learned from a plaster cast and the laws of perspective from a book, but it was only by being with and meditating on nature that they could really begin to learn what she was about. The information found in books and plaster casts, while essential, is not the same as knowledge: knowledge came only when they placed themselves like servants before the living motif, gave it their whole attention, and waited for it to speak. Moreover, they needed to see the motif not only by itself, but also in context, in its own environment, with all the nuances of bouncing color and moving light changing constantly the way it was perceived, yet not its essence. A similar thing happens in

medicine when the physician learns to see the patient "in context." As in painting, a changing perspective gives a changing view. Indeed, perhaps it would not be too farfetched to say that both the practice of painting and the practice of medicine are "the art of learning to see."

Two years after *Claude Monet*, in 1874, the Impressionists, including Renoir and Monet, held their first group exhibition and received the name that has come to cover a multitude of styles, not all faithful to the intent of the original few. Seven more exhibitions were held between then and 1886; well before the last, however, both Monet and Renoir had become disenchanted with the Impressionist technique they had developed. Renoir, in fact, confessed that he hated it. Monet was having such difficulty with his painting that he wondered if he might not be going crazy. In December 1883, the two men took one more trip together, to the Côte d'Azur, in search of new motifs. It was the last time they worked together. When they returned, each set out in a different direction, Renoir concentrating more on line and Monet going still deeper into color.

Monet and Renoir lived well into the twentieth century, Monet until 1926, Renoir until 1919. Both worked right up until the end of their lives, Monet in spite of eye problems, Renoir in spite of severely crippled hands. In order for Renoir to paint, in fact, someone had to fasten the brushes between his fingers. Renoir was seventy-eight when he died at Cagnes-sur-Mer; his genius was undiminished. Monet was eighty-six when he died in Giverny; he had just completed what may have been the most ambitious project of his life, a room of

*Continued on p 207*

# JAMA®

## The Journal of the American Medical Association

August 26, 1988

# HENRI MATISSE  〜

## *The Anemones*

When the French painter Henri Matisse (1869-1954) died at his home in Nice in November 1954, he was just a few weeks shy of his eighty-fifth birthday and doing some of his most innovative work. News accounts in the United States hailed him as the "master of pure color" and called him "one of the most joyous artists of the 20th century." Earlier, when at the age of eighty he had won the grand prize at the Venice Biennial Art Fair (the same year that John Marin, Jackson Pollock, and Willem de Kooning represented the Americans), he was called "a brilliant colorist." Yet, had it not been for the almost unbearable tedium Matisse suffered during a long recovery from appendicitis when he was a youth, the world would not be seeing color in quite the same fashion as it does today. Whereas the Impressionists began with the concept of light and tried to reproduce each of its colors on the canvas, Matisse started with the concept of color and, strictly by its placement on the canvas, tried to create light itself. In so doing he became identified as the leader of *Les Fauves*, or "the wild beasts," a group so dubbed by a Paris art critic when he saw the works of several Paris avant-garde painters hanging together in the same room at the Salon d'Autonme in 1905. By 1908, having little in common except the artificially imposed name, the group disbanded, each to go in his own direction. The label, however, survived and is a constant tribute to the risks Matisse took with color.

During his growing-up years as the son of a grain merchant in a town in the far north of France, Matisse showed no especial talent for or interest in drawing nor, apparently, in anything else. It was a given, however, that he would prepare for a professional career; accordingly, he studied

Latin and Greek at the local lycée. In due time he went to Paris to study law and, returning home at the completion of his studies, settled down to become a law clerk. It was then that appendicitis intervened; to ease his boredom during recovery, his mother gave him a box of paints. "Henceforth," Matisse said, "I did not lead my life. It led me."

And indeed it did. Always obsessive and full of anxiety, Matisse found that when he painted he could oftentimes, though not always, relieve those feelings. At other times he would face his easel in dread and in panic, with all the symptoms of acute anxiety: visible trembling, sweating, crying,

> *. . . he would face his easel in dread and in panic, with all the symptoms of acute anxiety . . .*

and violent impulses. Yet, with time, he learned that his feelings as he was working were often the best measure of how well he was succeeding at what he was trying to do, which was no more and no less than trying to give a visible form to the self he was experiencing at that particular time. By intensely observing his own reactions to the choice of a color or the placement of a line, he learned to express this concept. "I am unable to distinguish between the feeling I have for life and my way of expressing it," he said. Moreover, when he felt peace and harmony replace obsession and anxiety, he knew he had found release and that the painting was finished. "A moment comes," he said, "when every part has found its definite

relationship, and from then on it would be impossible for me to add a stroke to my picture without having to paint it all over again." He wished the same state of repose to his viewers: "What I dream of is an art of balance, of purity and serenity devoid of troubling or depressing subject-matter, an art which might be for every mental worker, be he businessman or writer, something like a good armchair in which to rest from physical fatigue." So confident, in fact, was Matisse of the ability of his paintings to calm an ill or troubled person that he would leave one with an ailing person as a proxy for his presence while he himself went off to paint.

One such painting of repose is *The Anemones*, painted when Matisse was in his midfifties and living in Nice. As always with a Matisse work, the painting is at once simple and sumptuous: simple because it is a vase of common flowers on a family dining table, sumptuous because of the richness of the color and the complexity of the design; simple with the clear, flat light of the south of France, sumptuous with the fussiness left over from the interior decoration style of the nineteenth century; simple in its three background colors of blue, green, and yellow ocher, sumptuous in the arabesques as sinuous as the lines of a woman's torso; simple as an orange and a lemon, sumptuous as the deep resonance of yellow against blue, orange against red and yellow. Geometrically, the painting is a study in contrasts: large, rectilinear shapes held together at their center by a fat, pear-shaped vase flanked on either side by a tall elliptical compote and spheres of fruit. In terms of color, however, the painting becomes more difficult. Two purple diagonal lines at the far left seem not to belong. In fact, they create a sense of tension or of uneasiness, of slippage

*Continued on p 208*

# JAMA®

The Journal of the American Medical Association

September 2, 1988

# JOAN MIRÓ

## The Farm

His name, the art critic Robert Hughes reminds us, is Spanish for "he looked." And look he did, for more than ninety years. Born in Barcelona, he was the son of a watchmaker and goldsmith and, on his mother's side, grandson of a highly successful cabinetmaker. In grammar school, he dreamed of being "a great engineer or a great doctor," though, by his own admission, he was a very poor student and "understood nothing about the practical sciences." His one solace during that period was drawing lessons, which he took after school hours. "That class was like a religious ceremony for me," he said. "The implements were like sacred objects, and I worked as though I were performing a religious rite." This feeling was to persist throughout his life. In the meantime, however, he failed his high school studies, and, because his parents did not consider painting or drawing a suitable choice for a life career, he was enrolled in a commercial school to learn business.

At age seventeen, he was placed at an import firm as a bookkeeping assistant and he dropped his art studies. For nearly two years he lived in increasing rebellion and despair until, finally, he had a mental and physical breakdown. During his long recovery, he stayed at the family farm near the village of Montroig, in a typically Catalan countryside not far from Barcelona. It was during this period of prolonged inactivity that he decided to make a firm commitment to art. Though they still failed to understand his choice, his parents dropped their opposition. Thus it was that the farm at Montroig became for him a second birth, this time into a world in which he felt he belonged. Ten years later, he would paint that world in *The Farm*. He was Joan Miró (1893-1983), Catalan, painter, poet, sculptor, ceramist, "last of the forefathers" (as Hughes has called him), first of the Surrealists, and the twentieth century's own Hieronymus Bosch.

Miró, who from 1919 on would divide his time each year among Montroig, Barcelona, and Paris, began work on *The Farm* in 1921, when he was in his late twenties and had just returned to Montroig after a failed one-man show in Paris. He continued work on it

> *. . . little things,*
> *that only children and*
> *invalids might see . . .*

in Barcelona, but did not finish it until the following year, in Paris. Art historians usually characterize this painting as belonging to the end of Miró's "first period," coming just before he moved into Surrealism, or "suprareality." On the other hand, as Jacques Dupin, Miro's principal biographer, notes, *The Farm* is not to be considered a summary or a résumé of Miró's work up to that point; it is, rather, a synthesis in which he is reconciling opposing forces within himself before moving to another level of awareness.

*The Farm* is, of course, Miró's remembered farm of childhood, of convalescence, of rebirth, of commitment to art. And, in spite of the appearance of an unforgiving earth, a merciless sun, empty ears of grain, and a scrawny eucalyptus tree, all of which become seared into the mind like some half-remembered catastrophe, there are happy and hopeful things to be remembered as well, little things, that only children and invalids might see: a lizard, a snail, some rabbits, a goat, a barking dog, a tiny woman working, a large child, pigeons, roosters, chicken wire, various buckets, a red spout on a watering can, a trestle table and a stepladder (each in the shape of the letter "A"), a donkey grinding grain. The footprints that end so mysteriously are part of Miró's special vocabulary and reflect the importance he attached to the foot. Humans, he often recalled, are rooted to the earth through their feet, but they are free of the earth the moment they lift a foot to walk. Especially remarkable is the extent and realism of the detail Miró lavished on each of the objects in the painting, detail that has caused some to liken him to Henri Rousseau or Hieronymus Bosch. The story is told of how he even carried grass from Montroig in his suitcase so as to be able to continue work on the painting when he was in Paris.

Later paintings would move more into fantasy and abstraction, but Miró always insisted that even the most abstract of his forms had its roots in a real object, an object that one could touch. *The Farm* is significant because it announces many of the directions he would follow. He himself believed it to be the source of all his later work. His colleagues realized its importance immediately. Dealers, however, were reluctant to take it and for several years the painting languished, until one day Ernest Hemingway, a friend of Miró, bought it for 5,000 francs.

Miró died in December 1983, aged ninety, of a respiratory ailment.

*The Farm*, 1921/1922, Spanish. Oil on canvas. 123.8 × 141.3 cm. Courtesy of the National Gallery of Art, Washington, DC; gift of Mary Hemingway.

# JAMA®

September 9, 1988

The Journal of the American Medical Association

# AUDREY FLACK ❧

## Royal Flush

In northern Europe in the seventeenth century, and chiefly in post-Reformation Holland, where the painting of religious figures was discouraged, there arose a type of painting known as *vanitas*, so called after Qoheleth's opening words in Ecclesiastes, "Vanity of vanities! All is vanity!" Basically a form of still life, in which humble, everyday household objects such as tableware, food, and flowers were celebrated in paintings for the common people, the *vanitas* painting narrowed its focus to include only those objects that would admonish the viewer to keep always in mind the briefness and uncertainty of life on earth: an hourglass to show the passage of time, a burning candle to show the irretrievability of time, a mirror to suggest that all that is seen is illusion, coins or jewelry to reiterate the message of the emptiness of power and possessions, flowers to remind the viewer that what springs up in the morning is withered by nightfall, a butterfly to recall that all, including the beautiful, return to dust, and a skull to reinforce the awareness that all die. In *Royal Flush*, a modern interpretation of the *vanitas* theme, the American painter Audrey Flack (1931-     ) has found new words for the expression of this centuries-old message.

Beginning as an Abstract Expressionist, during which time she was strongly influenced by the work of Jackson Pollock, Flack turned gradually to representational painting because she wanted to communicate with as large an audience as possible. "It is important for me that the objects I depict are easily recognized by the viewer," she says. Especially innovative, however, is the method she adopted for depicting these objects. Much as another artist might put a preliminary drawing on the canvas, Flack puts a camera image on the canvas. With the assistance of photographer Jeanne Hamilton, she takes numerous photographs of the still life arrangements she sets up; each photograph shows the objects in a different arrangement. When she finally has a photograph with the arrangement she wants, the image is projected onto a giant canvas. Using both filament brushes and airbrush, Flack then outlines and fills in the image with color until she has completed her message. With this method, it is possible to finish only three or four large canvases a year. As Flack herself defines her work, she is neither a Realist in the sense that she tries to faithfully

> *"Vanity of vanities!*
> *All is vanity!"*

mirror reality, nor a Photo-Realist in that she copies a photograph. Rather, she is a Super-Realist, one who "often exaggerates reality, bringing it into sharp focus at some points and blurring it at others."

In *Royal Flush,* one of these updated *vanitas* still lifes, the burning candle has been replaced by a lighted cigarette, as well as by a cigar, while a mechanical watch substitutes for the hourglass. The passage of time is further underscored by the melting ice cubes in the whiskey and by the beer that is going flat. Again, the position of the hands on the face of the watch suggests that for the players "the candle burns at both ends." The bills and coins remain as symbols of power, but the mirror has been transformed into the reflecting surfaces of glass, cellophane, metal, ice, and liquid. For poker fans, as Flack herself is, the pair of aces at top left is not a bad hand, but, with the ace of spades on top, it indicates death and thus takes the place of

the skull in the Dutch *vanitas* paintings. Moving to the right, the queens and eights are a full house, a good hand by any standard, but, as the viewer will see, still not good enough to collect the pot. Down and to the right, beneath the glass of beer, the cards are face down, indicating a player who has "folded," one who is saying in advance that he cannot win and therefore will not play. Finally, in the center of the painting, accented by the crossing diagonals of cigarette and cigar, is a royal flush, the very best hand it is possible to have in a game of poker. In hearts, the royal flush opposes the ace of spades, suggesting that although death does exist, it is overcome by love.

The symbolism of the painting as a whole may be read on many levels, depending on the viewer. For example, life is indeed, as is often suggested, a game of chance, but, like a poker hand, the outcome depends on not only what cards one has been dealt, but also how well one plays them. On another level, the viewer is shown a catalog of addictive behaviors and substances that can be harmful to health: gambling, tobacco, alcohol, salt, polluted air, and insufficient sleep. To escape unharmed from such behaviors would indeed be as rare as being dealt a royal flush. Or again, the viewer is reminded of the precarious nature of life and health by the cigarette, which balances on the rim of the ashtray. As time passes, the ash will lengthen until, finally, the cigarette will fall onto the table instead of into the ashtray.

Just as in a seventeenth-century *vanitas*, however, the weight of the message is lightened by the delight of the eye. *Royal Flush* is a maze of angles and circles, cylinders and cubes, a feast of surfaces. Lines oppose and parallel each other, shapes echo and complement one another (the

*Continued on p 208*

# JAMA®

The Journal of the American Medical Association

September 16, 1988

# PIETER DE MOLIJN

## Landscape With Open Gate

When the first golden rays of the seventeenth century broke across Europe, they focused on a tiny, newly formed republic on the North Sea. Less than a generation earlier, this country of some three million persons had been seven separate provinces of the northern Netherlands, vassals of the wide-flung kingdom of Spain. Now, self-determining in government, economics, commerce, banking, and politics, as well as in her religious, cultural, and social life, she joined England and Spain as a world power. With little land to plow, she made the most of it and fought the sea for more. But her genius was to plow the seas themselves, sending out ships with cargoes of colonists to settle new land and establish new trading companies and bringing back ships full of imports that would create European markets for such exotic goods as tulip bulbs and tea. The market economy in this new country was thriving and its citizens were prosperous; Holland, as she was called after the largest province of the union, would bask in the rays of this golden age for nearly one hundred years. In many respects, these united provinces of the seventeenth century were like the Florence of the fifteenth century, except for two important aspects: there was no large aristocracy and there was no institutional church.

Until this time, painters in most countries had been supported by the patronage of the wealthy, usually that of the church and of the royal court. Indeed, in other countries, for example in the case of Rubens in the Spanish Netherlands, artists were still supported in that manner. The loss of this royal and ecclesiastical patronage in Holland affected its painting in several ways. For example, large historical, mythological, or religious paintings were no longer

called for. What was wanted were paintings of the citizens of this rapidly developing country: their daily comings and goings, their homes, and their countryside with its wide skies and always present sea. If a painting pointed a moral, so much the better. These paintings should be small

> *. . . a Dutch sky that always carries in itself something of the sea.*

enough to be hung on the wall of a burgher's home. Large paintings had gone the way of the wealthy patron. The new patron was Everyman. Perforce, the painter became a small-business person, supplying products whose prices rose or fell as in the other markets, that is, according to the laws of supply and demand (though there was not the wild speculation that characterized some markets, such as the tulip bulb market). As noted by Simon Schama in *The Embarrassment of Riches*, a small landscape could sell for as little as one guilder (though most went for an average of three or four guilders), a price that could be doubled or tripled if the painting had a fine frame. By way of comparison, a lady's chemise or a man's shirt cost one guilder, while a midwife received about two-and-a-half guilders for attending a birth. If a painter specialized in painting only one or two scenes again and again, as many did, it was possible to turn out a landscape a day.

Among the many painters working in Holland at this time was Pieter de Molijn (1595-1661). Though he is ranked among the masters of seventeenth-century Dutch

landscape, the scant details of de Molijn's life can be pieced together only from what little has been left behind in official records. Baptized in London on April 6, 1595, by 1616 de Molijn was a master of the Guild of St Luke in Haarlem. Over the next thirty years, he would hold many administrative posts in the Haarlem Guild. He joined the local militia in 1624 and also married Mayken Gerards. He died at the age of sixty-five and was buried in Haarlem on March 23, 1661. At one time, de Molijn was thought to have been a pupil of Frans Hals, but now he is believed to have been a student of Esaias van de Velde and also to have had some contact with Jan van Goyen, both outstanding landscape painters. Among his own pupils was the genre painter Gerard Terborch.

*Landscape With Open Gate* is among de Molijn's earliest dated works, believed to have been produced about 1626, when he was in his early thirties. It is typical of his early work in that it retains the three-color scheme of sixteenth-century Mannerist landscape: brown foreground, green midground, and bluish background. On the other hand, the work reflects the new style of Dutch landscape in its low horizon line and wide sky. Most characteristic of de Molijn himself, however, are the strong, rising diagonals and the sandy, curving slope. The tiny figures, just barely seen at the crest of the road and in the shadow of the cottage and fence, are somewhat of a surprise; usually de Molijn painted his figures on a larger scale. However, he leaves no doubt as to the subject of the painting: shining full on the crest of the sandy road, on the open gate, and on the dying oak tree (the painting's moral?), it is light. It is specifically Dutch light, light reflected from a Dutch sky that always carries in itself

*Continued on p 208*

# JAMA

The Journal of the American Medical Association

September 23/30, 1988

# MATTHEW ARNOLD BRACY SMITH ✑

## Peaches

There is probably no English painter so widely admired among those who care for the plastic arts," wrote Sir John Rothenstein in his three-volume *Modern English Painters*. But the apprenticeship of Matthew Arnold Bracy Smith (1879-1959), third of five children born into a well-to-do Yorkshire family, was a long one and it was a difficult one. Sickly as a child (his biographer calls him "neurasthenic"), he turned to drawing to ease his loneliness, but he remained too morbidly shy to claim any special recognition for this talent. Indeed, his father discouraged his interest in art. When he left school, his father took him into the family business, but business was an occupation for which the young man proved to be singularly unsuited. Finally, when Matthew was in his midtwenties, his father gave him permission to enter the Slade School of Art in London for formal training, though neither his father nor the school's director expressed any faith in his talents.

Two years later, apparently because of the pressures he felt were on him to succeed, Smith suffered a breakdown and left the Slade. On recovery, however, he managed to secure his father's permission to study painting abroad, provided he did not go to Paris. Thus it was that at age twenty-seven Smith went to Brittany, to Pont-Aven, because he knew that was where Gauguin once had worked. "Here," he later told Rothenstein, "my life began." But it would be nearly another twenty years before Smith would achieve his mature style, a vision that he could call uniquely his own. And here,

*. . . the colors of an English summer . . . recollected into an autumn bowl of fruit.*

from Pont-Aven, except for one period between 1934 and 1940 when he lived in Aix-en-Provence, would begin an odyssey of frequent comings and goings and changes of studio and residence throughout Britain and France (including Paris) that would not end until Smith died in London, aged seventy-nine.

*Peaches*, completed when Smith was in his late fifties, belongs to his mature style. His harvest is abundant, a rich vintage ripened from the best of Postimpressionism, from the Fauves, van Gogh, Gauguin, Munch, and Cézanne; we see the sharp color contrasts of Derain and Vlaminck, the sinuous curves of Matisse, the heavy, almost leaded outlines of Rouault, the bold forms of Gauguin, the restless strokes and golden yellows of van Gogh's wheat fields, the lonely greens and blues of Munch, the awkwardness of Cézanne's apple still lifes. *Peaches* is all of these, and yet it is none of these; it is a new creation. For all its proclaimed boldness and expressionistic heritage, it yet has a subtle shyness that is unmistakably Smith's own. It is his invitation, muted, though nonetheless heartfelt, to share with him all the colors of an English summer of sea and sky and city recollected into an autumn bowl of fruit.

Smith died on September 22, 1959, after a lengthy illness. In his last years, this lonely but friendly and much-admired painter was knighted in recognition of his work. He left more than a thousand paintings, sketches, and drawings, which were later bequeathed to the Corporation of London.

*Peaches*, 1937, English. Oil on canvas. 60 × 73 cm. Courtesy of the Tate Gallery, London, England/Art Resource, New York, New York.

# JAMA®

The Journal of the American Medical Association

October 7, 1988

# JOHN MARIN ❧

## Grey Sea

Only now, thirty-five years after his death, are the oil paintings of John Marin (1870-1953) beginning to be fully appreciated. During his lifetime, and for nearly a quarter of a century thereafter, it was his watercolors that had pride of place among his works. They alone were enough to assure him of a permanent place as an American master. Often mentioned in the same breath as those of Homer, who worked a generation earlier, the only similarity between the two artists is that both had a special love for the seacoast of Maine.

Marin was born in Rutherford, New Jersey, two days before Christmas of 1870. By New Year's Day the infant's mother had died, and his father took him to Weehawken to be raised by his maternal grandmother and two maiden aunts. Marin's school years were undistinguished by anything except that he loved to roam the countryside near his home and sketch landscapes and animals. Eventually his sketching led, when he was in his late teens, to delicate water-color landscapes, but neither he nor anyone else apparently took his talent seriously. He was, as he often said of his painting in later years, just "playing around with paint." In his twenties, he tried several jobs, both in business and in architecture (he built six houses), but he seemed suited for none. Finally, when he was nearly thirty, he entered the Pennsylvania Academy of the Fine Arts; he stayed for two years. He also spent some time at the Art Students League in New York City. Again, however, there was nothing especially memorable about these years, except that he did at last decide to make a serious commitment to painting. In 1905, at the age of thirty-five, he left for what was to be five years in Europe, financed by his father. Marin's laconic summary of that time is that he learned to

play billiards; he also learned to make etchings and he exhibited several water-colors. An oil painting ("unremarkable," says his biographer) was bought by the French government for the Luxembourg Museum.

The real turning point in Marin's career came in 1909. Through a friend from art school, he met the American photographer Edward Steichen in Paris, who in turn showed Marin's work to his friend and fellow photographer Alfred Stieglitz. Steichen and Stieglitz owned a gallery in New York City where they were interested in showing "art-in-photography" photographs and the "anti-photographic" in painting. Marin's watercolors were exactly what they

> *"The wind has changed. Now the west wind blows. . . . Autumn is here—Enjoy it."*

wanted and a show was arranged. Reviews of the show compared Marin with Whistler and Matisse; his career was launched. He was forty. Meanwhile, he returned to New Jersey, where he married Marie Jane Hughes. Until she died in 1945, she accompanied him almost daily on his painting trips. The couple's only child, John Marin IV, was born in November 1914. The year is memorable in Marin's life for another reason as well: he had found his "spiritual home," the coast of Maine. For nearly forty years, the family would spend winters in New Jersey and summers in Maine. Marin even bought his own island.

During the summer of 1938, Marin was living in a house in Addison, Maine, on Cape Split, a place he was to love more

dearly than any other. His house was so close to the ocean that he could watch the "water abreaking on that ledge outside." After several decades of doing watercolors, he had resumed painting in oils, and it was sheer delight to him to work up the paint into its own little mountains of impasto. It was also a summer of especially bad weather and angry seas. In September, an "unusually destructive" hurricane, according to meteo-rologic records, ravaged Long Island and lower New England for nearly two weeks. Before it ended, its winds had topped 180 mph and it had claimed six hundred lives, as well as leaving $306 million in property damage. From his home in Maine, Marin captured the turbulent waters of that September in *Grey Sea*. Marin's creativity was far from spent. He was sixty-seven.

*Grey Sea* is painted in the often cryptic vocabulary Marin had developed: "Chinese hieroglyphics," as one critic called it. But always there are the triangles and parts of triangles, which are both mystical and structural. In some places, the sides of triangles are joined to form an *M*, his and his son's last initial and his wife's first initial. In other places, they are impastos of color, like forests of pine trees. Still others have peaks that have been worn down and flattened into flowing curves, like a land-scape of ancient mountains. Most mysterious is the large central triangle, built to enclose the small green triangles. It looms up in the center of the painting like a schooner under sail—the ghost of a schooner. But it is essential, for about its peak pivots the entire weight of the sea, like the weight of the centuries.

Marin thought musically and he painted musically. There is always rhythm, harmony, point and counterpoint, and, in the end, resolution. His favorite composer was Bach

*Continued on p 208*

# JAMA®

## The Journal of the American Medical Association

**October 14, 1988**

# PETER PAUL RUBENS

## Portrait of Clara Serena Rubens

For the sheer magnitude and range of its accomplishments, the life of Peter Paul Rubens (1577-1640) looms as large as, and can be as intimidating as, one of his giant history or mythology paintings. And, if as is often said (only partly in jest, one suspects), life does indeed sometimes imitate art, then Rubens' life may be called a tapestry of gods and goddesses as rich in texture and as intriguing in design as the most Baroque of any of his works.

Born in Westphalia, Rubens was the son of Jan Rubens, a Calvinist lawyer from Antwerp living in political and religious exile, and Maria (Pypelincks) Rubens. When the boy was ten, Jan died (having first been reconciled to the Catholic church) and Maria took Peter and his younger brother Philip back to Antwerp. There, at age thirteen, Rubens entered the royal court as page to the Countess Lalaing and was also, over the next several years, apprenticed to the painters Tobias Verhaect, Adam van Noort, and Otto van Veen. At age twenty-one, Rubens became a member of the painters' Guild of St Luke in Antwerp, signifying that he was a master and now could himself engage apprentices. Two years later, he went to Italy as court painter to the Duke of Mantua, beginning a series of journeys to courts in Italy and Spain, where he copied and delivered pictures to their royal members. With the death of his mother in 1608, however, Rubens returned to Antwerp, again working under royal patronage. A year later, he married Isabella Brandt, daughter of an Antwerp lawyer, and together they settled down to a life blessed with gifts of every sort.

Rubens' daily routine attests to his enormous energy, both physical and creative: he rose at 4 AM, attended Mass, worked until 5 PM, and then went riding for exercise and relaxation. His large studio, which employed many assistants (among them were van Dyck, Jordaens, and Snyders), attracted there probably as much by Rubens' personal magnetism as by his growing eminence, was equally well regulated. With the birth of his and Isabella's first child, Clara Serena, in early 1611, it seemed that little remained to be desired. But tragedy was not far behind. Shortly after Clara Serena's birth, Rubens' only brother and close companion Philip, by then a leading Stoic scholar in Antwerp, died. Whatever Rubens' personal grief may have been, however, his creativity and already enormous output were, if anything, enhanced. By 1615,

> *To Clara Serena . . . he was clearly and simply "Father."*

still short of his fortieth birthday, Rubens had become the leader of the Antwerp school of painting and the master of the Flemish Baroque. His studio turned out huge history paintings, some of them a roomful of scenes chronicling the entire life of a single royal personage, as well as allegories, myths, and religious subjects; both themes and subjects were larger than life and all were suitable to the prevailing Counter-Reformation mood of the Spanish Netherlands. Sometimes an entire room was dedicated to scenes from the life of a single royal personage.

But Rubens was not a history machine nor merely a studio manager. He could also paint small, delicate, intimate portraits intended for no other purpose than to express his joy. One such work is *Portrait of Clara Serena Rubens*, a picture of his oldest child,

painted when she was five and Rubens, at thirty-nine, at the peak of his powers. Painted on canvas hardly larger than a piece of today's business stationery, the portrait is as far from Rubens' giant goddesses and weeping Magdalens as David is from Goliath. With her untroubled brow and clear steady gaze, the child is as Rubens named her: Clara Serena. Yet there is an awareness about her that edges into the innocence, a sense of her own privacy, a sense of herself, a sense of her own growing knowledge and powers. Nonetheless, the look is one of utter trust in that what she sees is good. Even as he paints this beloved daughter, however, Rubens puts a hint of shadow across her brow as a kind of foreboding only he can see. Clara Serena, his only daughter, died when she was twelve. Nor was tragedy finished. Three years later, in 1626, Isabella died, leaving Rubens, however, with two sons.

Rubens grieved by working. From 1625 to 1630, he undertook a series of strenuous and highly secret diplomatic missions (in the form of what perhaps today might be called shuttle diplomacy) between the Spanish Netherlands, England, Spain, and Holland in efforts to secure peace. For these efforts, Rubens was knighted by Charles I of England and ennobled by the king of Spain. Nor did Rubens' appetite for personal happiness fail him. In 1630, at age fifty-three, he married Hélène Fourment, the sixteen-year-old daughter of an Antwerp tapestry merchant. (Had Clara Serena lived, she would have been three years older than her stepmother.) Over the next ten years, Rubens would immortalize Hélène in many secular paintings (some of which she subsequently wanted destroyed), while she bore him five children, the last born after his death in Antwerp at the age of sixty-three.

*Continued on p 208*

# JAMA®

The Journal of the American Medical Association

**October 21, 1988**

# PAUL CÉZANNE

## *Harlequin*

In 1888, when Paul Cézanne (1839-1906) began work on *Harlequin*, he was rapidly approaching his fiftieth birthday; he had yet to earn a living. Two years earlier, in 1886, his life had undergone a number of major changes. He had married the mother of his then fourteen-year-old son and his father had died. Tightfisted and tyrannical in life, the elder Cézanne had left his only son a sizable fortune. Also in 1886, Émile Zola, Cézanne's close friend—both when they were boys in Aix and students and artists in Paris—published his novel *L'Oeuvre*, an admitted roman à clef about the Impressionists and their followers in Paris. Many people, including Cézanne, believed that Sidney Lantier, the impotent protagonist of *L'Oeuvre* who kills himself in front of a grandly conceived canvas he is unable to complete, was in fact Cézanne. Actually, Lantier was a composite of many painters Zola knew, but as far as Cézanne was concerned the model was clear. The friendship was ruptured, never to regain its former intimacy.

Save for one time, when he was admitted through the offices of a friend on the jury, Cézanne had been consistently rejected at the Salon, year after year. When he showed his work at several of the Impressionists' exhibitions, it was ridiculed for its clumsiness and lack of drawing as cruelly as that of Manet at the Salon. Yet Cézanne slogged on, shutting himself up day after day, year after year, sometimes in Paris, more often in Aix, by turns exalting or despairing, cursing or quiet, overly aggressive or flatly timid, hopeful and full of doubts, arrogant and touchingly humble, suspicious of all and hopelessly naive. In a single day he could destroy fifteen canvases in a rage and then spend two years working on one.

Constantly, he complained that he could not express himself, that his brush could not put his sensations on the canvas. He was a battleground for wars of ambivalence. He was deserted by one-time supporters. Zola, for example, who had considerable influence

> *. . . hopeful and full of doubts, arrogant and touchingly humble, suspicious of all and hopelessly naive. . . . the protagonist of his own tragicomedy.*

by this time, had, in addition to his novel, concluded that while his boyhood friend had once showed promise, he had not realized it and would not ever realize it. Cézanne, however, was convinced that he had something new to say. He became the protagonist of his own tragicomedy.

*Harlequin*, painted during these critical years, 1888 to 1890, is in many senses a self-portrait. A harlequin, for example, was once a demon, either a spirit of genius or an evil spirit that caused undesirable emotions or traits. A demon could also be a supernatural force, driving its host to extraordinary accomplishments. In Cézanne's day, a harlequin was a tragic character in a play who was supposed to make people laugh, a sort of buffoon. He wore a mask, carried a wooden sword, kept his shaved head under a captain's hat, and acted in pantomime. But while he clowned on the outside, he wept on

the inside. Cézanne's *Harlequin* stands center stage, wearing the familiar variegated tights, patterned into diamond-shaped tears. The wooden sword, which could hardly protect *Harlequin* in a battle, is Cézanne's paintbrush and is a sham. The hat of authority (for did not Zola promise Cézanne that one day the two of them would rule a new school?) is askew, while the face mask has no mouth: Cézanne, like *Harlequin*, cannot express himself. Only the hands are not in costume. They are Cézanne's own, large and clumsy and awkward, unable to make a finished drawing or a polished Salon piece. But they are powerful and destined to open a whole new century of painting.

In spite of diabetes diagnosed about the time *Harlequin* was finished, Cézanne worked on, indefatigable as ever, for another sixteen years. The angles of his personality became less acute as he aged, widening into less frequent and milder emotional upsets, but his suspiciousness, if anything, increased. Yet on the rare occasions when he entertained, he was considered a generous and gracious host. For the most part, however, he remained in seclusion, leaning for emotional support on his sister Marie, his son Paul, and his religious devotions. He died at his home in Aix on October 22, 1906, aged sixty-seven.

*Harlequin*, 1888/1890, French. Oil on canvas. 101.1 × 65.7 cm. Courtesy of the National Gallery of Art, Washington, DC; collection of Mr and Mrs Paul Mellon.

# JAMA®

The Journal of the American Medical Association

**October 28, 1988**

# PIETRO LONGHI

## *The Faint*

As described by John Julius Norwich in *A History of Venice*, eighteenth-century Venice was the pleasure capital of Europe. Untroubled by wars that racked the rest of the Continent, she was the obligatory stop on everyone's grand tour. In Venice, the gambling was the most exciting and best organized anywhere and the courtesans the most accommodating. Venice was also the city of the *cicisbeo*, a kind of permanent escort for a married woman whose husband was often away, and of Giacomo Casanova and easy annulments. There were also churches to visit and plays, operas, painting, sculpture, and all kinds of music. Venice indeed provided a well-rounded, well-nourished life for residents and wanderers alike. One could feed the mind, stir the emotions, titillate the senses, rouse the passions, or salve the soul. The Inquisitors were lenient; they heard so few cases that their number had been reduced to one. For the English there were the *veduti*, or views of the Grand Canal, by Canaletto and Bellotto, which they took home in bunches. Meanwhile, however, as Venice played, the republic declined. In 1789, Venice saw its last election of a doge, the 118th in a nearly unbroken line from the year 726; before the century ended Napoleon's troops were in the piazza. It was the first time in over a thousand years that foreigners other than visitors had occupied Venice.

The beginning of the century had seen the birth of Pietro Longhi (1702-1785). If it is to Canaletto and his nephew Bellotto that we are indebted for their views of the eighteenth-century Venetian canals and buildings, then it is to Longhi and his son Alessandro that we are indebted for their views of Venetian citizens. While Alessandro is known primarily for portraits, his father is the master of the small genre scene,

showing the Venetians in activities of daily life. Unlike the Dutch genre painters of a century before, who painted scenes of humble folk at home or bawdy scenes of tavern low life, Longhi chose intimate scenes from the lives of the rich and aristocratic as well as the poor and humble. *The Faint*, which he painted about midway through the century, might in fact be called, in contrast to a Dutch low-life scene, a glimpse of high jinks in the drawing room.

The action in *The Faint* (at one time known as *The Simulated Faint*) is fairly straightforward. A lady in a pink dress with her hand to her heart swoons in a chair while her three companions anxiously attend

> *. . . a glimpse of high jinks in the drawing room.*

her. To her right a woman uncorks a bottle of smelling salts, while at her left an elderly man, presumably a physician, is entering and gesturing toward her. At the bottom left of the painting, a game table is overturned, cards and money are scattered about, and an open purse lies beside them. In the right background, a draped curtain suggests that perhaps a little play is being acted out. In the left background, in the picture above the sofa, a small angel appears to draw a curtain, suggesting that a larger drama also exists.

Longhi, however, who was ever mindful of his rich and influential patrons, is deliberately vague about the exact plot of this drawing room drama. Thus, he leaves us wondering whether the leading lady's swoon is due to an overheated room, a too-tight

dress, an excess of passion generated by the excitement of gambling, or attempts to end a losing streak at cards (or even, perhaps, one at love). Whatever the case, the surroundings are sumptuous and the ladies and gentlemen are as elegantly dressed as dolls, befitting their status as Venetians at play in the middle of the eighteenth century.

Whatever the plotting that produced this little drama, Longhi's own role as its virtuoso producer is secure. The composition is open, yet balanced and unified. For example, the central group of the cardplayers, which could be considered a closed group of four, is opened out and given a pyramidal shape by the addition of the two bulky pillows. Off to the side at the right, itself a pyramid, is the imposing and authoritative figure of the doctor, standing alone, yet joined to the central group by his fingertips. Balancing him on the left are a hierarchy of geometric shapes playing one off the other: large vertical and horizontal rectangles of picture and sofa, a smaller circle of a table, an accent of a triangular hat, and tiny rectangles and circles of cards and coins. But, as if to remind us that not all shapes are so straightforward, Longhi adds just the top and side of a curving mantelpiece and atop it a sphere and cylinder subtly joined into a flask of Venetian glass. Both the flask and the tabletop integrate all the colors of the painting: delicate pastel shades of pinks, blues, and yellows in the ladies' and gentlemen's clothing, graded greens in the wall covering and drape, an accent of black in the doctor's robe, and even smaller touches of brown in the woods.

Longhi is often compared with his English contemporary William Hogarth, but the grounds for the comparison are not firm. Longhi and Hogarth are similar in that

*Continued on p 209*

# JAMA®

## The Journal of the American Medical Association

**November 4, 1988**

# JEAN-BAPTISTE-SIMÉON CHARDIN

## *The Attentive Nurse*

The death of Louis XIV in 1715 came down on France like the final curtain of an expensive and lavish, but ultimately boring, production. Relieved of the burdens of court protocol and intrigue, actors and audience alike withdrew from the stuffy rooms of Versailles to giggle and romp in the town houses and salons of Paris. Whereas the seventeenth century had been baroque—overwhelming, if not downright intimidating, in its scale and abundance—the eighteenth century in contrast was rococo, so called after *rocaille*, the small shells and pebbles used to decorate the interiors of grottoes; their small, curving lines became the principal motif of artists. With a regent government, life in general for the aristocracy was acted on a smaller scale and in an easy, open, free, and even frivolous manner. Its mood was best characterized by Watteau, who painted a jester and titled it (aptly, it seems) *L'Indifferent*, or by Fragonard, who painted pastel-pretty ladies and gentlemen in leafy bowers of bliss. One day an Englishman would recall the century as the best of times—and also the worst of times.

Tucked quietly away in this eighteenth-century backdrop of Paris was another, lesser known, painter, Jean-Baptiste-Siméon Chardin (1699-1779), whose small, bourgeois genre works were quite unlike those of the rococo fantasy painters. Circumscribed by a century full of sudden shifts and dramatic contrasts, Chardin lived his entire life of more than eighty years in only three streets in Paris—Rue de Seine, Rue Princesse, and Rue du Four—and the Louvre, where he spent his last twenty-two years. And also unlike the century, his life was unnoted for any spectacular revolutions, in painting or otherwise.

In 1724, at age twenty-five, Chardin became a master painter of the Academy of St Luke in Paris, and before he was thirty he had been admitted to the Royal Academy. An oft-told story has it that academy members, including the director himself, were one day greatly admiring what they believed to be a work by an unknown Flemish master when Chardin stepped forward to admit that the painting was his, whereupon he was made an academy member on the spot. In 1731,

> *As she attends her patient, he . . . attends his painting, lavishing care with every stroke . . .*

Chardin married Marguerite Saintard, who bore him a son. Like many fathers before him, as well as many who would come after, he tried, but failed, to have his son follow in his own footsteps. In a statement to the academy, Chardin said his son had succumbed to a training too rigorous, and he warned fellow academy members to ease their examination procedures: "You can be sure that most of the high conditions of society would be empty if one were admitted only after an examination as severe as the one we must pass."

In the beginning of his academy career, Chardin was forced to accept tasks he did not like, and he soon turned to making the small, intimate, genre scenes, usually of mothers and children in domestic settings. One such scene, though without a child and with a maidservant instead of a mother, is *The Attentive Nurse*, painted probably in 1738. When Chardin painted *The Attentive*

*Nurse*, he was thirty-nine years old, the father of a seven-year-old boy, and a widower, his wife having died three years earlier. This last illness and care of his wife has something to do, perhaps, with the attention and care with which he paints a young woman absorbed in the simple task of peeling an egg. As she attends her patient, he in turn attends his painting, lavishing care with every stroke of his brush. Like the Dutch genre painters of a century before, he is a virtuoso of textures: pitcher, bowls, wineglass, ladle, egg, spoon, bread, chair, mantelpiece, table, dress, apron, tablecloth, hands, face. And he is a master of delicate colors and subtle harmonies: varieties of pink, white, green, blue, brown. But in Chardin's own words, even the purest and most perfect colors are not enough for a painter to paint with. In reply to a colleague who had asked what one paints with if not with colors, Chardin answered, "You use colors—but you paint with feeling." *The Attentive Nurse*, with the care and attention obvious in the young woman's hands and facial expression, confirms his statement. Since some of Chardin's most charming portraits of children date from the same period, is it too much to suppose that the object of the nurse's attention is perhaps Chardin's own son?

In 1744 Chardin married again. In the meantime, perhaps because his genre scenes caused him to be considered a "minor painter," he enjoyed the confidence and trust of his colleagues at the academy, so much so that they allowed him to hang the competitive Salon exhibitions. Only in 1770, when a new director of the academy was appointed, did Chardin's fortunes begin to decline. In his early seventies and with failing eyesight, he resigned from his various posts, but continued painting, turning to

*Continued on p 209*

# JAMA®

### The Journal of the American Medical Association

**November 18, 1988**

# ALBRECHT DÜRER ∾

## Portrait of a Clergyman

In the world of art, the year 1500 is generally used mark the end of the early Italian Renaissance and the beginning of the High Renaissance. To the people of that time, however, the year 1500 was notable chiefly because it marked the close of the first half of the second millennium and the opening of its second half. In Nuremberg, the "Hub of Germany" as it was called, a twenty-eight-year-old engraver and painter decided that he would observe the occasion in his own special way: he would record, permanently, "with indelible colors," all that he knew at that time about art and his relationship with it. But, he also cautioned, "Art derives from God. . . . Therefore, those without aptitude should not attempt it, for it all is an inspiration from above." The result of the young painter's inspiration was an iconlike, full-face portrait of a bearded young man with ropes of golden shoulder-length curls; he is strangely posed like the medieval images of Christ, but wears, incongruously, a fur coat. The sitter for the portrait was Albrecht Dürer (1471-1528), today acclaimed as the greatest of the German artists, the Leonardo of the North, and the artist who synthesized the Gothic Germano-Flemish style of the North with the Renaissance style of Italy. The painter of the portrait was Dürer as well, the same Albrecht who had first introduced the self-portrait into Western art some sixteen years earlier with an uncanny silverpoint work done when he was barely into his teens.

Dürer was born on May 21, 1471, in Nuremberg, a thriving intellectual center in Germany. He was the son of a goldsmith who had emigrated from Hungary and a mother from Nuremberg. One of eighteen children, he was nevertheless last of his line when his brothers and sisters either did not survive childhood or, like himself, remained childless. Trained as a goldsmith like his father and initially apprenticed to his father, he soon was apprenticed to the painter Michael Wolgemut. In Wolgemut's workshop, he learned to do woodcut illustrations for printed books. In the summer of 1494, Dürer married Agnes Frey, the daughter of a highly respected and well-situated coppersmith in Nuremberg; shortly thereafter, however, he left his nineteen-year-old bride while he made an extended trip to Venice. On his return in 1495, he had apparently found his métier. He entered into an intensive occupation with graphic works, which not only brought him fame and

> *. . . a psychological chef d'oeuvre of a man who is living his life on the cusp of the Reformation.*

income in his own day, but also are the chief work for which he is known today.

After a second trip to Italy, which lasted from 1505 to 1507, Dürer returned to Nuremberg and did paintings as well as woodcuts. From 1512 to 1520, he enjoyed the patronage of the Emperor Maximilian and was also entrusted with diplomatic missions, like Rubens after him. In the meantime, however, rather than settling down into the comfortable company of his fellow artisans, Dürer sought out humanistic circles and studied mathematics, geometry, Latin, and literature. Among his friends he numbered the humanist scholars Wilibald Pirckheimer and Erasmus of Rotterdam. Dürer was at the height of his powers. The fur coat painting had been his last and,

apparently, definitive self-portrait, but he continued to paint portraits of others. Characteristic of his work at this time is *Portrait of a Clergyman*, painted in 1516, when Dürer was forty-five.

The sitter for *Portrait of a Clergyman* is not known for certain. It could be Johann Dorsch, the first Protestant minister of Schwabach and later, in 1528, minister of St John's in Nuremberg. Regardless of the sitter's name, however (or even perhaps because it is unknown to us), and with the date prominently displayed, the painting becomes a psychological chef d'oeuvre of a man who is living his life on the cusp of the Reformation. Within the year, Luther would nail his ninety-five theses to the door of the Palast Church in Wittenberg. Unlike Dürer's last self-portrait, which suggested a veneered spirituality or even a faint dandyism, *Portrait of a Clergyman* shows a man with a firm chin, a resolute jaw, and clear, steady eyes. Above the clean-shaven chin (though with ever so faint the shadow of a beard), the lips flicker slightly on the edge of a smile or perhaps on a word. The mien is sober and austere, suggesting more contemplation than action, though the sun-weathered face suggests an outdoor worker or perhaps a traveler newly arrived from a journey on horseback. Again, the small shoulders that slope in a gentle physique suggest a life devoted more to study than to deeds of physical prowess. His figure, completely cloaked in black, is set against a rich, deep, emerald color, dark like the green of a forest, flecked with a blue like that of an autumn sky. The blue in turn is carried around the collar of the robe and down its front. Suggestive of the detail required in Dürer's engravings, each hair from under the cap is individually stroked, like the individual grasses in a piece of turf or the

*Continued on p 209*

# JAMA®

The Journal of the American Medical Association

December 2, 1988

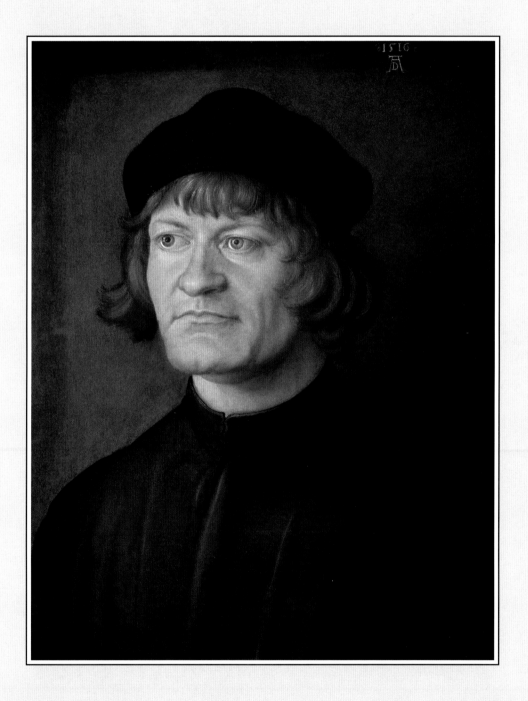

# FRANS HALS

## Portrait of an Elderly Lady

Like morning stars that are outshone by the rising sun, a whole company of seventeenth-century Dutch and Flemish masters shine invisibly within the light of their two contemporaries and compatriots, Rembrandt and Rubens. Of these, the brightest was, perhaps, the Haarlem painter Frans Hals (c 1580-1666). He was called the "genius of the comic"; few are the facts and rich the rumors that emerge from his life. He was born to Flemish parents in Antwerp, but while he was still a youth the family moved to Haarlem. In his late teens or early twenties, he studied with the Flemish painter Karel van Mander, who had an academy in Haarlem. Hals is notable in that he did not go to Italy to study and, indeed, except for one trip to Antwerp, never seems to have strayed far from Haarlem. By 1610, which is the date of his earliest known work, Hals was a member of Haarlem's Guild of St Luke. In 1611, his first son, who would also become a painter, was baptized. Shortly thereafter, when his wife died, he remarried. Hals' second wife bore him eight more children, at least two of whom, a feebleminded boy and a wayward daughter, brought him much grief. In 1616, when he was in his mid thirties, Hals received his first important commission. By 1644 he was sitting on the Council of Haarlem, but shortly thereafter his fortunes began to decline. He was always short of money, in debt, and in 1654 his assets were seized; in 1662, when he was in his eighties, he is recorded as asking for help from the municipality. He died in the Old Men's Home in Haarlem on September 1, 1666, penniless.

Always poor, often on welfare, and forever besieged by creditors, Hals yet painted jolly scenes of roistering, swashbuckling, carousing drinkers. This, coupled with his

### She could be, in fact, the Mona Lisa grown old.

chronic poverty, led to the suggestion that Hals was himself an alcoholic. It is told that after many a night in the taverns of Haarlem, his students would have to see him home and put him to bed. But Hals had another side to himself as well, a side that could solve the fiendish difficulties—political as well as aesthetic—of the group portrait and still make it touching, or he could take an individual fellow citizen and make him or her live forever. An example of the latter is *Portrait of an Elderly Lady*.

*Portrait of an Elderly Lady* was painted perhaps as a commemoration of the sitter's sixtieth birthday. She poses self-consciously and stiffly in clothes that, though somber in tone, are grand in texture and detail. From the cap with its starched buttresses to the meticulously pleated ruff, the multibuttoned bodice, the lace cuffs, the book, the widow's band, and the betrothal ring, we have a Dutch woman typical of the well-to-do middle class of seventeenth-century Holland. But then Hals breathes a spirit into her and she begins to live. She is amused at something off to her left—perhaps the antics of a grandchild, perhaps an image of herself dressed in such unaccustomed finery, perhaps even at Hals himself. The lace at her wrists and hair becomes lace that she has made, the ruff a ruff that she has pleated and starched, the buttons buttons that she has fastened, every one, in spite of her gnarled and swollen fingers. The rings, one of which fits only on her forefinger, betoken a part of her life that is over, but one that was happy, while the book is likely a book of devotions. And all the while she continues to smile as she looks on (or beyond) the passing scene, with a smile that is as enigmatic as that of the Mona Lisa. She could be, in fact, the Mona Lisa grown old.

Hals was around fifty years old when he painted *Portrait of an Elderly Lady*. He would go on for nearly thirty-five years more; some of his greatest work, namely, two group portraits, belongs to his last two years, when he was in his eighties and living in the Old Men's Home.

*Portrait of an Elderly Lady*, 1633, Dutch. Oil on canvas. 103.0 × 86.4 cm. Courtesy of the National Gallery of Art, Washington, DC; Andrew W. Mellon Collection.

# JAMA®

## The Journal of the American Medical Association

**December 9, 1988**

# WASSILY KANDINSKY ∽

## Improvisation 31 (Sea Battle)

Like so many others of the time, the Russian painter Wassily Kandinsky (1866-1944) came to painting by way of the law. But, unlike most, he was already well established in his career of political economics when he gave it up in favor of painting. The decisive moment seems to have come when he saw one of Monet's paintings of the *Haystack* series and became intrigued with the idea that it was actually a painting without a subject, or that at least the haystack was not the subject. At age thirty, already a professor of law in Moscow and the chosen candidate for the chair of law at the University of Dorpat, Kandinsky gave up both appointments and went to Munich to study painting. During the next dozen years he studied and traveled, visiting or temporarily settling in Venice, Odessa, Moscow, Tunis, Dresden, and Sèvres. Returning to Munich in 1908, Kandinsky had a sudden flash of insight one evening when he failed to recognize one of his own paintings; he saw only forms and colors on the canvas that were "indescribably beautiful." Finally realizing that what he was seeing was one of his own paintings tipped on its side, he also realized that paintings did not always need a subject to be intelligible; they could instead be pure distillations of form and color. Like music, they could communicate directly with the emotions without the need for the intermediary of an object. Three years later, in 1911, Kandinsky published his seminal *Concerning the Spiritual in Art* in which he set forth his opinions.

According to Kandinsky, certain colors and shapes, freed from the necessity of residing in an object (for example, shape in the figure of a woman, color in the red of her hair), could instead express directly, without the intermediary, the emotions or "inner need" of the artist. In a sensitive viewer, emotions akin to those of the artist would be evoked, thus setting up between the two spirits, painter and spectator, a resonance or sympathy. Certain colors had certain attributes, Kandinsky said, that would produce certain (predictable) sensations in the viewer. In Kandinsky's lexicon, colors could be warm (yellow) or cold (blue), light (white) or dark (black),

*. . . as jazz dazzles the ear . . . so does Improvisation 31 delight the eye . . .*

they could move (red) or be still (green), be active (orange) or passive (violet), and, finally, have motion within themselves (red) or move either in an eccentric direction (yellow and orange) or in a concentric direction (blue and violet).

These attributes, moreover, in their varying degrees could be put together in an almost infinite variety of combinations to give an almost infinite number of meanings. Thus, yellow is earthly, sour, shrill, insistent, aggressive, not profound, and the color of lunacy. Blue is heaven, rest, and—in shades from light to dark—like a flute, a cello, a double bass, or an organ; in its darkest form, blue is the color of inexpressible grief. Green is motionless, passive, wearisome, restful, self-satisfied, "bourgeoisie," and in its pure state like the middle notes of a violin. Black and white are each colors of silence, white the silence before birth, black the silence after death. Red glows. It is power, concentrated deep within itself. In its

various combinations, it can be strong, harsh, ringing, sharp, or determined. Mixed with brown, it can ring like a trumpet or thunder like a drum. Violet is a cooled red, sad and ailing, and has the sound of a bassoon or an English horn. Orange, on the other hand, is a red warmed by yellow and sounds like the bells of the Angelus or a note on an old violin.

As for his own work, Kandinsky recognized three sources of inspiration, again taken from musical forms: *impression*, which is "a direct impression of outward nature"; *improvisation*, which is "a largely unconscious, spontaneous expression of inner character, the non-material"; and *composition*, which is "an expression of a slowly formed inner feeling, which comes to utterance only after long maturing." Although "reason, consciousness, purpose, play an overwhelming part," the result is seamless. "Nothing of the calculation appears in the finished painting, only the feeling."

*Improvisation 31 (Sea Battle)* is one of some forty paintings of the second type Kandinsky completed between 1909 and 1914. The English critic Roger Fry called them "pure visual music." Like its musical counterpart, it is a spontaneous expression of the artist's inner feelings. Just as jazz dazzles the ear and excites pleasurable feelings without necessarily calling up any concrete images in the mind, so does *Improvisation 31* delight the eye and rouse the emotions without the need for an image (though one is hinted at in the title).

For his work in pure form and pure color, divorced from or not actually existing in an object, Kandinsky is often called the first abstract painter. Though others were traveling in the same direction at that time and may have even "arrived" before

*Continued on p 209*

# JAMA®

The Journal of the American Medical Association

**March 10, 1989**

# HANS HOLBEIN THE YOUNGER ❧

## *Edward VI as a Child*

The documented life of Hans the Younger (1497-1543) (his father, Hans the Elder, was also a well-known painter) is as bland as life at the court of Henry VIII, where Holbein worked, was spicy. Although Hans the Younger was in his day the most famous northern European painter living, dominating the first half of the sixteenth century, there are no contemporary accounts of his life and few biographic facts beyond what exist in public records.

Born in Augsburg, an international center in southern Germany that was a crossroads for trading ideas as well as merchandise, Hans and his brother Ambrosius were trained in the Late Gothic style by their father. In 1515 the brothers went to Basel, Switzerland, where, at age eighteen, Hans executed his first work, a tabletop in medieval style. The following year he illustrated a copy of Erasmus of Rotterdam's *Praise of Folly*, which brought with it not only the later friendship of Erasmus, but also Holbein's introduction into humanist circles. In 1519, when Ambrosius died, Hans, who had been in Italy, returned to Basel and took over his brother's studio. The same year he also joined the Zum Himmel painter's guild and married Elsbeth Schmid. Supporting himself and his family with commissions from the town and from wealthy merchants, Holbein painted murals and did woodcuts, but he was especially noted for his portraits, including three of Erasmus. With the religious situation becoming uncomfortable on the Continent, however, Erasmus advised Holbein to go to England; he gave him a letter of introduction to his friend, Sir Thomas More, then speaker of the House of Commons and later, succeeding Cardinal Wolsey, lord chancellor. Although his portraits had become very popular in England, two years later, Holbein was back in Basel. His stay in Basel was not long. In 1529 the town council banned religious painting, a major source of Holbein's income. In 1532 he left Basel once again and settled permanently in England. His wife and four children remained in Basel. Since More was by then in disfavor, Holbein worked on commissions from the Hanseatic League, but by 1536 he was in the king's service, doing not only portraits, but anything else the king desired: book illustrations, miniatures,

*Before midsummer he was dead, subject, like all the children of his time, to the scourges of infectious disease.*

drawings, woodcuts, and designs for everything from jewelry to stained glass to festivals. One of the portraits of that period was *Edward VI as a Child*, painted in 1538, when the future king of England was a year old.

The situation at the court of Henry VIII at the time of Edward's birth was anything but reassuring. Henry, nearing fifty, had been on the throne for nearly thirty years. From a promising start, he had grown self-indulgent, paunchy, and demanding. Two of his chief advisers, Wolsey and More, had been charged with treason and both were dead, More by the sword, Wolsey in bed. Henry's queen, Catherine of Aragon, had been banished from court along with their daughter Mary, and Henry had married one of Catherine's maids-in-waiting, Anne Boleyn. Already pregnant with Henry's child at the time of their marriage, Anne, too, was now dead. Convicted of infidelity to Henry and sent to the scaffold, she left a child, Elizabeth. Less than a day after her death, Henry had married another of the maids-in-waiting, Jane Seymour. That union produced a male child, Edward, and though his mother died less than two weeks after his birth, Henry was happy; he had an heir.

At the age of a year, Edward is, as Holbein shows him, already regal. Dressed in scarlet and gold, with a plumed hat much like his father would wear in a later portrait, Edward gazes down at his subjects while he raises his right hand in a gesture of royal recognition. In his left hand is the royal rattle, suggesting his future scepter, with which he could rattle a kingdom whenever he chose. Beneath the draped parapet on which he leans, Holbein has included verses written by the influential Richard Cardinal Morison. Addressed to Edward, they pay tribute to his father: "Little one, emulate thy father, be the heir of his virtue, the world contains nothing greater. Heaven and earth could scarcely produce a son whose glory would surpass that of such a father. Thou but equal the deeds of thy parent and men can ask no more. Shouldst thou surpass him, thou has to have outstripped all kings the world has revered in ages past."

Every inch a prince from the day of his birth, Edward would be king by the time he was nine. Coached by his advisers, whose opinions he presented as his own, he would be applauded for his precocity and praised for a wisdom beyond his years. But he was not to surpass his father, nor even to equal him. In delicate health for most of his life, in the spring that he was sixteen he had measles, followed by smallpox. Before midsummer he was dead, subject, like all the children of his time, to the scourges of infectious disease.

*Continued on p 210*

# JAMA®

The Journal of the American Medical Association

**March 24/31, 1989**

PARVVLE PATRISSA, PATRIÆ VIRTVTIS ET HÆRES
ESTO, NIHIL MAIVS MAXIMVS ORBIS HABET.
GNATVM VIX POSSVNT COELVM ET NATVRA DEDISSE,
HVIVS QVEM PATRIS, VICTVS HONORET HONOS.
ÆQVATO TANTVM, TANTI TV FACTA PARENTIS,
VOTA HOMINVM, VIX QVO PROGREDIANTVR, HABENT
VINCITO, VICISTI, QVOT REGES PRISCVS ADORAT
ORBIS, NEC TE QVI VINCERE POSSIT, ERIT.

# JEAN-HONORÉ FRAGONARD

## A Young Girl Reading

In an earlier time and in a different place she would have been a Botticelli Madonna or, if a bit later and farther north, a full-hipped Rubens goddess. But in France, three fourths of the way through its century of Enlightenment, she comes from the brush of Jean-Honoré Fragonard (1732-1806) as *A Young Girl Reading*. Born to a haberdasher's assistant and his wife in the southeast of France, Fragonard grew up in Paris, to all intents destined to be a notary's assistant. The lawyer to whom he was apprenticed, however, suggested that the young Fragonard would do better to study art. Accordingly, he was placed first with the genre painter Chardin and, after he had mastered the techniques of painting, with the leading artist of the day, François Boucher. Together with Watteau, who lived a generation earlier, Boucher and Fragonard gave France nearly a century of rococo art.

Rococo was born when Louis XIV died. Stifled by the ceremony and dwarfed by the Baroque magnificence of Versailles, when Louis finally died in 1715, the court paused only for the space of a sigh and then turned to decorating their apartments in Paris. Their taste, which favored smaller and more intimate settings, soon spread to the upper bourgeoisie as well. In contrast to the Baroque, the new style was friendlier; it was based on a delicate balance of curves and countercurves placed in various, usually asymmetric, arrangements. Because it was much like rock work or grotto work, it was called rococo (from *rocaille*, the French term for "pebble"). Intended primarily as a style of interior design, rococo soon spread to painting; Fragonard continued in the style long after newer trendsetters had moved their interest to the neat and tidy lines of Neoclassicism. His *A Young Girl Reading*,

> *... curves and countercurves ... an intriguing labyrinth of C's.*

which dates from his midforties, is an example of rococo at its best. It is one of a series of such paintings of young girls, small in size, intimate in feeling, apparently in the hope that they would be found suitable for the smaller, more private, apartments of Parisians.

Typical of the rococo style, the painting is an intriguing labyrinth of *C*'s. Taking their form from the fingers and thumb of the model, they are repeated throughout the painting: in the collar and cuffs, in the ribbons in the hair and on the bosom, in the folds of the dress, and even, quite strikingly, in the contrasting brush strokes of the pillow. The only vertical is that of the wall and the only horizontal the arm of the chair. With the light pouring over her like liquid gold, it is a very feminine picture of a young and restless girl. It is prophetic as well, for she sits with her back to the future, as though not to see the coming deluge. But Fragonard himself, though he paints a dying rococo, looks to a future of a hundred years hence and more: his young sitter has the skin tones of a future Renoir, the yellow of a van Gogh, and the sharply contrasting colors—yellow/violet, umber/blue—of a Fauve.

Enormously popular at the height of his career and well-to-do besides, "bon papa Frago," as he was affectionately called, went into eclipse as the result of changing tastes, but he survived the Revolution. He died in 1806, aged seventy-four, virtually forgotten, but with an oeuvre of more than 550 paintings and several thousand drawings. With Watteau, he has been called "one of the two great painters of the unpoetical 18th century in France."

*A Young Girl Reading*, c 1776, French. Oil on canvas. 81.1 × 64.8 cm. Courtesy of the National Gallery of Art, Washington, DC; gift of Mrs Mellon Bruce in memory of her father, Andrew W. Mellon.

# JAMA®

## The Journal of the American Medical Association

April 14, 1989

# ROGIER VAN DER WEYDEN

## *Portrait of a Lady*

Until the beginning of the fifteenth century, Western art follows a fairly smooth progression of styles, the characteristics of the newer identifiable in those of the former. Then, the road forks: though not completely without connection to the other, one road goes south to Italy and is called Early Renaissance; the other goes north to the Netherlands and is called Late Gothic. The northern route is dominated by two painters, Jan van Eyck, often called the father of Netherlandish painting, and his slightly younger contemporary and countryman, the Flemish Rogier van der Weyden (1399/1400-1464), often called the most influential European painter of the fifteenth century. Together—van Eyck in Bruges, van der Weyden in Brussels—they made the century the golden age of Flemish art.

Born in Tournai, a commune of what is today southwest Belgium, Rogier entered the workshop of Robert Campin (probably the same person known as the Master of Flemalle) in Tournai in 1427, where he studied for four years. In 1432 van der Weyden emerged in city records as "Maistre Rogier" of the painters' guild of Tournai, and by 1435 he was listed as official painter to the city of Brussels. Except for a religious pilgrimage to Rome during the Jubilee Year of 1450, Rogier spent most of his life in Brussels. He was married to Ysabel Goffaerts, also of Brussels, sometime around 1425.

Although Rogier left no dated works, on the basis of style his life and work can be divided roughly into three periods. In the first, up to about 1430 and consisting of various religious works, he shows some influence of his elder contemporary, van Eyck. In the middle or mature period, lasting from about 1430 until his Holy Year

trip to Italy in 1450, Rogier concentrated his religious works into scenes of the Passion and of the suffering of Christ and the Virgin. The best known of these, indeed of all his works, is the *Descent From the Cross*, now at the Prado Museum in Madrid, which was to become the paradigm for centuries of future *Descents*. Another is what could have been a painting for the Guild, *St Luke Painting the*

> *. . . the tension between spirit and flesh, between intellection and passion, between contemplation and action.*

*Virgin*, now at the Boston Museum of Fine Arts. Particularly notable in the *Descent* was Rogier's investiture of his subjects with highly charged emotions, manifested not only in facial expression, but even more so in bodily posture, a feature new to painting at that time. Finally, Rogier's third period comprises the last fourteen years of his life, from his first awareness of the early Italian Renaissance during his 1450 pilgrimage until his death in Brussels in 1464. Among these works is a series of secular portraits noted for their sensitivity; in their psychological expression, they would move Netherlandish, indeed European, painting into a new dimension. *Portrait of a Lady*, painted when Rogier was in his early sixties, is one of these.

*Portrait of a Lady* is, at first glance, a work of great beauty and simplicity, carrying with it the Gothic notion of lofty spirituality. Yet, as has been pointed out, none of the lady's

features, when considered individually, is beautiful. For example, the hair is sparse, the forehead too high, the eyebrows too light, the ear too large, the lips out of proportion. Nor is the design as simple as initially believed. On further looking it becomes a pattern as intricate as the weave on the lady's cap. Rogier's genius lies in the presentation; like the effect of a simple tale compellingly told, it works its magic on the viewer. It is illusion, into which the viewer readily buys. For example, appearing as delicate as the sheer fabric of her wimple— she is extraordinarily thin, as one may see in the narrow shoulders and cinched waist— the lady is nonetheless a tower of strength. The diagonals of the wimple, meeting above her brow, give her the stability of an isosceles triangle; the pattern is inverted in the V of the sheer fabric at the neck and turned on its side in the material of the girdle. She is also tender, as is shown by the soft rounding of the crown of her cap, a shape that is answered by that of the dark fabric at her bosom. The décolletage is further emphasized by a dark ribbon hanging from her neck that draws the viewer to the red girdle, to its intricately designed gold clasp, and thence to the hands, ornamented with gold and tightly clasped. It is but a glimpse to return from the red horizontal of the waist to the face again and to wonder over the red horizontal of the full, sensuous lips. Ever so subtly Rogier marks the tension between spirit and flesh, between intellection and passion, between contemplation and action.

The identity of the lady remains unknown. Because of a similarity to a Rogier portrait of Philip the Good, Duke of Burgundy, whose court was in Flanders at the time, the portrait was once thought to be that of his daughter, Marie de Valengrin.

*Continued on p 210*

# JAMA®

The Journal of the American Medical Association

April 28, 1989

# DIEGO RODRÍGUEZ DE SILVA VELÁZQUEZ

## *The Needlewoman*

**H**urt and discouraged by the public ridicule heaped on him for his entry at the Paris Salon of 1865, Édouard Manet went to Madrid to nurse his feelings. There, on a Sunday morning, he wrote to Fantin-Latour how he had found at the Prado the astonishing works of a painter who, it was said, could "make the scales fall from the eyes" and who, in a rare accolade, he called "the painter of painters." Dead for more than 200 years, this painter was Diego Rodríguez de Silva Velázquez (1599-1660); he had anticipated much of the work the nineteenth-century French artists such as Manet and others were doing.

Velázquez was born in Seville to Juan Rodríguez de Silva of a noble Portuguese family and Geronima Velázquez of Seville. His early studies were humanistic; he excelled in languages and philosophy. When, already at age twelve, his extraordinary talent for painting became evident, he was accordingly apprenticed to the painter, poet, humanist, and theoretician of art (as well as inspector of art for the Inquisition of Seville) Francisco Pacheco. Young Velázquez was soon Pacheco's favorite pupil and in 1617, when he was eighteen, he became an independent master of the Guild of Painters in Seville. The following year Pacheco "married him to my daughter," Juana, "moved by his virtue, integrity, and good parts and by the expectations of his disposition and great talent." The union was fruitful and Pacheco turned out to be prophetic: by 1621, the couple had two daughters and, in 1623, as a young man of only twenty-four, Velázquez was appointed court painter to Philip IV in Madrid. Now not only were Velázquez' talent and training secured, but his social and financial future as well. Philip would grow increasingly attached to Velázquez over their nearly forty-year association; he gave him a studio in the palace, an apartment in the city, free medical care, a regular salary above and beyond payments for individual paintings, bonuses, and a pension. Antonio Palomino, Velázquez' seventeenth-century biographer, writes of how the lonely king had a key to the studio and "used to come and sit there for a while to watch Velazquez paint, much as Alexander the Great often visited Apelles in his workshop, according to Pliny." In exchange, Velázquez was forbidden to take

> *. . . the lonely king . . . "used to come and . . . watch Velazquez paint . . . "*

any commissions other than those from the king. As the years passed, however, Velázquez did a series of personal paintings; the subjects were of his choice and the paintings were intended to please only himself. They were often daringly original, anticipating movements in art that would not occur for another 200 years. An outstanding example is *The Needlewoman*.

The subject is thought to be Velázquez' daughter Francisca, then in her early twenties, who was married to his pupil Juan Bautista del Mazo. She is absorbed in her task: her hands work busily on a piece of white cloth, perhaps part of an infant's layette. The triangle of the cloth she sews is repeated in the white triangle over her left shoulder, while the other two pieces of white cloth balance each other diagonally. The dark square of the pillow in the left foreground is answered by the light square of bosom above the neckline of the dress.

The cleavage above the fashionably tight bodice is at the geometric center of the painting. Soft light caresses the hair, the forehead, the side of the nose, the bosom, the left shoulder, the right fingers, and the left hand, directing the viewer's gaze and contrasting the stillness of the body with the motion of the hands. Most important, however, is the unity achieved by the color harmonies. Characteristic of Velázquez by this time, they are delicate blendings of grays, greens, and ochers, accentuated by a moon crescent of red, not unlike the gray-green harmony and red accent that would be used by his countryman Goya in a painting of a young Madrid industrialist a century and a half later.

Velázquez worked for the king for another twenty years, continually rising in Philip's esteem until he became gentleman of the bedchamber in 1643 and chamberlain of the imperial palace in 1651. His two greatest paintings, the well-known *Las Meninas* (*The Maids of Honor*) and *Las Hilanderas* (*The Spinners*), in which he successfully combined ancient Greek mythology with contemporary Spanish life, were completed after 1656, when he was by then in his late fifties. In 1659 he was awarded the Order of Santiago. Though given only after a lengthy inquiry into his background that concentrated on his bloodline and on whether any of his family had ever engaged in trading, it was nevertheless the first time a painter, who was considered a manual worker, had ever been so honored. In early spring 1660, helping to arrange the prenuptials between the Infanta Maria Theresa and Louis XIV, Velázquez went ahead of the king's party to Irun, on the border between Spain and France. There he oversaw the decoration of the conference hall, where the meeting

*Continued on p 210*

# JAMA®

The Journal of the American Medical Association

May 12, 1989

# LAUREN FORD

## *The Country Doctor*

Details of the life of the American artist Lauren Ford (1891-1973) are as scarce as those in her paintings are abundant. Only the broadest sketch is possible. Born in New York City nearly a hundred years ago, she studied at the Art Students League. Between the two wars she lived in Europe, where she became greatly attracted to the Benedictines, studying Gregorian chant and the medieval art of manuscript illumination. In the late 1930s, she returned to the United States and settled in Bethlehem, Connecticut, where she specialized in Nativity scenes. She has been characterized as "a painter of whimsical Connecticut scenes," as painting in a combination of genre and American naive, and as an American Brueghel. *The Country Doctor* is one of these Connecticut works.

A garden of visual delights, the painting is a catalog of life at the close of a summer day on the farm, an illuminated page in the Book of Hours of a country doctor at the turn of the century. Children spill across the canvas: riding on the hayrack, climbing a fence, swinging in a hammock, hammering croquet balls, feeding chickens, watching pigs, fleeing from a goose (a girl) or from a goat (a boy), teasing the dog, worrying the cat, and running to the outhouse. A lone adolescent girl dreams on a hill above a lily pond. In the barnyard, a Noah's ark of animals strut, cluck, quack, gobble, root, bark, or go to be milked. Men and horses work silently, on the wagon, among the corn shocks, riding the plow, going to milking. In the garden cabbages are set out, and hollyhocks drowse in the sun. Smoke rises from the chimney of the summer kitchen. Nearby is the town, with churches, post office, and cemetery, and, across the valley, the schoolhouse with its American flag. Beyond the river the quilted hills fade into pale green and then into an eternity of bluish purple, like the landscape beyond the window of a fifteenth-century Florentine portrait.

> *. . . an illuminated page in the Book of Hours of a country doctor at the turn of the century.*

But all this is but prologue to the real drama, which is about to begin. Down from center stage stands a horse and buggy, tended by a small boy. Through the gate and just beyond walks the doctor, black bag in hand. And, at the exact, geometric center of the painting is the door to the farmhouse, a curtain that is about to rise on the drama to be played out behind it. Perhaps it will be one of a life beginning or a life ending or of a life helped over a rough place. But, like the medieval morality play, the drama will center on three characters: the doctor, the patient, and the illness. And, when the doctor exits and the curtain closes once again, life outside will go on much as shown, though with a little more joy or with a little more sorrow, one cannot guess.

The country doctor of a hundred years ago is today an anachronism. On the other hand, perhaps not. For while the mode of transportation and the contents of the black bag have changed, the task has not. Nor has the drama ended.

*The Country Doctor*, c 1930-1940, American. Oil on canvas. 137.2 × 182.9 cm. Courtesy of the Canajoharie Library and Art Gallery, Canajoharie, New York.

# JAMA®

The Journal of the American Medical Association

May 19, 1989

# GILBERT CHARLES STUART ⟿

## Catherine Bras(s) Yates (Mrs Richard Yates)

In a fledgling republic that, although high in ideals, was still short on experience, good intentions were not enough to educate its people. The eighteenth-century American physician had to look to England and beyond if he aspired to anything but the most rudimentary training. Likewise the artist who aspired to any role greater than that of itinerant painter of children's portraits. Thus it was that, shortly after the Battle of Breed's (later Bunker) Hill in 1775, the twenty-year-old Gilbert Charles Stuart (1755-1828) found himself on the way to London to learn to paint.

The son of a Scottish immigrant, Stuart was born in North Kingstown, Rhode Island, but moved with his family to Newport when his father's snuff mill failed. There, at age fourteen, his native artistic ability attracted the attention of a visiting painter, the Scottish Cosmo Alexander, who took him back to Edinburgh with him. But Alexander died unexpectedly before Stuart's training had been completed and the sixteen-year-old was left to work his way back to America on a sailing ship, an experience he never cared to recall in later life. For a time the young Stuart painted portraits in Newport, but, recognizing the inadequacy of his work, at the beginning of the Revolutionary War he went to England to further his training, as had John Copley and Benjamin West before him. Befriended by West, living in his house in London and working with him, and through the generosity of a medical student from Rhode Island, Benjamin Waterhouse, as well as by his own hard work and not inconsiderable charm, Stuart had soon surpassed his master. Along with the English painters Reynolds, Gainsborough, and Romney—and learning from each—Stuart was by his late twenties making portraits of fashionable London society. At age thirty-one he married, and the following year, 1787, he and his wife moved to Dublin. There followed six more years of success, during which time he painted most of Dublin society. But, in addition to professional success, his easy charm led him to financial extravagance; in 1793, to escape his creditors, Stuart and his wife left for the United States. What he found was startling.

> . . . Mrs Yates sews,
> not because she must,
> but because Yankees
> are never idle . . .

The loose confederation of colonies he had left was now a young, prosperous, energetic republic with its own Constitution and Bill of Rights and, in place of George III, George Washington, newly elected by the people to lead the country for a second four-year term. Stuart's stated goal was to paint the president's portrait, a coup he felt would assure him of both financial and social success if he could manage it. While trying to secure his commission, however, Stuart was not idle. He settled in New York City, where his English training, his social graces, and his charm, as well as the yen of wealthy Americans to record their own success, once more assured his success. Thus it was that Richard Yates, a senior partner in Yates and Pollock, New York importers of European and East Indian goods, commissioned Stuart to do five portraits of family members: himself, his wife Catherine, his brother Lawrence, and his daughter and her husband, George Pollock. *Catherine Bras(s) Yates*

*(Mrs Richard Yates)* is an outstanding example of this group, indeed of any of Stuart's work.

Seated in a Federal scoop-back chair, the fifty-seven-year-old Catherine Brass Yates, a native of New York City, is carefully shown as a woman who is as progressive in her sympathies as she is up-to-date in her dress. As befits a prosperous merchant's wife, the dress is of imported silk with fashionably tight sleeves and tight bodice, the kerchief is organdy, and the intricately made cap is muslin, pleated to perfection. The cap is actually a mobcap, patterned after those worn by the women of the French Revolution and worn by American women of that time to show their solidarity. Most important, however, is Stuart's decision of how to portray the simple values of the new republic: Yankee energy and Yankee industriousness. Thus, Mrs Yates sews, not because she must, but because Yankees are never idle, not even while sitting for a portrait. Meanwhile, Mrs Yates casts on Stuart a glance at once amused and skeptical, as though to wonder how so idle a profession as painting can be tolerated by a grown man. What Mrs Yates thought after she saw the finished portrait has not been recorded, but it has been recorded that Stuart was both a "most accurate painter" and "never a favorite portrait painter with the ladies." Stuart for his part has managed to combine the Yankee values into a classical harmony of grays and whites against a continuo of olive green with accents of red, gold, and brass.

It took only little more than a year after his return to the United States for Stuart to receive his coveted invitation to paint George Washington, and it came through the offices of no less a figure than Chief Justice John Jay. Although Stuart would

*Continued on p 210*

# JAMA®

The Journal of the American Medical Association

May 26, 1989

# JOHN SINGER SARGENT

## The Four Doctors

When The Johns Hopkins Hospital opened on May 7, 1889, its "Famous Four"—William H. Welch in pathology, William S. Halsted in surgery, William Osler in medicine, and Howard A. Kelly in gynecology—were already in place, having been recruited as early as 1884 with the promise of similar faculty positions in the soon-to-be-opened medical school. However, financial reverses in the investment income from the endowment fund delayed groundbreaking for the medical school for the foreseeable future. A sum of at least $500,000 was needed. The outlook remained bleak until, thanks to the Women's Fund Committee, a national effort organized by Miss Mary Garrett and several other daughters of the Hopkins trustees, the sum—of which $306,977 came from the personal funds of Miss Garrett—was raised and presented to the trustees on Christmas Eve, 1892. The women had only two requests: that the proposed medical school be a four-year, rather than the planned three-year, school with an AB degree or equivalent required for admission and that women be admitted on the same terms as men. Both conditions were met, although with one casualty: Welch's assistant, William Councilman, moved over to Harvard, which did not yet admit women, causing Osler to quip that while Harvard got the man, Hopkins got the money. The school opened in October 1893, with fifteen men and three women in its first class.

But that was not to be Miss Garrett's only bequest to the medical school. Thirteen years later, in 1905, she commissioned John Singer Sargent (1856-1925), the most famous portrait painter of turn-of-the-century Europe and America, to paint the Famous Four. Presented by her to the university on January 19, 1907, *The Four Doctors* has been called "the acme of formal and official medical portraiture in American art." (Gerdts, 1981) When Sargent came to paint *The Four Doctors*, he was no stranger to illness, death, or the medical profession. The second child of six, only he and two sisters lived beyond the age of four years. His father, Fitzwilliam Sargent, was a physician, although he was inactive by the time John was born. Prior to his marriage, Fitzwilliam had had a promising career in the United States. A graduate of the University of Pennsylvania, he was an attending physician at the Wills Eye Hospital in Philadelphia and a fellow of the College of Physicians of Philadelphia. He was the

> *. . . Osler and Sargent had to go through several frustrating sittings.*

author of *On Bandaging and Other Operations of Minor Surgery*, a work that went into several editions, including Japanese, and was a standard work on the battlefields of the American Civil War. It was illustrated with his own drawings. Fitzwilliam had also edited two textbooks in the field of surgery. John's mother, Mary Newbold Singer, was a talented musician and watercolorist, who, however, for some reason was unable to live in the United States. For nearly thirty years after her marriage to Fitzwilliam, the family lived a nomadic existence in Europe, traveling from spa to spa seeking the mother's and elder daughter's health and relief from the weather. John was born during one of the family's sojourns in Florence. He saw the

United States for the first time in 1876, when he was twenty.

When Welch, Halsted, Osler, and Kelly gathered in Sargent's Tite Street studio in London, England, for their initial portrait sittings, one of the immediate problems that faced Sargent was composition. He grouped and regrouped the four men until at last he had the desired effect. Thereafter he could work with each individually. Welch's face he got right away. Osler's was the most difficult, and both Osler and Sargent had to go through several frustrating sittings. Another difficulty was color. Although Osler wanted to wear his red Oxford robes, Sargent would not permit it because, as he said, the red was simply too red. Welch, on the other hand, was permitted to wear his Yale robes. Finally, when the painting was nearing completion, Sargent grew discouraged. "It isn't a picture," he said. Then, recalling a large Venetian globe he had in his other studio, he had it brought over to Tite Street (even though it meant chopping away part of the studio door to get it in) and placed it in the background. "We have got our picture," he said. And indeed he had. The globe, besides unifying the composition in its echo of the arch above it, provides a contrast for the head of Osler and brings together the figure of Osler with that of Halsted, standing. Welch, seated at the left, and Kelly, seated at the right, balance the composition on either side. Or, looked at another way, the painting in the background, El Greco's *St Martin of Tours Dividing His Cloak With the Beggar*, besides providing an allegory, changes the number of figures in the painting from four to five, an easier number to deal with, and also forms the apex of a triangle with Welch, Halsted, the globe, and Osler as its sides. Kelly, asymmetrically placed off to the right,

*Continued on p 210*

# JAMA®

The Journal of the American Medical Association

June 2, 1989

# ANONYMOUS

## *The Dog*

Just as overzealous cultivation can sometimes kill the very blooms it seeks to foster, so too can training sometimes stifle a talent before it can be expressed. Conversely, a garden let grown wild will bloom perhaps not with the most beautiful of the flowers, but certainly with the sturdiest. Likewise, a sturdy talent left untrained will certainly also express itself, although usually not in the expected and conventional forms. Thus, throughout the history of painting, and in American painting in particular, there have appeared those individuals, untrained and often even unschooled, whose fire burned so intensely that it demanded expression despite its raw and primitive form. Sometimes the names of these artists are known, as are the nineteenth century's Edward Hicks, Erastus Field, Joseph Pickett, and Joseph Davis and the twentieth century's John Kane, Horace Pippin, and Anna Mary Robertson (Grandma) Moses. But frequently the painter is known simply as "Anonymous" and the viewer is left to guess at who made the painting, where it was made, and when it was made. Such is the case with *The Dog* by an unknown painter thought to be of the late nineteenth or early twentieth century.

Heavy-coated in long, reddish-brown hair, with a blocky body, a broad head and muzzle, tiny ears, and small feet, the dog has all the essentials of a chow chow, a breed that first appeared in the United States in 1890 and that was at the height of its popularity in the 1920s. Done in the typical fashion of the naive artist, the painting is lacking in all the sophistications taught at the academies—perspective, foreshortening, modeling, chiaroscuro, spatial impression, atmosphere, three-dimensionality—in short, all the conventions of expression that had come to be expected by the nineteenth- and

> *. . . feelings not . . . filtered through a mesh of instruction.*

twentieth-century viewer. Instead, we are confronted directly, even bluntly, by the artist with feelings that have not been filtered through a mesh of instruction. Nothing the artist sees is less significant than any other feature. Care and attention have been lavished equally on every detail. Each hair of the coat has been carefully brushed, each blade of grass, each leaf of the vine, each potted plant, each rock, each brick individually pictured. The colors have been carefully observed, matched, and harmonized, blues with blues, greens with greens, reds with reds. The shapes have been diligently observed and faithfully rendered. The artist's attempt at perspective, his efforts to show the distant view in relation to the near subject, is indicated by the juxtaposition of the small wall with the large dog. Pots of flowers on either side suggest a drawn curtain, while the grass suggests a stage and the seven carefully arranged potted plants, footlights (National Gallery of Art, unpublished notes, 1989). Finally the contrast of the gentle flowers belies the malevolent eyes and the fierce-looking fangs flanking the blue-black tongue. Far from inspiring fear, the dog becomes the faithful family pet, lovingly preserved in a family portrait.

What academic training would have done for this artist one cannot say. Like the works of other naive artists before and after *The Dog*, the work is painted with more affection than skill, with more heart than hand, but it is precisely for that reason that it charms the viewer. A literal rather than a free-flowing translation of the reality the painter experiences, the work reaches openly, like the work of a child, and goes directly to the heart of the viewer.

*The Dog*, early twentieth century, American. Oil on canvas. 89.5 × 105.4 cm. Courtesy of the National Gallery of Art, Washington, DC; gift of Edgar William and Bernice Chrysler Garbisch.

# JAMA®

The Journal of the American Medical Association

**June 9, 1989**

# ANTHONY VAN DYCK

## Isabella Brant

Anthony van Dyck (1599-1641), one of the most influential portrait painters of all time, had what some might call the misfortune to be a contemporary and compatriot of Peter Paul Rubens. Twenty-two years his junior, van Dyck was born into a middle-class family of Antwerp. When he was eight, his mother died, and two years later the boy was apprenticed to the Antwerp painter Hendrick van Balen, where he remained for some six or seven years. Rubens was then at the height of his popularity. Van Dyck's early talents must have been considerable, for in 1618, at only age nineteen, he was made a master of the Guild of St Luke in Antwerp. (Rubens had been twenty-two when he was admitted to the same guild in 1598.) Like other masters, van Dyck was now allowed to accept commissions and to train apprentices. The same year, 1618, van Dyck entered the workshop of Rubens, soon becoming his chief assistant, and also began his career as a portrait painter. In the autumn and early winter of 1620/1621, van Dyck spent four months at the English court of James I, and although he got along well with the young Charles, Prince of Wales, who was his own age, London was not to his liking. He returned to Antwerp in February 1621, but it was not to be for long. Before the end of the year he was off for what eventually proved to be a six-year stay in Italy. Before he left, however, in the few months' interlude in Antwerp between London and Genoa, he painted *Isabella Brant*, a portrait of the thirty-year-old wife of Rubens. Van Dyck was twenty-two.

Isabella Brant was the eldest daughter of Jan Brant, an academician and humanist who, with Rubens' brother Philip, was one of the four secretaries of the city of Antwerp. At age eighteen, she married Rubens, twelve years her senior, and became the mistress of a large and busy household. At the time of the painting, she was also the mother of three children, Clara Serena, age ten, Albert, age seven, and Nicholas, age three. Little else is known of the facts of her life. When she died five years later, possibly of tuberculosis, Rubens eulogized her in a letter to a friend: "I have lost my most intimate companion, whom I could and must in reason always love; for she had none of the

> *. . . Isabella of the mysterious smile and the abstracted gaze . . .*

faults of her sex. She was neither morose-tempered nor weak; but so kind, so good and so filled with all womanly virtues that everyone loved her during her life and mourns her since her death."

Shortly after his marriage to Isabella, Rubens had bought a large and expensive house and garden in the fashionable section of Antwerp, on the Wapper Canal. Over the next ten years he had two studios built on the property, one very large and ornate, the other smaller. Then, further indulging his taste for the Italian architecture he had seen in Genoa and Mantua, he connected the buildings with a large triumphal arch, adorned with every kind of decorative device. Van Dyck has posed Isabella in the courtyard of this house, beside the arch. Dressed sumptuously in brocade, satin, velvet, and filigreed lace, as befits her husband's status, she nonetheless appears ill at ease. It would not be difficult, in fact, to imagine Isabella as just having dusted the flour from her hands before hastily pulling back her hair and donning the costume for the portrait. Posing for her husband's assistant would be, after all, as much a part of her duties as overseeing the menu for the entertainment of her husband's business associates. And van Dyck undoubtedly wished to impress his master with the setting of the arch and Isabella's queenly pose and rich costume. But it is a portrait designed to show not so much the soul of Isabella Brant as the virtuosity of the young studio assistant. Typically, he tries to put all he knows into a single painting as though he will never have a chance to paint another. Yet, for all the opulence that threatens to outshine Isabella, the spirit triumphs and we have Isabella of the mysterious smile and the abstracted gaze, a woman who is only impatiently patient and indulgent, while what she wants really is to get on with business that truly matters.

Van Dyck returned from his six-year stay in Italy in 1627, his work much matured. Immediately he was immersed in many commissions, especially for portraits. He also tried his hand at religious painting and even at scenes from mythology. In 1632 his earlier friendship at the English court with the Prince of Wales bore fruit and Charles, now Charles I, invited him to London. There he was appointed principal painter to their majesties and was also knighted, an honor already conferred on Rubens before him. In 1640, after eight years in London, van Dyck married an Englishwoman, Mary Ruthven. Shortly thereafter Rubens died in Antwerp and, as heir apparent of Flemish painting, van Dyck hurried back across the Channel to claim the throne. But there was to be no "The King is dead! Long live the King!" In little less than a year and a half, van Dyck also was dead. Graced, but destined to live always in the shadow of the

*Continued on p 211*

# JAMA®

### The Journal of the American Medical Association

June 16, 1989

# MARJORIE ACKER PHILLIPS ⟿

## Night Baseball

In a search for a truly American art, most painters have gone to the country's landscapes: to its Rocky Mountains, its Hudson River Valley, and its New Mexican desert. Others have concentrated on its faces: those of its founders, pillars, dowagers, and immigrants. Still others have chosen to record its industries: steel, automobiles, and bridges. And finally, others have gone to its streets: to their skyscrapers, their ash cans, and their patriotic processions. Remarkably few have gone to sport. Yet, what could be perceived as more typically American than a baseball game? Indeed, the English language itself, as adopted by the United States, is studded with expressions that are part and parcel of its daily commerce, a whole lexicon of "baseballisms," such as *hit a home run* (succeeded); *got a three-bagger* (did well); *struck out* (failed); *strike three* (ditto); *couldn't get to first base* (was frustrated); *three and two* (critical); *two out in the bottom of the ninth* (last chance); *play ball* (cooperate); *batter up* (begin); *ballpark figure* (an estimate); *grandstanding* (showing off); *out in left field* (not with it); and *in a different league* (not to be compared). Marjorie Phillips (1895-1985) with *Night Baseball* is one of the exceptions.

Born Marjorie Acker in Bourbon, Indiana, Marjorie Phillips grew up in a well-to-do family in Ossining-on-the-Hudson, New York, where her father was a chemical engineer and inventor. Two of her uncles, Reynolds and Gifford Beal, were well-known artists. From 1915 until 1918, she commuted daily from Ossining to the Art Students League in New York City, where she studied with Boardman Robinson and Kenneth Hayes Miller. Her preferences were for landscapes and family scenes. In 1921, Marjorie married the art collector Duncan Phillips and moved to Washington, DC. There she assisted Duncan in developing a museum of modern art he had begun a short time earlier as a memorial to his father and his brother. Housed in a four-story Victorian mansion at Twenty-first and Q streets since its beginning, The Phillips Collection, as it is known, today contains some 2,000 works

> ## *DiMaggio is at bat and a storm is imminent.*

by artists such as Bonnard, Degas, Monet, Picasso, Goya, Matisse, Klee, Cézanne, O'Keeffe, and Rothko. Its centerpiece is Renoir's *Luncheon of the Boating Party*, acquired in 1923 for $125,000 and considered today to be his finest work. Mrs Phillips served as associate director of the collection from 1925 until 1966 and as director from 1966 until 1972. During the 1930s, Mrs Phillips had work in three major expositions: the 1933 Century of Progress in Chicago, the 1939 World's Fair in New York, and the 1939 Golden Gate Exposition in San Francisco. In addition to The Phillips, where she has a special room, her work is owned by the Whitney Museum, Yale University, and the Boston Museum of Fine Arts.

For *Night Baseball*, Marjorie Phillips has chosen the Washington Senators' Griffith Stadium in Washington, DC. Her vantage point is just behind the home-team dugout, where she frequently occupied a box with her husband and sketched the games. Crowded to the front of the opposite dugout are the New York Yankees, who are at bat. The night is sultry and still, with a lowering sky. The flag hangs limp. The crowd is hushed, the moment tense. DiMaggio is at bat and a storm is imminent. The first base coach is on the alert, the infielders are poised, the plate umpire, his chest protector ballooning in front of him, is crouched behind the catcher, and on the mound the pitcher is about to release the ball. Above it all, banks of light, like diamond clips, hold back the dark.

*Night Baseball* recalls a moment that was legendary even as it was happening and that today, less than forty years later, evokes a wistful yearning for another time of such innocence. Things then were neither as standardized nor as regulated as now and thus the center field wall of the old Griffith Stadium could accommodate itself to five houses and a large tree, and if right field was not as deep as left field, then no matter, that was easily remedied simply by making the right field wall a little higher. Baseball was, after all, hardly a business; it was a game. And while the giant candelabra atop the grandstands and in the bleachers were signaling that baseball would eventually become another commodity, night baseball in 1951 was still somewhat of a novelty. The first baseball game had been lit up as early as 1880 in Hull, Massachusetts, but it was not until the 1930s that lights began to appear in the major leagues, and it was only after World War II, in the late 1940s and early 1950s, that their use accelerated. And it was only recently, in 1988, that the last major league park was finally electrified and baseball was free to join the growing list of consumer items.

Marjorie Phillips gives no hint of the final outcome of the game that sticky night

*Continued on p 211*

# JAMA®

The Journal of the American Medical Association

June 23/30, 1989

# LUCAS CRANACH THE ELDER ～

## A Princess of Saxony

They have been called "the great trinity of German painters": Dürer, Cranach, and Holbein, men born in the last third of the fifteenth century who were destined to carry German art from its Late Gothic period into the period of the northern Renaissance. Of the three, Dürer was the eldest by a year and Holbein the youngest by almost a generation. Nearly an exact contemporary of Dürer was Lucas Cranach the Elder (1472-1553), so called to distinguish him from his son, Lucas the Younger.

Little is known of Cranach's early years. Born at Kronach, a Franconian town under the sovereignty of the electors of Saxony, his family name could have been Sunder ("sinner," "criminal") or Müller ("miller"). His father was known as Hans Maler ("artist," "painter") and it was in his father's shop that Lucas learned engraving. In 1500 he was in Vienna, where his earliest surviving works show the marked influence of Dürer, as well as that of the Danube school, a style transitional between Gothic and Renaissance. In 1505 Cranach was called to Wittenberg, where Frederick the Wise, Elector of Saxony, appointed him court painter, a position once held by Dürer. He was also given a salary two-and-a-half times greater than that paid to his immediate predecessor; within three years he had his own coat of arms, granted by Frederick. Cranach stayed in Wittenberg almost to the end of his life, serving three successive electors, Frederick the Wise, John the Steadfast, and John Frederick the Magnanimous. At age seventy-eight he went into voluntary exile with John Frederick, first in Augsburg and later in Weimar, where he died at age eighty-one.

During his forty-five years in Wittenberg, Cranach did well for himself, becoming,

after the chancellor of Wittenberg, its wealthiest citizen. Besides running a large studio that employed up to ten journeymen, Cranach sold wine and ran an apothecary shop. Alchemist formulas are said to be encoded into some of his paintings. He also owned a book and stationery shop and a printing press on which he printed the writings of his close friend Luther as well as

> *. . . for all the formality, she remains a child just at the threshold of adolescence.*

Luther's translation of the New Testament into German. From 1519 on Cranach held the office of town councilor and was burgomaster from 1537 to 1543, when he declined further service. In about 1512 he married Barbara Brenghier of Gotha and the couple had three daughters and two sons. Both sons became painters, but Hans died in 1537, while Lucas the Younger became his father's successor, both as court painter and as heir to his talent.

Cranach's early works are mainly religious, and he never missed an opportunity to portray a nude, whether in a biblical (Adam and Eve) or classical mythology (Venus) setting. Beginning in Vienna, Cranach also painted a large number of portraits and was in fact the originator of the full-length portrait. Besides the various electors of Saxony and members of their courts, Cranach painted a large number of portraits of reformers and scholars of the day, including those of Luther and Melanchthon. Indeed, today's image of the Reformation world of Witten-

berg comes largely from Cranach. On the other hand, he managed to keep himself nonpartisan in the religious controversies and could paint for Protestant and Catholic princes alike, including not only those of Saxony, but also Cardinal Albert of Brandenburg, who liked to be seen praying or studying. Cranach himself was fond of the double portrait and often portrayed husband and wife or two colleagues as pendants. One such work is *A Princess of Saxony*, pendant to one of her brother, the prince.

It is uncertain who the princess is, but one source names her as Princess Christine, daughter of Duke George the Bearded, born in 1505 and about twelve years old at the time of the portrait. Perhaps intended as a portrait that would show her off to the family of another royal house as an eligible bride, the child is portrayed in all the trappings of a royal princess. The heavy red dress is elaborately embroidered in gold, her neck is collared with a multijeweled necklace, and about her shoulders she bears a burden of gold links that speak for the wealth of her dowry. Her principal natural adornment, her waist-length hair, is carefully arranged about her shoulders, its scrupulously painted waves echoed in the arabesques of the dress design and the twisted links of gold. The minute filigree pattern of each of the links is repeated in the broader lacing of the bodice of the dress. The hands are awkwardly rendered, as in most of Cranach's portraits, for he considered them insignificant to a portrait. In contrast, the facial features, especially the eyes and the lips, are lovingly portrayed, and while they announce the princess' individuality, they also proclaim that she is the daughter of this family and no other. But for all the formality, she remains a child just

*Continued on p 211*

# JAMA®

The Journal of the American Medical Association

July 7, 1989

# LUCAS CRANACH THE ELDER

## A Prince of Saxony

To the south, in Florence, the Italian Renaissance was well under way when, in 1513, Niccolo Machiavelli presented his literary portrait, *The Prince*, to the reigning monarch, the "Magnificent Lorenzo de Medici." To the north, in Wittenberg, the Protestant Reformation was just getting under way when four years later, in 1517, Martin Luther nailed his ninety-five theses to the door of the castle church, and his friend, Lucas Cranach (1472-1553), completed the portrait *A Prince of Saxony*. One in prose, one in pigment, Machiavelli and Cranach both testify to how man saw his world at the beginning of the modern era. "One looks to the end," says Machiavelli. "Let a prince then win and maintain the state—the means will always be judged honorable and will be praised by everyone; for the vulgar are always taken in by the appearance and the outcome of a thing, and in this world there is no one but the vulgar." Thus, although it would be desirable for a prince actually to be "full of pity, faithful, human, open, religious," such a mode is not always necessary nor even advisable, nor, indeed, even possible at all times. But, he concludes, it is essential that a prince appear to have these qualities, for the vast majority of people have only the appearance of a thing on which to base their judgments.

Cranach's prince, on the other hand, we do see, though not in the appearance of his deeds. Rather we see him in his persona, or at least we have the illusion of seeing him, if only as Cranach saw him or as Cranach wished him to be seen. His identity is not known, but it is suggested that he is Prince Frederick, son of Duke George the Bearded of Saxony, born in 1504 and thus about

*. . . little more than a child, but already burdened with the heavy robes of state.*

thirteen years old at the time of the portrait. He is the brother of Princess Christine, whose portrait at age twelve is pendant to this one. As portrayed by Cranach, this prince is little more than a child, but already burdened with the heavy robes of state. On his head the jeweled wreath, which surely must be uncomfortable, has slipped to the side. The robes are elaborately patterned with arabesques, while the curls of the shoulder-length hair are carefully arranged to harmonize. Characteristically, the hands are awkwardly painted. By contrast, attention is lavished on the face until the boy begins to live. The prince, with a properly sober expression, looks out at us, but beneath it all, barely suppressed, is the boy. At one moment he sits for Cranach. At the next, he will doff the robes into a heap and run to join the latest game or hunt. Although he is trained to be a prince, one doubts whether even giving the appearance of being concerned with such things as pity, faith, humanity, openness, and religion are uppermost preoccupations at the moment. Rather, his desire is simply to get on with things.

It is to Lucas Cranach the Elder that we owe our visual impressions of the world of Wittenberg and the early days of the Reformation. His numerous portraits of the reformers and humanists Luther and Melanchthon, as well as of the three successive electors of Saxony—Frederick the Wise, John the Steadfast, and John Frederick the Magnanimous—whom he served from 1505 until his death nearly fifty years later, leave us a heritage we otherwise would probably have lost. All told, in spite of even what has been lost, Lucas Cranach the Elder left some four hundred paintings from this very important period, the beginnings of the modern era.

*A Prince of Saxony*, c 1517, German. Oil on panel. 43.7 × 34.4 cm. Courtesy of the National Gallery of Art, Washington, DC; Ralph and Mary Booth Collection.

# JAMA®

The Journal of the American Medical Association

July 14, 1989

# MARIE-LOUISE-ÉLISABETH VIGÉE-LEBRUN

## *Portrait of Marie-Gabrielle de Gramont, Duchesse de Caderousse*

Witty, beautiful, intelligent, and artistically precocious, Marie-Louise-Élisabeth Vigée-Lebrun (1755-1842) was, at the age of fifteen, already supporting her widowed mother and younger brother with earnings from her work. At age twenty she was fully established as a professional portrait painter, at age twenty-four she became a member of the Academie de Saint Luc in Paris, and at age twenty-eight she became official painter to Queen Marie Antoinette. For the next decade, she would document vividly the dying French regime in hundreds of portraits, until, on October 5, 1789, the very night the king and queen were arrested and brought to Paris, she and her nine-year-old daughter dramatically escaped from Paris at midnight in a jolting stagecoach, while a fellow passenger, a Jacobin, muttered imprecations at her side. For the next twelve years, until 1802, Vigée-Lebrun would remain an exile from France.

*Portrait of Marie-Gabrielle de Gramont, Duchesse de Caderousse* dates from five years before the beginning of the Revolution and the artist's escape from Paris. Although Vigée-Lebrun's lifetime output would total some eight hundred portraits, in 1784, pregnant for the second time (the pregnancy, her last, would end in miscarriage), she turned out only five portraits, this being one of the two women's portraits. It was shown at the Salon of 1785 to much acclaim and became one of the artist's most celebrated works. Today, it is considered to be among her six or seven finest. With hair loose and unpowdered, the Duchess is shown as a shepherdess who has just returned, flushed and happy, with a basket of fruit. Laughingly, she tempts the viewer with a grape. Her costume of a deep-blue velvet bodice over a red skirt with a white scarf calls attention to the colors of France. Thus, Vigée-Lebrun presents the Duchess as a woman who, although a member of the aristocracy, is also at once nurturing, fruitful, seductive—and patriotic. Writing some fifty years later, in a passage as chatty as her portraits, Vigée-Lebrun recalled the painting as follows:

"As I detested the female style of dress then in fashion, I bent all my efforts upon rendering it a little more picturesque, and was delighted when, after getting the confidence of my models, I was able to drape them according to my fancy. Shawls

> " *. . . I detested the female style of dress then in fashion . . .* "

were not yet worn, but I made an arrangement with broad scarfs lightly intertwined round the body and on the arms, which was an attempt to imitate the beautiful drapings of Raphael and Domenichino. . . . Besides, I could not endure powder. I persuaded the handsome Duchess de Gramont-Caderousse to put none on for her sittings. Her hair was ebony black, and I divided it on the forehead, disposing it in irregular curls. After the sitting, which ended at the dinner hour, the Duchess would not change her headdress, but go to the theatre as she was. A woman of such good looks would, of course, set a fashion: indeed, this mode of doing the hair soon found imitators, and then gradually became general. This reminds me that in 1786, when I was painting the Queen, I begged her to use no powder, and to part her hair on the forehead. 'I should be the last to follow that fashion,' said the Queen, laughing; 'I do not want people to say that I adopted it to hide my large forehead.'"

Partly the victim of her own success, partly the product of her times, Vigée-Lebrun was both praised and maligned during her lifetime, not only for her painting, which was considered to be anywhere from brilliant to vapid, but for her personal life as well. Her husband, whom she had married reluctantly and at her mother's urging, gambled away her not inconsiderable earnings for twenty years. Her work critically acclaimed, she was yet refused membership in the Academie Royale de Peinture et de Sculpture because her husband was a picture dealer. She was finally admitted only when the queen intervened. On another occasion, her submission to the Salon of 1787 was initially refused exhibition because of the unpopularity of the subject. It was a portrait of Marie Antoinette. In her personal life, she was accused simultaneously of being the mistress of the French finance minister, a Parisian count, and a painter. She was also accused of extravagance, various reports claiming that she had spent from 20,000 to 80,000 francs on one of the suppers she gave for small groups of friends. In her memoirs, she said the actual cost had been fifteen francs.

While in exile, Vigée-Lebrun was far from idle. Painting the aristocratic heads of Rome, Naples, Moscow, and St Petersburg, she amassed a second fortune. In Russia, where she stayed for six years, she was a great favorite of Catherine II. In 1802, with her French citizenship rights restored, Vigée-Lebrun returned briefly to Paris, but went on to London, where she painted Lord Byron and the Prince of Wales, among others. Finally, in 1805, at age fifty, she

*Continued on p 211*

# JAMA®

**July 21, 1989**

The Journal of the American Medical Association

# PIET MONDRIAN

## Tableau No. IV: Lozenge Composition With Red, Gray, Blue, Yellow, and Black

Wherever artists gathered in Paris in the latter part of the nineteenth century, a favorite topic of argument, often loud, was the importance of line versus color in painting. Those with a classical bent insisted that line was more important and allied themselves with Ingres, while those who were more romantically inclined insisted, just as vociferously, that it was color that made a painting a painting and allied themselves with Delacroix. Indeed, a widely publicized caricature from the period shows Delacroix and Ingres, each astride a miniature horse, jousting in front of the Institut de France, their paintbrushes aimed like lances. "Line is color," announces Delacroix's banner. "Color is Utopia," answers Ingres' shield. "Long live line."

To the Dutch painter Piet Mondrian (1872-1944), who arrived in Paris a generation later at the age of forty, there was no such dichotomy. To him line and color were equally important, each being only the means to an end. But, each had to be freed from its conventionally accepted forms (line as outline or contour, for example, and color as taken from nature) so that in their new roles they would express neither classicism nor romanticism, neither figure nor landscape, but rather essence, or, as the intensely religious Mondrian put it, the absolute. Particulars had to be gotten rid of so that the universal could be expressed. The right angle was the universal line, and the pure primaries red, yellow, and blue were the universal colors (plus black and white, since one was the presence and the other the absence of all colors). Writing about his ideas almost as extensively as he painted them, Mondrian called his theory "neoplasticism." It was the watershed of his life. Changing his name from "Mondriaan" to "Mondrian," as if to signify that henceforth he would confine himself to essentials only, he devoted the next thirty years of his life to the pursuit of his idea of the absolute. In the process he was, along with Wassily Kandinsky, to carry modern painting into its abstract mode.

Born in Amersfoort, Holland, to strict Calvinist parents, Mondrian was one of four brothers and a sister. The usual parental tug-of-war was waged in his boyhood when his father wished him to train for teaching, whereas Piet wished to be a painter. A treaty

> " . . . when one does not represent things, . . . a place remains for the divine."

of sorts was arranged when Piet agreed to study for a diploma in art instruction. After he had qualified, however, he refused to accept a teaching assignment. Thus, at age twenty, henceforth providing his own financial support (although sometimes subsisting just barely), he entered the Academy of Fine Arts in Amsterdam. Disciplined and industrious, Mondrian received a thorough grounding in academic art over the next several years. In 1903, at age thirty-one, he visited Dutch Brabant and was so impressed with the simple and deeply religious life of the peasants that he settled there (much as his fellow countryman and idol, van Gogh, also for religious reasons, had settled among the coal miners of the Belgian Bourinage a generation earlier). But bothered, as he said, by too many visitors from the city, Mondrian returned to Amsterdam a year later and set up his studio there.

In Amsterdam, although he was seeking to free his painting from academic constraints, his work still contained the everyday images he knew: the polders, windmills, church facades, lighthouses, canals, willows, and chrysanthemums and the sea. In 1909, intensifying his search for the absolute, Mondrian joined the Dutch Theosophical Society, a heavily mystical movement then very popular in the Netherlands. It was from there that he eventually progressed to his own theory of neoplasticism, in which only straight lines and primary colors could express a "pure image of the absolute." Gradually, he ceased altogether using images, for "when one does not represent things," he wrote in his notebook, "a place remains for the divine." Moreover, he theorized, the right angle is the meeting place of opposites, the horizontal and the vertical line, the masculine and the feminine, movement and repose, the material and the spiritual. And finally, he concluded, colors should never be mixed because the colors of nature cannot be duplicated. Rather, they should be used pure, along with white and black. With this elementary vocabulary as his vernacular, Mondrian changed modern painting in the measure that Homer, Dante, and Shakespeare had changed language.

Among the classical images of modern art left by Mondrian is a series of paintings in a diamond format, always a square turned forty-five degrees, a shape virtually unknown to art until his work. Mondrian left only sixteen of these diamonds, and, of these, fewer than half are done with color and black lines. Of these latter, *Tableau No. IV: Lozenge Composition With Red, Gray, Blue, Yellow, and Black* (formerly *Diamond Painting in Red, Yellow, and Blue*) is considered by some to be his finest. Deceptively

Continued on p 211

# JAMA®

July 28, 1989

The Journal of the American Medical Association

# REMBRANDT VAN RIJN

## Portrait of a Lady With an Ostrich-Feather Fan

What more can be said about a man whose name is synonymous with painting that has not already been said in a thousand biographies and half a hundred self-portraits? Said the French painter and writer Eugène Fromentin, "His life is, like his painting, full of half-tints and dark corners." And so it is. At one moment it is bathed in light, as in his marriage to Saskia and the birth of his beloved son Titus, and at the next it dissolves into shadow with the death of Saskia and the loss of his property. Said his fellow countryman van Gogh, "Alone or almost alone amongst painters he has . . . that heartbroken tenderness, that glimpse into a superhuman infinitude that seems so natural there; you come upon it in many places in Shakespeare." The French minister of culture, Malraux, likened him to Dostoyevski, saying his art has no predecessors and will have no successors: "It is singular that the dialogue with God of one lone soul responds so powerfully to the great call of men to communion." But most of all, we know him, or we think we know him, because his face looks out at us in more than sixty self-portraits, now young and vigorous, then with Saskia, next in an introspective mood, again in a funny hat or an outlandish costume, or, at the end, tired and old and rheumy, but, finally, at peace. He is indeed the archivist of the human condition, himself the least heroic and most human of all. It is fitting that few would recognize his surname. He is simply Rembrandt (1606-1669). That is enough.

*Portrait of a Lady With an Ostrich-Feather Fan* was painted in about 1660, when Rembrandt was in his midfifties. Behind him were hundreds of paintings, drawings, and etchings of single figures, groups of figures, landscapes, and history, mythology, and religious scenes, including the well-known *Night Watch* and *The Anatomy Lesson of Dr Nicolaas Tulp*. Behind him also were success and prosperity, his marriage to Saskia, the deaths of three of the four children she bore him, her own death, his financial extravagance, his bankruptcy, an ill-fated liaison with his son's nurse followed by a lawsuit for breach of promise, and another, happier liaison with his housekeeper Hendrickje Stoffels, who was, however, excommunicated when she bore a daughter in 1654. Yet in all this his creative powers were not only not

> *. . . a sonnet in light and shadow. . . . a middle-aged woman . . .*

diminished, they were still expanding. Although his subsequent work would not be to the popular taste as much as previously, he was yet to produce some of his best.

John Walker, formerly director of the National Gallery of Art, has called *Lady With an Ostrich-Feather Fan* "the greatest portrait of a woman ever painted." The identity of the sitter is not known, but the painting is pendant with a portrait of a man, presumed to be her husband, holding gloves. She is striking in her simplicity. Sad, with sunken cheeks that might suggest a wasting illness, she is nevertheless at peace, a wistful peace perhaps, but peace. None of her individual features—her high, broad forehead, her widow's peak, her scant eyebrows, her heavy-lidded eyes—are especially beautiful, yet Rembrandt composes them in such a way that they speak of her own inner composure. And lending stability and reinforcing the sitter's own sense of repose is the larger, overall composition: the upper and lower lighted areas—the head and the collar above and the cuffs, hands, and plume below—form mirror images of two triangles, their bases meeting across her bosom. Moreover, this double triangle is echoed in the bowlike fastening at the center of the collar. Again, the sense of harmony is enhanced in the jewelry, with the globe earrings, the globe pendant, the circles of rings and bracelets. Finally, the textures of the hard, metallic gold ornaments and the cutting edges of the jewel on the finger contrast with the softness of the feather in the hand.

In its measured rhythms, *Lady With an Ostrich-Feather Fan* is a sonnet in light and shadow. Featuring a middle-aged woman wasted with illness and wearing jewels that will last longer than she, the painting becomes a type of the *vanitas* or memento mori work so popular in the Calvinist society of Rembrandt's day. Yet, the primary sense is still one of peace, peace with herself and with those around her. Like all of Rembrandt's subjects, himself perhaps most of all, he paints not heroes, but humans, yet in their very humanity they become heroic. When we look into the shadows and moving lights of a Rembrandt painting, what we see is not only images, but in the end, all of us, from cradle to tomb. "He is there when the cradle lights up," says Elie Faure, " . . . he is there when we are old, when we look fixedly at the side of the night that comes. . . . He does not pity us, he does not comfort us, because he is with us, because he is us." He is Rembrandt.

*Portrait of a Lady With An Ostrich-Feather Fan*, c 1658/1660, Dutch. Oil on canvas transferred to canvas. 99.5 × 83.0 cm. Courtesy of the National Gallery of Art, Washington, DC; Widener Collection.

# JAMA®

**August 11, 1989**

The Journal of the American Medical Association

# FRANCISCO JOSÉ DE GOYA Y LUCIENTES ~~

## Yard With Madmen

Toward the end of 1792, Francisco José de Goya y Lucientes (1746-1828), court painter to Charles IV and, at age forty-six, the most acclaimed portrait painter in all of Madrid, went to Cádiz to do a portrait of his friend and chief treasurer of Cádiz, Sebastián Martinéz. On the return trip to Madrid, while in Seville, Goya was stricken with a mysterious illness, during which he was thought to be dying. While the exact nature of the illness has never been fully explained, it did leave Goya temporarily paralyzed on the right side of his body, partially blind, and subject to dizzy spells; permanently, he was left profoundly deaf, with "roaring noises" in his head and headaches. Months after the onset of the illness, at the end of March 1793, he was still in Cádiz, and Martinéz wrote to Martín Zapeter, another friend of Goya's, that "the noises in his head and the deafness have not improved, but his vision is much better and he is no longer suffering from the disorder which made him lose his balance. He can now go up and down stairs very well and in a word is doing things he was not able to before." One of the "things he was not able to do before" is *Yard With Madmen* (formerly *The Madhouse of Saragossa*), one of eleven cabinet pictures Goya painted on tin plate while he was convalescing. Noting that paintings of these "various popular diversions" (several of the other scenes were of bullfights) were a departure from his usual work, Goya explained that his commissioned paintings allowed for no observations outside those expected, while these little paintings, done on his own time and for his own personal satisfaction, gave him scope for "caprice and invention."

Without preaching a homily, Goya turns *Yard With Madmen* into an eloquent parable of not only his own suffering, but, indeed, of all human suffering. Center stage, two

> *an eloquent parable of . . . all human suffering.*

figures, without clothes, contend in mortal combat, much as the human psyche, shorn of its defenses, must contend with its personal demons. To either side, two figures, oblivious to all around them, grimace, each into his own private hell. In the right background a third figure grovels, while in the doorway a fourth, with upraised arms, offers enthusiastic comment. In the midst of it all, his identity secured by his street clothes, an attendant raises a whip to deal yet another blow to the already defenseless combatants. It is a story of darkness, despair, violence, and alienation. Yet, Goya leaves the viewer not without hope. Stretching across the entire top of the canvas, and even penetrating downward into the dungeon, he has painted almost pure light. Living as he did at the end of the eighteenth century, it is his paean to the Enlightenment, then sweeping across Europe. It is also his tribute to reason, which he believed would restore sanity. But most important, the light is his own affirmation of life, given in spite of his own loss. In the isolation of his deafness, it is as though, missing one sense, Goya could concentrate himself more deeply on the mystery of the human condition, whether in the realm of the intellectual, the social, or the personal.

For Goya, the experience of his illness was a turning point into new possibilities. His deafness was total and permanent, but in the remaining thirty-five years of his life he went on to produce some of his greatest works, including the well-known series of etchings, *Los Caprichos* (1796-1798) and *Los desastres de la guerra* ("The Disasters of War") (1808-1814). It was as though his illness had freed him from his shackles, now to paint not what convention expected, but what truth told him. In a sense, deafness had become Goya's light.

*Yard With Madmen*, 1794, Spanish. Oil on tin. 43.6 × 32.4 cm. Courtesy of the Meadows Museum, Southern Methodist University, Dallas, Texas; Algur H. Meadows Collection.

# JAMA®

The Journal of the American Medical Association

August 18, 1989

# BARTOLOMÉ ESTEBAN MURILLO

## *Two Women at a Window*

So brilliant in so many countries was so much of the painting of the seventeenth century that one whose name is not Rembrandt or Rubens or Velázquez comes to be obscured by the light that is cast by them. Such is the case with Bartolomé Esteban Murillo (1617-1682), who rounded out the golden age of Spanish painting. Yet at one time he was more highly regarded than his countryman Velázquez. Indeed, his reputation as the "Spanish Raphael" persisted for 200 years, right up until the 1880s.

Born in Seville, Murillo was the son of the barber-surgeon Gaspar Esteban and María Murillo. With both parents dead by the time he was ten, the young boy became the ward of an uncle who in turn apprenticed him to another relative, the comparatively obscure Sevillian painter Juan del Castillo. By age twenty-one Murillo was independent, earning his living by painting small religious pictures for export to Spain's possessions in the Americas. In 1645, at age twenty-seven, he was apparently successful enough to marry, and his wife, Beatriz de Cabrera Sotomeyer, eventually bore him nine children. In 1660 he founded the first academy of fine arts in Seville and became its director. He died in Seville in 1681, aged sixty-three, several months after a fall from a scaffold in a church he had been decorating in Cádiz. So great was his modesty, said a contemporary biographer, that he would not allow himself to be examined after the accident, his modesty thereby resulting in his death.

Whereas his contemporary Velázquez worked in the capital city of Madrid on royal commissions, supported by a pension and painting portraits and other subjects as the king desired, Murillo worked in Seville, drawing his income more or less freelance from commissions from religious groups for decoration of their churches and monasteries. Mindful of the Council of Trent's statement on art of 1563 and also of a lengthy work published in Seville in 1649 by Pacheco, the inspector of art for the Inquisition (and Velázquez' father-in-law), Murillo, as did other artists who painted religious subjects, strove to hold to the ideals of painting as officially set forth. Subjects had to be presented in a manner that was

> *. . . unique individuals whom we will remember as much as if we had spoken with them . . .*

theologically correct according to the canons of the time. Murillo concentrated on religious cycles from the Old and New Testaments, but especially he painted saints performing one of the several corporal acts of mercy, such as feeding the hungry, sheltering the homeless, burying the dead, and caring for the sick. It is based largely on this oeuvre that his reputation rests. Thus, once highly praised, mostly because of the edifying content of the paintings, today he is equally in disrepute, again because of content, which is found to be "saccharine." But Murillo had another side to him, best seen in his portraits and landscapes and in such genre paintings as *Two Women at a Window* (formerly *A Girl and Her Duenna*). It is in these works that his truly painterly qualities can perhaps best be judged.

From an age heavy with Baroque, Murillo is seen in a simpler, almost classical style. With the window itself forming a frame within a frame in its strong vertical and horizontal lines, the two figures, one triangular, the other rectangular, each occupy their own space, the young girl pushing boldly forward, over the sill, the older woman ducking back, behind the shutter. Their heads lie on a diagonal from lower right to upper left, with all the space above and to the right empty and mysterious. The colors are warm, being all tones of brown accented by red, while the white highlights anticipate the naturalism of 150 years thence. Most striking, however, is a feature that immediately sets the women apart from the more familiar sanitized beggar boys and saccharine saints: each has a distinctive personality. They are unique individuals whom we will remember as much as if we had spoken with them—the girl impish, impudent, bold, saucy, the woman shy, retiring, modest, but still able to appreciate what is evidently a good joke. What the source of the amusement is, however, remains somewhat uncertain, for there is disagreement over the correct title of the painting. When first engraved around the beginning of the nineteenth century, the painting was known as *Galician Women* after an area of Spain noted for its courtesans. It has also been suggested that the painting, which is life-size, was meant to be seen at the level of a ground floor window so that passersby would be deceived into believing that they were being watched. Finally, a Spanish art historian says the scene is simply one of feminine curiosity and "does not portray women for whom love is a profession." But whatever the case, this charming portrayal of young and old, wise and simple, fear and adventure surely belongs, as another critic has noted, to the genre of the Spanish picaresque novel, an association that has yet to be widely discussed or appreciated.

*Continued on p 212*

# JAMA®

The Journal of the American Medical Association

August 25, 1989

# GRANT WOOD

## Death on the Ridge Road

Though his work is today synonymous with Midwest America, it took Grant Wood (1891-1942) three trips abroad and the first thirty-five years of his life to realize that what he wanted to paint was all around him and had been for all of his life: his mother, his sister, his dentist, his friends and neighbors in Cedar Rapids, the local farmers and townspeople, and the houses and cornfields of the Wapsipinicon Valley of east central Iowa. Influenced and encouraged by the stories and essays of Ruth Suckow about rural Iowa, and especially by the poet Jay Sigmund, who would be also his friend and mentor, Wood became not only a regionalist painter, but also an active voice for the regionalist movement in all of American art, literature included. Two of his best-known works in this genre are *Woman With Plant* of 1929 and the much-parodied, but nonetheless enduring, *American Gothic* of 1930.

Born on a farm near Anamosa, Iowa, a small town twenty-five miles northeast of Cedar Rapids, to Francis Maryville Wood and Hattie D. Weaver Wood, Grant lost his father when he was ten and moved with his mother, older brother, and younger brother and sister to Cedar Rapids. In Cedar Rapids' grammar school he was encouraged by the art teacher, and in June 1910, after graduation from high school, he went north to study for the summer at the Minneapolis School of Design and Handicraft with the designer and architect Earnest Batchelder. Back in Cedar Rapids, his art studies over the next few years were desultory, consisting of various night, summer, and correspondence courses. Part of the time he studied at the University of Iowa and at the Art Institute in Chicago. He supported himself, and later his mother and sister as well, by teaching in a country school and making

jewelry and lamps of his own design. Toward the end of World War I he served in the US Army designing camouflage. In 1919 he began what eventually became six years as an art teacher in the Cedar Rapids public school system. During the summer of 1920 he made his first trip to Paris, and in 1923, on leave from teaching, he spent eleven months in France and Italy. Like so many other American students in Paris, he studied at the Académie Julian. In 1926, at age thirty-five, Wood made his final trip to Paris.

> *. . . a single steep hill and two cars and a truck . . .*

Hitherto painting in the quasi-Impressionist style he had learned in Europe, it was after this trip that he adopted the definitive style that came to be known as Regionalism.

Wood had been established as a region-alist painter for some time when, in 1935, he painted *Death on the Ridge Road*. A year earlier, Wood, who distrusted automobiles and, indeed, machinery and mass-produced items of all kinds, had reluctantly bought his first car. Promptly, as if to fulfill a self-made prophecy, he smashed it into a milk truck. Then, his friend and mentor Jay Sigmund, while driving on the Ridge Road just north of Stone City, Iowa, was seriously injured in an auto accident. Wood marked the event, first with a drawing in 1934, and the fol-lowing year with the painting. Wood noticed as he was completing the painting, initially put on canvas, that the paint had already begun to peel. He redid it on panel much in the manner of the fifteenth-century Flemish masters he so admired. This final version was widely used at the time in campaigns for auto safety.

*Death on the Ridge Road* is a marked departure from the usual content and feel of a Wood painting. Instead of an idyllic scene of planting or harvest or of drowsing, halcyon days in summer, it is a menacing scene that forebodes disaster. Missing is Grant's usual panorama across miles of gently rolling hills, the intricate web of roads, rivers, and bridges, the round, friendly trees, the plodding horses, the earnest working people. In their place is a single steep hill and two cars and a truck, the one car small, slow, sedate, and dutiful, the other sleek, low-slung, fast, and law-breaking, and the truck big, lumbering, and innocent. The highway slashes diagonally across the hill, while the treeless landscape is dominated by stark utility poles that stand like Gothic crosses. To the right a dark cloud is pulled across the sky like a curtain opening on the tragedy about to be played. The principal colors are a violent clash of red and green. Yet this work is not com-pletely divorced from his other paintings. Wood was fond of using a Gothic-arch motif that he worked into his paintings in the design of a window or in the joining of the tines of a pitchfork or even in the rick-rack trim on a woman's apron. Here, the characteristic zigzag design is seen in the fence posts with their shadows and, expan-ded, in the planted land to the right. Even the cloud pattern suggests a zigzag, but even more of a clincher is the zigzag position of the vehicles.

Besides the obvious theme of auto safety and the personal reference to the two recent auto accidents in Wood's life, *Death on the Ridge Road* can be seen in many other ways, all of them either violations of what Wood considered sacrosanct or collisions of values. For example, there is the invasion of the privacy of the Iowa countryside by the

Continued on p 212

# JAMA®

September 1, 1989

The Journal of the American Medical Association

# MICHELANGELO MERISI DA CARAVAGGIO

## The Cardsharps (I Bari)

His name was Michelangelo Merisi, Michelangelo not for the sculptor, who had just died, but for the archangel, and Merisi for his father Fermo, a well-to-do stonemason; but he came to be known simply as Caravaggio (1571-1610) for the town near Milan in which he was born. His short and tempestuous life—he did not reach his fortieth birthday—has provided an endless supply of anecdotes, while his work, denounced in his day as inappropriate and immoral, is today recognized as truly innovative and a major influence on subsequent painters, Rembrandt, Velázquez, Murillo, and Rubens among them. Born in a century in which only the ideal was acknowledged, Caravaggio dared to paint not what he imagined ought to be, but what he actually saw with his eyes. Nature makes no particular thing beautiful in all its parts, said the prevailing wisdom; thus, "the painter desiring natural beauty in each form ought to take from diverse bodies all that which in each single one is most perfect, and ought to join it together since it is difficult to find a single one that is perfect." Caravaggio, either from genius or lack of ability, or even perversity, did not or could not do this. If "the model was taken away from his eyes his hand and his imagination remained empty," said another contemporary. It was essential for him to work from a model, and he always reproduced it faithfully. Thus, if the model had dirty feet, then so did Caravaggio's St Matthew; if the peasants toiling along the road had sweaty headbands, then so did his pilgrims; and if the corpse of the strumpet fished out of the Tiber was bloated, then so was the body of Caravaggio's dead Virgin. But even more distressing to the Establishment of Caravaggio's time, perhaps, was the startling manner in which he handled light. For

Caravaggio, light was the bearer of truth, and he used it to show his subject in sharp relief. Not only did the light reveal every detail of the subject, but it often shattered the rigidly held notions of his viewers as well. Finally, and perhaps most annoying to his peers, Caravaggio painted directly on the canvas with a facileness that did not require a preliminary drawing or squaring of the canvas. He was a "monster of genius and talent, without rules, without theory, without learning and meditation," the "Anti-Michelangelo," said one.

> " . . . monster of genius and talent, without rules, without theory, without learning and meditation . . . "

For all the antagonism he aroused, little is known about Caravaggio's early life or training, except that when he was about thirteen years old his father apprenticed him for four years to the Milanese painter Simon Peterzano, who claimed to have been a pupil of Titian. At about age twenty Caravaggio was in Rome hustling living expenses with crude works he produced quickly and sold cheaply, meanwhile saving his real efforts for works that might produce commissions. Apparently he was successful, for he first worked in the studio of the Cavaliere d'Arpino, and later he settled into the household of Cardinal del Monte in Rome. In 1599 he received a commission to do a chapel, but, after completion, it had to be done over because the works were "indecorous." Other altarpieces were rejected the following year. It is also about this time, perhaps following an

illness, that Caravaggio began to appear with depressing regularity in Rome police records. The offenses were varied, but seemingly impetuous, antiauthority, and usually violent: inflicting sword wounds (on several occasions), throwing stones at the police, writing obscene verses, wounding a notary, dumping a plate of artichokes over a waiter's head. (It is recorded that there were eight artichokes, four of them cooked in oil and four in butter.) The culmination came in 1606, when Caravaggio killed his opponent in a sword fight in a dispute during a game of tennis, albeit accidentally. Forced this time to flee the city, Caravaggio went to Naples and eventually to Malta. Yet he contrived to paint, even while in flight, and from these years come some of his most profoundly religious works. Finally, in 1609, Caravaggio decided to end his flight and return to Rome (occasioned, no doubt, by a violent incident in Malta) in the hope of a pardon. En route from Naples to Rome, he was taken from the ship at Port'Ercole, a Spanish garrison, and imprisoned. Ironically, this arrest was a result of mistaken identity and he was soon released. The ship, however, had sailed without him and, as Caravaggio believed, with all his belongings. Weakened by his frantic efforts to rejoin the ship, Caravaggio died of malaria in Port'Ercole a short time later. In one final irony, his belongings were found after his death in the customs shed at Port'Ercole. Meanwhile, the pardon he sought had been announced in Rome on the very day his death was announced.

*The Cardsharps* was painted during Caravaggio's early years in Rome when he was in his midtwenties and had as yet no known involvement with the police. But he is familiar enough with fraud and deception to paint it convincingly. The gull, an

Continued on p 212

# JAMA®

The Journal of the American Medical Association

**September 8, 1989**

# MICHAEL SWEERTS ❧

## *Head of an Old Woman*

While Rembrandt and Rubens dominated the Dutch and Flemish painting of the seventeenth century, a small group of expatriates from Holland and Flanders worked in the south, in Rome. Known as *Bentvueghels* (birds of a flock) because they grouped together, they painted mainly *Bambocciate*—small, realistically rendered scenes of peasants, soldiers, or tavern lowlife. Their realism was undoubtedly influenced by the recently deceased Caravaggio, many of whose works were in Rome, although the name given their work derives from the Italian for "trivial." The name could also have come from *Bamboccio* (fat and lively baby), the nickname given to Pieter van Laer, an early member of the group. The *Bentvueghels* were, at any rate, a rowdy group who refused to obey the Roman law or to pay dues to the Roman Academy of St Luke. Eventually, in 1720, they were outlawed by the Pope.

Joining the group sometime around 1646 was Michael Sweerts (1624-1664), a twenty-two-year-old painter from Brussels. Becoming an associate member of the Guild of St Luke in Rome, he was charged with collecting the dues owed by his fellow expatriates. Typical of Sweerts' smaller portraits, and thought to have been painted about this time, is *Head of an Old Woman*. Sweerts shows the woman, once a flower that sprang up and bloomed, as one who has come now to the withering time. In tones of earth brown and sky gray, he paints her as one who has reached the November of her life. No longer does she look outward but, rather, inward, to the coming winter, recalling pleasures past, struggles won, and peace to

> *. . . one who has reached the November of her life.*

come. She has seen epidemics of plague, typhus, typhoid fever, scurvy, dysentery, and diphtheria. Leprosy and syphilis have somewhat waned, but that is small solace when nearly half of all other deaths occur in children who have not yet reached age two. She has had to fear anthrax, ergotism, influenza, smallpox, scarlatina, measles, rubella, and puerperal fever. And she has survived. What she looks to now with her averted eyes is perhaps to those who did not survive—to ghosts of mother, father, friends, siblings, husband, children—leaving her alone in a world peopled by an alien generation that she no longer recognizes. Until this moment, that is, when a young stranger takes a piece of wood and some colors and breathes a likeness of her out of the darkness. Re-created, she lives, no longer old, but eternally young, three and a half centuries later. Indeed, a survivor.

Whether Sweerts was successful in collecting the dues from his fellow expatriates is unknown, but the task surely must have been thankless. He left Rome sometime after 1654, and in 1656 he accepted the post of director of a school of drawing in Brussels. In 1659 he was made a member of the Brussels Guild of Painters. Two years later, at age thirty-seven, he became a lay member of a French missionary order whose chief task was caring for the sick and traveled with them to the Far East. However, because of complaints about his quarrelsome nature and general unsuitability for missionary work, Sweerts left the order sometime after they had reached Persia; he went to Goa, where he joined a Jesuit group. It was there that he died in 1664, of unknown causes. Like Caravaggio, whose work was neglected for centuries, he has, in the past fifty years, come back into favor.

*Head of an Old Woman*, c 1650, Flemish. Oil on wood. 49.2 × 38.1 cm. Courtesy of the J. Paul Getty Museum, Los Angeles, California.

# JAMA®

The Journal of the American Medical Association

**September 15, 1989**

# FERDINAND HODLER ⟿

## *The Disillusioned One*

To the Swiss painter Ferdinand Hodler (1853-1918), death was not some abstract, romantic notion from the pen of a poet. Rather, it had a form that was as real and as concrete as any tubercle bacillus in the laboratory of Robert Koch. Nor was death an occasional intruder in Hodler's life; it was a perpetual visitation. At age seven he lost his father, at fourteen his mother, and by the time he was in his midthirties his five siblings and three half-siblings, all to tuberculosis. Like his slightly younger Norwegian contemporary, Edvard Munch, whose childhood and youth were also blighted by tuberculosis, Hodler would say of this time, "It seemed that there was always a corpse in the house, and that it just had to be that way."

An exact contemporary of Vincent van Gogh, Ferdinand Hodler was born on March 14, 1853, in Bern, the eldest of six children. His father Johann was a carpenter, his mother Margarete a cook-housekeeper. After the death of his father, his mother married Gottlieb Schüpbach and the couple had three children. The following year, when he was nine, and continuing until he was thirteen, Ferdinand assisted his stepfather in the sign-painting business. After the death of his mother in 1867, he was apprenticed to Ferdinand Sommer, who taught him how to paint Swiss views for tourists. In 1872, at age nineteen, he went to Geneva with the intention of entering the École des Beaux-Arts but did not know enough French to pass the entrance examination. Instead, he began copying at the Musée Roth, where he attracted the attention of Barthélemy Menn, a follower of the French painter Corot. Two years later, while studying with Menn, Hodler won the first of many awards for his painting, and in 1881, at age twenty-eight, he opened his own studio. Desperately poor, he slept in the studio using a cupboard door, which he removed each

evening and rehung each morning, as his bed. In 1887 his son Hector was born to him and Augustine Dupìn, a Geneva seamstress who was also his model and his mistress. In 1889, with his entire family save Hector dead of tuberculosis, Hodler, aged thirty-six, married Berta Stucki, the twenty-one-year-old daughter of a Bern watchmaker. The couple separated almost immediately and were divorced in 1891.

It was in 1890, after the separation from his wife and the death of the last member of his family, that Hodler began a series of paintings on the basic existential themes of love and

> *. . . a mountain of misery, an island of grief.*

death, faith and despair, fin de siècle themes that would also attract other artists, notably Munch in his *The Frieze of Life* series and Gauguin in *Where do we come from? Where are we? Where are we going? The Disillusioned One* is one of those in Hodler's series. Painted when Hodler was not yet forty, *The Disillusioned One* captures nevertheless the isolation and loneliness, the alienation and despair, that comes at least once to Everyman, if not in youth then perhaps in midlife, and most certainly in age. Head bowed, hands clasped, shoulders slumped, the figure is completely enclosed in its outline, an outline that could as easily be the contour of a vulture brooding over death as that of a melancholic man. So withdrawn into himself and so divorced is he from what surrounds him that he casts not even a shadow that would prove his existence. He is a mountain of misery, an island of grief. He could be a man old and ill and out of work or he could be a man for whom God has died, it does not

matter. Grief is grief, regardless, and mourning has no degrees. Yet "No man is an Island, entire of itself; every man is a piece of the Continent, a part of the main." Thus, closed off in his outline, his face nevertheless reflects the same green with which the grass grows, and the yellow of the landscape informs his robe. Flowers bloom beside the bench, not dying flowers of an aging summer, but first flowers of a newborn spring. For whenever Hodler painted death he also painted life, and whenever he painted despair he followed it with hope. For every night he painted, he painted a day, for every autumn a spring, for every darkness light, and for every disillusioned one, a chosen one. Indeed, one of his best-known paintings, completed the year after *The Disillusioned One*, shows the six-year-old Hector standing in a meadow filled with blooming flowers.

Except for a few trips, notably to Spain, Italy, Antwerp, Paris, Brussels, and Vienna, Hodler remained in Switzerland all his life, largely isolated from the art community of the rest of Europe. In 1898 he was married a second time, to Berthe Jacques. In 1908 he met Valentine Godé-Darel, a young woman who became his model and who, in his old age, bore him a daughter, Paulette, later adopted by his wife. In a remarkable series of paintings he chronicled Valentine as she wasted away from cancer after Paulette's birth. In his later years Hodler was honored by the Swiss government when it accepted his design for its 50- and 100-franc notes. In 1910 he received an honorary doctorate from Basel University. In 1914 the German government banned his works when he protested the shelling of Rheims Cathedral. In 1915, the same year that Valentine died, it was discovered that his beloved Hector, not yet thirty, had tuberculosis (he would die of the disease in 1920), while Hodler himself, in 1917, began

 *Continued on p 213*

# JAMA®

### The Journal of the American Medical Association

**October 6, 1989**

# JEAN ÉTIENNE LIOTARD

## Portrait of Marie Frederike van Reede-Athlone at Seven Years of Age

In seventeenth-century Europe, as commissions from the Church and the government for decoration of their religious houses and royal palaces fell off, so too did the market for the great history and religious paintings. Painters who once could be secure for a lifetime on an income from a prince of either house now had to scrabble in the marketplace. Fortunately, there grew at the same time a demand for portraits, not only for the "official" or the royal portrait, but for the private portrait as well, a demand that was swelled by an enlarging middle class. Thus, any artist who could paint a satisfying likeness could find steady employment, although, as expected, some painters were better than others, and income did not necessarily measure worth. But one who was successful both financially and artistically was the eighteenth-century Swiss painter Jean Étienne Liotard (1702-1789).

One of twin sons of Antoine Liotard, a religious refugee from Montélimar, France, who became a small tradesman in Geneva, Jean Étienne showed his talent early and began his art studies as a boy in Geneva. (His twin, Jean Michel, also studied art and later became an engraver.) At age twenty-two, he went to Paris, where he studied with Massé and Lemoyne and where, according to early biographical accounts, he was a sensation, his work being much sought after. Beginning in 1735, when he was in his early thirties, and continuing for the next forty years, Liotard made a series of lengthy journeys that took him to Rome, Vienna, Paris, Holland, and London. Most notable among Liotard's travels, however, was the four-year trip he took to the Levant, where he adopted Turkish dress and a long beard, affectations that he continued long after he returned to Western Europe and that earned him the lifelong epithet of "The Turk."

Immensely popular, he did likenesses of many of the important personages of the time, including Pope Clement XII and several of the Roman cardinals, the Empress Maria Theresa and her eleven children, and the Princess of Wales and other members of the English aristocracy. Much of his work was done in pastels, a medium that had recently been made popular in Paris by the Venetian artist Rosalba

> *Outwardly still a child, she has learned nevertheless to keep secrets . . .*

Carriera. Pastel was often favored over oils in that it worked up more quickly, did not incommode the sitter with lengthy sessions or unpleasant smells, and allowed for frequent interruptions during sittings, qualities especially suited to children's sittings.

According to critics, some of Liotard's best paintings date from 1755/1756, the year he spent in Holland. Of these, one of the most admired is *Portrait of Maria Frederike van Reede-Athlone at Seven Years of Age*. Done at the request of her mother, the Countess van Reede, whose own portrait Liotard had just completed, the portrait of the seven-year-old Maria Frederike is painted with all the fineness of porcelain and delicacy of lacework. It is characteristic of Liotard's work in its brilliant blues (he used the same velvet and ermine cloak with several other sitters as well), in its pastel medium, and in the fineness of the finish. His work was greatly admired by Flaubert and Ingres, although the English writer Horace Walpole said, in what was probably a euphemism for "unflattering," but a

tribute nevertheless, that his portraits were "too like to please."

Though Liotard's works are often said to lack psychological insight, Maria Frederike is nonetheless a true child of the aristocracy. She feigns indifference, but she is clearly aware of, and accepts as her due, the admiration of others. And, unlike the unknown four-year-old in Renoir's *A Girl With a Watering Can* or the five-year-old *Clara Serena Rubens*, who still live innocently in the kingdom of childhood, Liotard's Maria Frederike, at seven, stands at the threshold of the adult world. Outwardly still a child, she has learned nevertheless to keep secrets, or, if not to keep them, then to tell only the part that she chooses. It is a bit of calculation or deviousness that has entered her world, which, if it signals the end of innocence, at the same time signals an awakening ability to defend herself. Actually, few details are known of Maria Frederike except that at age twenty-one she married Sigismund Pieter Alexander Count van Heiden-Reinestein and that she probably had children, since the portrait is recorded as having passed to her descendants. She died at age fifty-nine, cause of death unrecorded.

In later life Liotard retired to his birthplace of Geneva. When the public's taste began to change and his portrait commissions fell off, he turned to painting still lifes and to writing. In some parting advice given in a treatise on painting written near the end of his life, he urged fellow painters always to heed the remarks of those he called the "ignorarts," those who knew nothing about art. Whereas those knowledgeable about art could be fooled by the artistic qualities of a work, he said, the ignorart cannot be fooled because he does not see the art; he sees only the truth. As many before him had also said, painting is, after all, the art of deception.

*Continued on p 213*

# JAMA®

The Journal of the American Medical Association

October 13, 1989

# QUIRINGH VAN BREKELENKAM

## *Interior With Woman Scaling Fish*

In a country where nights are long and days are gray, light is precious. Nowhere, perhaps, has this light been more celebrated than in the works of the seventeenth-century Dutch painters, who, as Lord Byron said of Rembrandt, could make even darkness equal light. One of the most popular motifs for the seventeenth-century genre painter was the Dutch interior, where the darkness of a room is pierced by just enough daylight to discover its inhabitants at their various occupations: peeling apples, scraping parsnips, making pancakes, pouring milk, scaling fish, tailoring a vest, reading a letter. Notable among these Dutch painters of domestic interiors is Quiringh van Brekelenkam (c 1620s-1667/1668).

Born probably in Zwammerdam, van Brekelenkam entered the Guild of St Luke in nearby Leiden in 1648, the year it was founded, and died in Leiden some twenty years later. He is noted primarily for his paintings of workshops and kitchens whose cheerful, industrious occupants concentrate over their work, often moving their task close to a window to take advantage of the last of the daylight. According to critics, his dark and light contrasts are well managed, and, in his best pictures, his coloring is unequaled. He is noted for his delicate grays, luminous reds, and warm whites and browns.

> *Even the woman's spectacles contribute to the notion that this painting is a celebration of light and vision.*

A good example of van Brekelenkam's work is *Interior With Woman Scaling Fish*, a tiny (its dimensions are only slightly larger than those of a business letter) gem of a work done when he was in his forties. Typical in its genre aspect—the mistress of the house preparing a meal—it is also a chance for him to show his virtuosity in handling light and color: the brilliant red plate and sleeve; the lesser reds of the wooden chair and stool; the more subtle reds of the woman's complexion; the glint of light off the plates, the kettle, and the fish scales, which sparkle about the woman's fingers like jewels. Even the woman's spectacles contribute to the notion that this painting is a celebration of light and vision.

Little else is known about van Brekelenkam's life beyond his meager vital statistics. He is thought to have been a pupil in Leiden of the Dutch genre and portrait painter Gerard Dou, who was himself a pupil of the young Rembrandt. His work is also judged to be reminiscent of that of Gerard Metsu, also a pupil of Dou and also a painter of interiors and genre scenes. Van Brekelenkam's gift was, like that of the other artists of the Dutch golden age of painting, to bring light out of darkness.

*Interior With Woman Scaling Fish*, 1665, Dutch. Oil on panel. 46.4 × 36.5 cm. Courtesy of the Los Angeles County Museum of Art, Los Angeles, California; gift of A. Popper.

# JAMA®

## The Journal of the American Medical Association

October 20, 1989

# JAMES SIDNEY ENSOR

## *Skeletons Warming Themselves*

The Belgian painter James Sidney Ensor (1860-1949) plumbed the depths of the absurd and returned with more than most of his viewers were prepared to accept. From one pole of human identity to the other, from the extreme of the mask to the extreme of the skeleton, his works were images of the fantastic: grinning, leering, grimacing grotesqueries of the human face, or bones, dry, rattling bones, without sinew, flesh, skin, or spirit, that played billiards, studied chinoiseries, fought over a herring or the body of a hanged man, and tried to warm themselves beside a stove whose fire, like theirs, had gone out. Often he is a reminder of Goya, but with a brighter palette and without the cruelties.

Ensor was born in Ostend, the Belgian seaside town that is Dover's port across the straits linking the English Channel with the North Sea. His mother was Maria Catharina Haegheman, who kept a curio shop full of seashells and, at carnival time, masks, as her family in Ostend had done for generations. His father was Frederic James Ensor, Brussels-born but English, who could adjust neither to life in a provincial sea town nor to an occupation of selling kitsch. Though he lived long enough to inspire his son's artistic bent and to oversee his training, he died at age fifty-two, the town drunk. James by that time had completed three years at the Brussels Academy, returned to Ostend where he had taken over the attic of his parents' home as a studio, and was deep into his most creative period. Meanwhile, his mother failed to understand why her son did not become a shopkeeper rather than waste time in the attic.

To this highly creative period, near its end, belongs *Skeletons Warming Themselves*,

painted in 1889, when Ensor was twenty-nine. His father had died of alcoholism two years earlier. The same year as *Skeletons*, Ensor's masterwork, *The Entry of Christ Into Brussels*, had been rejected for exhibition by his colleagues, who also voted to expel him from the avant-garde group Ensor had helped to found, Les XX. But because the vote failed one of being

> *"The fire is out. Will you find any tomorrow?"*

unanimous (Ensor voted for himself), he was permitted to stay, but not to exhibit. This event may have been commemorated in *Skeletons Warming Themselves*, in which the skeleton of the artist, discarded palette and brush at his feet, lies at the feet of music and literature, his head on an empty wood box. Meanwhile music, a silent violin at his side, and literature, with an unlit lamp, try to warm themselves at a stove in which there is no fire. At the base of the stove is written the words *Pas de feu* and beneath them *en trouverez vous demain?*— "The fire is out. Will you find any tomorrow?" To the upper right, watching from a doorway, stands an ambiguous figure that some interpret as a woman knitting in another, more fruitful attempt to get warm, while others see it as a man in clerical garb serving as a commentary on the failure of the Church, along with the arts, to have any relevance for modern society. Meanwhile, at the left, in what is perhaps Ensor's tribute to his Flemish forebear Teniers the Younger, another skeleton pokes his head through the door and observes the whole scene, just as did

Teniers' disembodied heads poke through windows. Thus, the painting also becomes a kind of *vanitas* or commentary on the human condition as seen by the artist. Most remarkable, however, are the colors chosen to complement this macabre scene: far from the somber tones one might expect, they are light, delicate, beautiful, iridescent pinks, greens, and blues, reminiscent of the colors of the shells Ensor grew up with in his mother's shop. His colors remind one of what he called the "pearly haze" of the North Sea, the sea whose opalescent mists were in his blood like saltwater, put there, as he said, by Venus at his birth.

Like the sea mists, which rise in the dawn and disappear in the sun, Ensor's creative period was over almost as soon as it had begun. All told, it lasted from the time he finished his studies at the Brussels Academy in 1880, at age twenty, to about 1893. He would outlive his creativity by nearly sixty years; what he did from age thirty-three on was only a variation on what he had done before. But gradually his work was discovered, and late in his long life he was the recipient of many honors from the very Establishment he had once scandalized, including a baronetcy and the cravat of the Legion of Honor. When he died at the age of eighty-nine, for all purposes a recluse in his house in Ostend, all of Belgium accompanied him to his grave site: government ministers, ambassadors, church dignitaries, generals, critics, magistrates, schoolboys, fishermen, fishwives. Such a turnout was perhaps only fitting for one who said that to paint one must always look with both eyes and that to look thus is to love. But just as the poet becomes eventually wordless, and the musician silent, so too does the painter one

114

*Continued on p 213*

# JAMA®

## The Journal of the American Medical Association

**October 27, 1989**

# GEORGE CLAIR TOOKER, JR ❧

## *Highway*

George Clair Tooker, Jr (1920-    ), was born in Brooklyn, New York, the elder of two children of a municipal bond broker and his Cuban American wife. The family moved to the south shore of Long Island shortly thereafter, and it was there, in Bellport, that George grew up. He began painting lessons at age seven and attended Bellport High School and Phillips Academy, Andover, Massachusetts, graduating from the latter in 1938. In 1942 he graduated from Harvard with a major in English literature. It was at Harvard that he became interested in the work of the Mexican painters David Alfaro Siqueiros and José Clemente Orozco, especially as they commented on social conditions. Following his Harvard graduation, Tooker enlisted in the US Marine Corps, where he was assigned to Officer Candidate School. However, he was medically discharged shortly thereafter when an old stomach ailment flared up. In 1943 he enrolled in the Art Students League in New York City, where he studied with Reginald Marsh, Kenneth Hayes Miller, and Harry Sternberg. In 1949 he spent six months traveling in Italy and France, returning to settle in New York City. In 1954, already the author of some of his best-known works, Tooker was commissioned to do the set designs for the Gian Carlo Menotti opera *The Saint of Bleeker Street*. In 1960 he established his home and studio in Vermont, but returned to New York City to teach at the Art Students League from 1965 to 1968. Thereafter he lived for a time in Malaga, Spain, but returned to Hartland, Vermont, where he now lives and works.

Tooker's work is unique in that it applies a traditional fifteenth-century medium and technique—egg yolk tempera on board prepared with half a dozen coats of gesso sized with rabbit glue—to a twentieth-century social commentary done in Surrealist fashion. Most often he comments on the anonymity of modern life, on faceless bureaucracy, on the depersonalization of the individual, and on the difficulties of meaningful communication. Together with this painstaking preparation of his materials, detailed and careful preliminary drawings, and slow and thoughtful painting, Tooker's output is limited to five or six paintings a year.

*. . . disquieting in a way one cannot quite finger, like . . . a dream one cannot quite remember . . .*

*Highway* was painted when Tooker was in his early thirties. Enigmatic and dark, it is disquieting in a way one cannot quite finger, like the sense of sinister foreboding that is left by a dream one cannot quite remember in the daylight. Anonymous men and women, empowered in the only way they know—by their automobiles—are now suddenly disenfranchised and made impotent by a black-booted, black-shirted, black-gloved faceless figure holding the ultimate symbol of authority, a scepter that says "Stop." The drivers acquiesce. Only the cars snarl. Meanwhile, the entire scene is closed to the viewer by arrows that point downward, like falling bombs. Overhead, useless lights float off to the horizon like toy balloons. The drivers are enclosed in a labyrinth of striped barricades from which there is no exit, while the atmosphere surrounding the rest of the industrial-urban landscape is that of a spectral smog. In another context, the black, faceless figure could be death, which marks the end of the road for all human plans. Not even with the power of their machinery can humans prevent it from eventually stopping them. Inexorable in every life, it may be delayed, but never denied.

Though many have tried to label Tooker's work, calling it "Magic Realism" or "Surrealism" or any of many other avant-garde names, and though Tooker has been likened to Magritte or has even been called a latter-day Brueghel, his work cannot be categorized. Like all poetry, it is ultimately about the human condition: about fear, terror, isolation, loneliness, difficulties of communication, powerlessness. Its specifics are as old as humanity, but they are translocated to a twentieth-century setting and set down in a fifteenth-century medium: specifics such as prejudice against the handicapped, the abuse of children, the absurdities of war, and the bureaucratic dehumanization of the individual. But, as in all of his work, Tooker's people overcome and, eventually, love in a relationship that, though it may be as fragile, is also as lasting as his tempera medium.

*Highway*, 1953, American. Tempera on panel. 58.1 × 45.7 cm. Courtesy of the Terra Museum of American Art, Chicago, Illinois; Terra Foundation for the Arts, Daniel J. Terra Collection; photograph courtesy of the Terra Museum of American Art.

# JAMA®

The Journal of the American Medical Association

November 3, 1989

# THOMAS EAKINS ❧

## The Wrestlers

Anatomist, mathematician, scientist, artist: Thomas Eakins (1844-1916) was all of these. But he paid dearly. Dismissed from one teaching post after another because of his insistence on truth, his insistence that students, even women, study from the nude male model rather than from plaster casts, Eakins was much misunderstood, not only by the Philadelphia community in which he lived, but even by the art community. His paintings were refused exhibition because of their "realism," or else they were banished to an obscure location. When a niece who had studied with him committed suicide shortly after her release from a mental hospital, her father blamed Eakins and severed family relations with him. In a despondent moment, when he was fifty, Eakins wrote to a friend, "My honors are misunderstanding, persecution, and neglect, enhanced because unsought." But another friend, Walt Whitman, would pay him the ultimate tribute: "I never knew of but one artist and that's Tom Eakins who could resist the temptation to see what they thought ought to be rather than what is." Dispassionate observer, passionate artist, Eakins became, along with Winslow Homer, one of the two greatest American realist painters.

Eakins' interest in anatomy, and in particular in the actions and delineation of the large muscles, was long-standing. As an eighteen-year-old student at the Pennsylvania Academy of the Fine Arts he attended lectures on anatomy, and the following year he drew from the live model. At age twenty he enrolled as a special student at Jefferson Medical College, where he studied practical anatomy with the surgeon Dr Joseph Pancoast and general anatomy with Dr William Pancoast. In 1871, after he returned from four years of art study and travel in

Europe, he undertook a series of rowing paintings, which are especially good at depicting the muscles of the arms and back at work. In 1873 he again studied anatomy at Jefferson. In 1884 he devised a system of motion photography whereby he could stop muscles in action, especially muscles of locomotion, for closer study at leisure. Among his results were serial photographs

*Dispassionate observer, passionate artist . . .*

of men walking, running and jumping, and pole-vaulting. An outgrowth of this project was another study, this one on the locomotion of the horse, in which he sought to determine whether the flexors of a horse pulling a cart were not also active at the same time as the extensors. On May 1, 1894, before the Academy of Natural Sciences in Philadelphia, Eakins presented his first (and only) scientific paper, "The Differential Action of Certain Muscles Passing More Than One Joint," and illustrated it with models constructed of wood, catgut, and rubber bands. Based on earlier dissections of the leg of a horse, on his street observations of cart horses, and on his working models, he concluded that "the tightening of the rubber bands representing all the principal muscles, both the so-called flexors and the so-called extensors, *at the same time,* caused the upper part of the limb to spring forward when released, and proved to me that I was not mistaken in my observation on the living horse." The study was later published in the academy's *Proceedings.*

In 1898, through the offices of a sportswriter friend, Eakins entered a new

world that would become his laboratory for study of the human body, the prizefighting and wrestling rings. The prizefighting paintings, while superb anatomic renderings, show the fighters in static positions—between rounds, taking the count, or proclaiming victory. The wrestling pictures, on the other hand, show the figures in action. *The Wrestlers* belongs to this latter group and is actually an oil study for a much larger, near–life-size, final version. As is often the case, the study is much freer and more spontaneous and thus closer to the actual event than the more highly finished, but stiffer, final version. For this painting, Eakins, with the help of his sportswriter friend, chose two wrestlers from the Quaker City Athletic Club, of which Eakins was a member. Again with advice as to holds, he photographed the wrestlers with one pinning the other to the floor in a half nelson and a crotch hold. From this he copied the wrestlers in a preliminary study, slightly altering the positions of the head and shoulders of the upper wrestler and the right leg of the lower wrestler. In the next version (shown) he added, for balance in the composition, the cutoff figure of the referee and, in the upper left background, a man at a rowing machine, in addition to marking off the ring boundaries. In the finished version, which is at the Columbus (Ohio) Museum of Art, the size of the canvas has been increased, the figures are more detailed, the background is clear, and a fifth figure, the cutoff figure of a man wearing a jockstrap, has been introduced behind and to the right of the referee. *The Wrestlers* is generally accepted as one of Eakins' most complete representations of the human body.

Eakins remained controversial nearly to the end of his life, and, while he had many

*Continued on p 213*

# JAMA®

The Journal of the American Medical Association

November 10, 1989

# PAUL A. SEIFERT ⟶

## Residence of Mr E. R. Jones

From the caves of Lascaux to the twentieth-century kindergarten, it has been the human impulse to leave a pictorial record. Whether to celebrate what is, to recall what was, or to pass a message to those to come, the urgency of the picture making, the desire to record, often took precedence over what technical skill the artist may or may not have had. And while such works are often called "naive" or "primitive," it is this very lack of guile that gives them direct entry to the heart of the viewer. Such an artist was the American itinerant painter Paul A. Seifert (1840-1921), and such a painting is *Residence of Mr E. R. Jones.*

Seifert was born in Dresden, Germany, and studied engineering at the University of Leipzig. At the age of twenty-seven, finding military service in his country onerous, he immigrated to the United States and reached northern Wisconsin. From there he traveled downstream on the Wisconsin River on one of the logging rafts until he came to Richland City. There, befriended by Laurence Kraft, the only resident of the town who spoke German, he stayed. Within a year he had married Kraft's daughter Elizabeth, and the couple settled on an eighty-acre farm at Bogus Bluff, on the Wisconsin River. Eventually the couple had four daughters. On his farm Seifert raised flowers, fruits, and vegetables, which he took on foot each day and sold to townspeople. As a hobby Seifert took to painting watercolors of local farms and gradually ranged farther and farther afield. Tramping the roads of Richland, Grant, Sauk, and Iowa counties in southern Wisconsin with his watercolors and colored papers on his back in a bag his wife had made for him, he painted dozens and dozens of farm scenes that he sold to the owners of the farms for not more than $2.50 each. Later he opened a shop near Gotham, Wisconsin, on a farm

> *A large barn, well filled, is of the greatest importance during a Wisconsin winter, and a cause for great thanksgiving.*

where a granddaughter now lives. A true craftsman, Seifert also did glass painting with scenes of churches and castles. These sold for $5 each. Often he accented his works with metallic paints, adding the reflection of sun from a window, for example, with gold paint. He also practiced taxidermy, an art he had learned in Germany.

*Residence of Mr E. R. Jones* is typical of Seifert's work, except that in addition to recording an actual farm near Dodgeville, Wisconsin, it also records the sudden change of a midwestern season. Still wearing her brilliant autumn gown, the shivering Mother Earth now pulls a white coverlet about her to warm her until she births the spring. Meanwhile, the house has also bedded down, its summer kitchen empty, its vegetable cellar closed. The only signs that time itself has not ceased are a harnessed cutter waiting for its passenger and cows waiting to be milked. Two other figures approach the house, whether with good news or bad news or no news at all, we cannot tell. Typical of the naive style is the blue sky arched across the top of the painting as a child would do and the handling of perspective—or lack thereof. An attempt is made to show the trees in proper relationship, the more distant being smaller than the near, but, by contrast, the more distant barn is far larger than the house. Here, perhaps, Seifert has lapsed into a kind of psychological perspective. A large barn, well filled, is of the greatest importance during a Wisconsin winter, and a cause for great thanksgiving.

Seifert died in southern Wisconsin at age eighty. His explanation of why he painted was as simple and as direct as his watercolors: "People like my work and I like to paint for them." Indeed, though some of Seifert's one hundred or so works have made their way to museums, many more are still kept by later generations of the family for whom they were done, guarded religiously, like icons. They are, after all, a record, the more precious because personal. Only a century old, they record a time that is as different from today as autumn is from winter. But it is a hopeful winter, for the sky is blue and the barn is large and full. Moreover, "If Winter comes, can Spring be far behind?"

*Residence of Mr E. R. Jones,* 1881, American. Watercolor and tempera on paper. 54.6 × 69.8 cm. Courtesy of the New York State Historical Association, Cooperstown.

# JAMA®

## The Journal of the American Medical Association

**November 17, 1989**

Residence of Mr E. R. Jones. Town Dodgeville. Wis. 1881.

# JOHN SINGLETON COPLEY

## *Watson and the Shark*

In June 1774, the American colonial painter John Singleton Copley (1738-1815) embarked in Boston Harbor on a ship bound for London. At age thirty-six, the largely self-taught Copley was already the author of some 275 highly successful portraits of American colonials, and he proposed now to further his self-study by looking at works in Italy. (Some of today's critics say that in the entire history of American art, these portraits are second only to those of Eakins.) It was a trip Copley had long planned but had always put off because not only was he a timid and hesitant man, but he was also fearful of the sea. Even for such a relatively easy sea voyage as from Boston to New York, he always went by the longer and more arduous land route. Whether the threatening political situation in the colonies finally tipped the balance in favor of the trip is not known, but the voyage to London was to result in one of Copley's most famous paintings, for Brook Watson, an Englishman only slightly older than Copley, happened to be a fellow passenger. Walking with a limp because of a wooden leg, Watson repeatedly recounted the circumstances of the loss of his limb, even though the event had occurred more than a quarter of a century earlier, while, fascinated, Copley made sketches based on the narration.

Watson, born of a good family in northern England, had lost both his parents while he was still a child. Raised by an aunt, he went to sea at age fourteen. While swimming one day in Havana Harbor, he was attacked by a shark, which took the lower portion of his right leg. Then, just as the shark was coming in for the kill, his jaws almost closing on Watson's head, his frantic companions rescued him. Four years after his meeting with Watson, Copley turned his story into *A Youth Rescued From a Shark*, now known simply as *Watson and the Shark*. The painting was an immediate success in London, with everyone, high to low, uneducated as well as educated, offering comments. A housemaid said, "I cannot take my eyes off that painting," while a political rival of Watson, noting that the monster took the leg and not the head, added, "The best of workmen and the best of wood/

> *. . . what passes between the eyes of the terrified boy and the eyes of the shark as they look into each other's souls?*

Could scarce have made a head so good." Such jibes, however, did not seem to hurt Watson, for he became an alderman of the City of London, a member of the House of Commons, Lord Mayor of London, and, eventually, a baronet of the United Kingdom. Two hundred years later he still lives, a legend in the history of American art and the hero of a sea story to rival all.

While *Watson and the Shark* is generally acknowledged to be among Copley's best, and certainly his most arresting, the critics of 1778 found several errors of logic in it, namely, that the shark does not look like a shark and its tail is not lashing the water, that the figure of the boy is too large, that the men are not rowing correctly if they are trying to reach the boy, that their fingers are not in proper position for grasping the boy, and that the wind that blows the harpooner's hair should also affect the sails of the ships in the harbor. And while the scene is the entrance to Havana Harbor, Copley has taken liberties with its environs. For example, Morro Castle, on the right, has been raised, while the city wall, on the left, has been lowered. But Copley was not interested in literal fact as much as in poetic truth. For example, what higher drama can there be than in what passes between the eyes of the terrified boy and the eyes of the shark as they look into each other's souls? Or in the broken boat hook floating at the extreme right of the painting, a record of at least one failed rescue attempt and testimony to the strength of the shark? Or in the stump of the leg, with the boy's blood already mingled forever with the sea? Or in the faces of the boy's fellow seamen, all united in a single effort: to save the life of a boy in mortal danger?

Copley never returned to the United States. After his arrival in London in 1774, he was befriended by two of his admirers, the American Benjamin West and Sir Joshua Reynolds. When war in America became imminent, Copley sent for his wife and children and the family settled in London for good. The following year, 1776, Copley was elected an associate of the Royal Academy, and, in 1779, an academician. Unfortunately, except for *Watson and the Shark* and a couple of large history paintings, his work never equaled that of his colonial days. After 1800, he sold little. He became known instead for his contentious spirit and his political squabbling, not, as might be expected, over the war, but over matters within his profession. At age seventy-seven he had the first of two paralytic strokes. He died of the second, on September 9, 1815.

*Watson and the Shark*, 1778, American. Oil on canvas. 182.1 × 229.7 cm. Courtesy of the National Gallery of Art, Washington, DC; Ferdinand Lammot Belin Fund.

# JAMA®

**November 24, 1989**

The Journal of the American Medical Association

# ALFRED SISLEY

## First Snow at Veneux-Nadon (Premiere Neige à Veneux-Nadon)

The fall of 1878 did not bode well for Alfred Sisley (1839-1899). Married for twelve years and the father of two children, he had been painting for all of that time and more, but with little financial success. In the beginning it did not matter, for the young family was being generously supported by Sisley's father, who directed an export business in Paris. But with the Franco-Prussian War and the Siege of Paris, the father's business failed, and shortly thereafter he died. Disastrously poor, Sisley moved his family to the countryside, where over the next several years they lived in a succession of villages, each farther from Paris than the last in the hope that living would be cheaper, though still near enough to afford business trips to the city on occasion. Now, in 1878, the family was threatened with eviction from their house in Sèvres. In desperation Sisley turned to Théodore Duret, one of the few journalists in Paris sympathetic to Sisley and the other Impressionists, with a plan that he hoped would alleviate his financial situation and allow him to paint freely, unconstrained by the pressure for immediate income. If, he told Duret, someone could be found who would pay him 500 francs a month for six months, he would in exchange give him thirty canvases. Sisley felt certain that at the end of this time he would be on his feet, able to paint and to sell. Duret could produce no such sponsor, although he did find someone who bought seven paintings. The family was eventually evicted anyway. What kind of painting Sisley would have done had Duret come up with the 3,000 francs that fall can never be known. On the other hand, ample evidence exists of what he could and did do despite his worries. *First Snow at Veneux-Nadon (Premiere Neige à Veneux-Nadon)* was painted that fall.

Sisley was born in Paris on October 30, 1839. Both parents were British, but the family lived in Paris for business reasons. His father's firm did a lucrative business exporting artificial flowers to South America. Sisley himself was never naturalized and retained his British citizenship until the end of his life. At age eighteen, he was duly sent to London to learn the coffee and cotton brokerage business, but he spent most of his four years there in London's art galleries,

*"Every picture shows a spot with which the artist himself has fallen in love . . . "*

where he was especially taken with the work of Bonington and Turner, and in particular that of Constable. Sisley demonstrated little aptitude for business, and on his return to Paris his parents gave him permission to enter the studio of Gleyre to study painting. There he met fellow students Monet, Renoir, and Bazille, with whose names his would be linked, and who were to remain his friends, Bazille until he was killed eight years later in the Franco-Prussian War, Renoir and Monet until the end of Sisley's life. Well-off and generous with his father's money, Sisley often helped out his friends when they were in financial straits (as they often were), even bringing Renoir to live with him for a time. But, genial, generous, and full of good humor as he was, Sisley was at the same time timid and reserved. Thus, he seldom, if ever, joined the noisy group of nascent Impressionists who frequented the Café Guerbois in Paris, where Manet held forth each evening, or, later, the Café de la Nouvelle-

Athenes, famous for a painting of a dead rat on its ceiling, when Manet moved over there after the war. While the group argued this or that manner of painting or complained about the Salon's attitude toward them, Sisley was at home with his family, painting.

With the coming of the Franco-Prussian War in 1870, Sisley's quiet, comfortable life was abruptly ended. Along with the dramatic reversals in his life—his income stopped, his father dead, Bazille, his friend, also dead, his friends dispersed, his life in Paris ended—his painting underwent equally dramatic changes, but in the opposite direction. Paradoxically, as his life darkened, his palette lightened. It was as though, light being the ground of his being, if he could not live in it, he would preserve it on canvas. At the same time he also began using the broken touches and juxtapositions of small strokes of color that later came to be called Impressionism. Living now outside Paris, in Louveciennes, he loved the open spaces and, especially, the sky. In fact, as he noted, the sky was always the beginning point of any painting he made. He was also fond, as was Monet, of painting the same spot at different seasons of the year, recording the various depths and movements and colors of the autumn, spring, summer, and winter skies. Also typical, as in *First Snow at Veneux-Nadon,* was Sisley's composition. Unlike the work of the other Impressionists, a Sisley painting was strong in its compositional lines, which were usually built on a road or lane that receded diagonally into the painting. By this simple device, Sisley hoped to lead the spectator along the road indicated by the painter, the viewer being made to notice what the artist himself had felt. "Every picture shows a spot with which the artist himself has fallen in love," wrote Sisley to a friend. "The artist's

Continued on p 213

# JAMA®

The Journal of the American Medical Association

December 1, 1989

# EDVARD MUNCH

## *The Sun*

To celebrate its upcoming centenary in September 1911, the University of Christiania (Oslo) planned to build a new great hall, or aula, and to decorate it with murals to be done by a Norwegian artist, selected in competition. The competition, which was announced in March 1909, could not have come at a better time for the forty-five-year-old Edvard Munch (1863-1944). Several months earlier, suffering from severe alcoholism accompanied by general quarrelsomeness, ideas of persecution, hallucinations, brawls, and other outbursts of violence, Munch had been admitted to the clinic of Dr Daniel Jacobsen in Copenhagen, which specialized in nervous conditions of Scandinavian artists. Now, about to be released from the clinic, the competition gave Munch the stimulus he needed to embark on his new life of sobriety (which would last permanently, until he died some thirty-five years later). Going to the south coast of Norway, he settled in the isolated, but scenic, town of Kragerø, there to begin his planning. The competition itself, however, did not go smoothly. Beginning with some twenty-five painters and sculptors, the jury narrowed the count to six. Still there were difficulties, and in 1911 a second competition was held. This time the jury chose Munch, but the university's building committee, dominated by conservatives, refused to give him a contract. Finally, in May 1914, bowing to the pressure of Munch's enormous popularity in Europe and no doubt influenced by the rising prices of his work as well, the university board accepted the designs. Two years later, in September 1916, they were finally unveiled in the Great Hall.

Munch's original idea for the murals had been to honor poets and other intellectuals. Socrates, Nietzsche, and Ibsen would be on the center wall, facing the spectators, while Bjørnson and Jonas Lie would occupy either

> *. . . each year, on December 10 . . . The Sun is the backdrop for the presentation of the Nobel Prize for Peace.*

side wall. Later, Munch decided that the murals would be allegorical instead and that he would take all his motifs from the Norwegian people and landscape: from the people and scenery of Kragerø, where he was then living, and from Hvitsen, where he later lived while working on the murals. "My aim was to have the decorations form a closed, independent ideal world, whose pictorial expression should be at once peculiarly Norwegian and universally human," he said in a letter to the Committee for the Decoration of the Great Hall.

The murals, as finally unveiled, consisted of three large and eight smaller paintings. The main (center) panel, facing the hall's occupants, is *The Sun*, rising over the rocky landscape of Kragerø, its rays embracing the other panels and inviting the viewer to walk toward its light. On the wall to the left is *History*, where an old blind man from the fjords, steeped in memory, sits beneath an ancient oak tree as he relates the past to a wide-eyed boy. On the wall to the right of the center panel is *Alma Mater* (in the beginning called *Researchers* and *The Scholars*), where, in the summer landscape of Hvitsen, a woman, the Great Mother, feeds her baby from her abundance, while an older child stands beside her. The eight smaller panels, also allegorical, portray variously chemistry, wisdom, youth, power, industry, autumn, and sowing.

When they were unveiled, the paintings were an immediate popular and critical success. Nearly seventy-five years later they remain so, and, while not often reproduced in books, are probably more familiar than most viewers realize. In an added twist that not even Munch could have foreseen, each year, on December 10, in the Aula of the University of Oslo, Munch's center panel, *The Sun*, is the backdrop for the presentation of the Nobel Prize for Peace. In his wish that his murals have universal human significance and for an ideal world, Munch could not have come closer.

*The Sun*, 1909-1916, Norwegian. Oil on canvas. 455 × 780 cm. Courtesy of the Munch Museum, Oslo, Norway; © 2001 The Munch Museum/The Munch-Ellingsen Group/Artists Rights Society (ARS), New York, New York.

# JAMA®

December 8, 1989

The Journal of the American Medical Association

# AMMI PHILLIPS

# Girl in Red Dress With Cat and Dog

In some respects, the training of physicians and painters in early nineteenth-century America paralleled each other. Finding few opportunities for professional training in the United States, the elite of both groups went to Europe to study, returning to the States to practice and often to become the leaders of their respective professions. On the other hand, a far greater number, unable to afford study abroad, and seeing advantage in the rapid expansion and the spirit of individualism existing in the young country, set up in practice after only the most rudimentary training. To the latter group of painters belongs Ammi Phillips (1788-1865). Thanks to the work of art historian Mary Black and collectors Barbara C. and Lawrence Holdridge, Phillips is one of the most thoroughly researched of the nineteenth-century American folk artists.

Ammi Phillips was born in Colebrook, Connecticut, to Samuel Phillips, Jr, and Milla Kellogg Phillips, the third or fourth in a group of seven brothers and sisters, and spent his entire life traveling about the three-state area of Massachusetts, Connecticut, and New York, with one trip into Vermont. Among the towns he lived in were Troy, Rhinebeck, Fishkill, and North East, all in New York State, and Interlaken, Massachusetts. Largely self-taught, he is recorded as selling portraits as early as 1811, when he was twenty-three. In 1813 he married Laura Brockway of Schodack, New York, and the couple had five children. When Laura died in 1830, Phillips, then forty-two, married the twenty-two-year-old Jane Ann Caulkins, and the couple had four more children. Phillips' patrons were the local farmers, the townspeople, especially the professionals, and, in the 1830s, the wealthy landowning Dutch and English families along both sides of the Hudson River. Because of markedly different styles in different periods of his life, Phillips was once thought to be two separate unknown painters, the "Kent Limner" and the "Border Limner," the first so called because so many of his portraits turned up in 1924 at a fair in Kent, Connecticut, the second because so many of his subjects lived on either side of

> Like the rural-style physician, he had been replaced by technology.

the Massachusetts–New York state line. Recent research, however, has shown that both the Kent Limner and the Border Limner are indeed one person: Ammi Phillips. Phillips was nothing if not prolific. Some 500 portraits are known; at least one source puts his oeuvre at perhaps 1,000 portraits. Phillips died at Interlaken, Massachusetts, on July 11, 1865, and is buried in Amenia Island Cemetery in New York State. His estate, which he left to his widow Jane Ann, was valued at $850.

*Girl in Red Dress With Cat and Dog* is thought to have been painted in the mid 1830s in the Amenia area of New York State. Typically, for folk painters, it is a "formula" painting: the artist painted an individual head of the sitter, but then completed the rest of the painting in a more or less standardized fashion he had devised. Standard for Ammi Phillips in this case were the pose, the arms forming parallel diagonals, the adult-type, off-the-shoulder red dress, the coral beads, even the dog. Variations might consist in the number of ruffles on the pantaloons (one or two), how the sleeves would be edged (white piping or lace), the color of the slippers (red or black), and, for girls, the number of strands in the coral necklace (from two to four). In the children's hands he might place a favorite object or, more often, sprigs of strawberries. Mary Black has identified six portraits, four of girls, two of boys, that make use of this formula, although in two instances the figures have been reversed and one of the boys wears a blue, rather than a red, dress. Both boys, however, wear the same off-the-shoulder, bell-skirted type of dress with pantaloons. Only the girl in the Amenia portrait holds a cat—whether at her insistence or at the artist's is unknown, but one likes to think it is at hers. No matter at whose insistence, however, the cat makes hers the most distinctive of the personalities in the six portraits.

In 1837, shortly after *Girl in Red Dress With Cat and Dog* was painted, one of the artists returning from Europe was Samuel F. B. Morse. With him he brought the very latest from Paris: the new invention of Louis Jacques Daguerre. It would spell the beginning of the end of Phillips' occupation and of those of hundreds like him. The increasingly wealthy Americans demanded the newest and found the daguerrotype to be much the preferred method of preserving memories of themselves and their children. Twenty years later the country was buying three million daguerrotypes a year. As noted, when he died in 1865 at age seventy-seven, Phillips' lifetime output of oil portraits had been perhaps a thousand. Like the rural-style physician, he had been replaced by technology.

*Girl in Red Dress With Cat and Dog*, c 1830-1835, American. Oil on canvas. 81.3 × 63.5 cm. Courtesy of the Museum of American Folk Art, New York, New York; promised anonymous gift.

The Journal of the American Medical Association

December 15, 1989

# ALBERT BESNARD ❧

## *The First Morning (Albert and Charlotte Dubray Besnard With Their Son, Robert)*

He was the rage of the 1886 Paris Salon, the same Salon that in previous years had so consistently rejected the works of Manet and the Impressionists, and that, again, this year, had once more turned down an entry by Cézanne. But the same critics who vied with each other in ridiculing Manet and the Impressionists could not find words enough to praise this versatile young artist, Paris' own, winner of the Prix de Rome, the current new sensation. But even those words were modest compared with what was yet to come. By 1905, the same year that Braque and Picasso were experimenting with Cubism, a critic called him "the greatest force in French painting of the day," one who handles light like Turner, a "son of Rubens, a rival of Ingres, a direct descendant of Watteau and Fragonard." By the time another decade had passed, a writer for one of the international art journals was calling him one of the last, if not, indeed, the last, of the Old Masters, and established an artistic pedigree for him that extended back to the early fifteenth century, coming in a direct line through Cabanel, Picot, Vincent, David, and so on, to Caravaggio and, ultimately, to Squarcione, who was born at the end of the fourteenth century. Once the rage of Paris and the toast of London, today he is virtually unknown. He is Albert Besnard (1849-1934), landscapist, portraitist, muralist, and decorator, who painted and drew equally well, whether in oils, watercolors, or pastels or with etching stylus.

Born in Paris the same year that Delacroix was painting a ceiling of the Louvre, Besnard was the offspring of an artistic couple: his father was a painter who had studied with Ingres, and his mother was a prominent miniaturist who had studied with Mme Mirbel. Thus, apparently destined for a career in art, at age seventeen Albert entered the École des Beaux-Arts, where he studied in the studio of Alexandre Cabanel. A lackluster student, and disliking the academic training, he nevertheless won an Honorable Mention in the Salon at only age nineteen and the coveted Prix de Rome in 1874, at age twenty-five. In 1879 he married Charlotte Dubray, daughter of a well-known sculptor and herself a sculptress

> *... the parents admire and show concern for the child but do not touch him.*

of note. The couple spent the next two years in London, where the Pre-Raphaelite movement was then at its height. Returning to Paris, Besnard accepted a commission to decorate the vestibule of the École de Pharmacie in Paris, for which he chose subjects in the sciences and in medicine. Other mural projects included the dome of the Petit Palais, the ceilings for the Hôtel de Ville, the Comédie Française, the Sorbonne Lecture Hall for chemistry, the hospital of Cozin at Berck, and the French embassy in Vienna—all in addition to his easel work. He even turned his hand to decorating a grand piano and to designing stained glass windows.

*The First Morning (Albert and Charlotte Dubray Besnard With Their Son, Robert)* was painted when the couple was in London and shows the midwife holding up the Besnards' first child for their admiration. Typical of many of the academic paintings of the time, even though the subjects are not impov

erished, the setting is nevertheless that of a quasi-religious, rustic poverty. Typical also of the child-rearing customs of the upper middle class in the late nineteenth century, the parents admire and show concern for the child but do not touch him. Thus, while *The First Morning* becomes a painting of an intimate moment in the life of the artist and his wife, it yet fails to engage the emotions of the viewer. The whole setting has a quality of the staged about it, like a carefully arranged tableau. Moreover, the tableau gives the air of having been researched to the smallest detail, even to the wedding rings on the mother and the midwife. Thus, much as the parents admire the child, but only at a distance, one may admire the painting for its color and its draftsmanship and its superb handling of light, but also only at a distance. It fails to enter the personal experience of today's viewer. It is not "touchable."

In addition to his artistic successes in Paris, Besnard went on to become director of the École Français in Rome in 1914 and, in 1922, of the École des Beaux-Arts in Paris. He was a member of the Académie Française and a commander of the Legion of Honor. He died in Paris on December 15, 1934, aged eighty-five. He remained, as one obituary writer noted, a continuing source of astonishment to his critics because of his versatility, but also a source of puzzlement because he seemed to be able to change his style at will. Like the Impressionists, his forte was light, especially as portrayed in reflections and shadows, but he combined it with an academic style that made his work palatable to the critics. At times his style hinted at Art Nouveau. But, although, as in *The First Morning*, many of his scenes were of intimate moments, even of times of sickness and dying, they lacked the personal

*Continued on p 213*

# JAMA®

The Journal of the American Medical Association

December 22/29, 1989

# ERNEST LAWSON ❧

## *Melting Snow*

White, silent, deep. Snow falling quiet as feathers dropping. Knife-cold. Nights long, sunshine brief. The earth, stuck on its axis. It is January, deep into winter, and going deeper still. Yet, not without hope. Sooner or later, sometimes early, sometimes late, sometimes just at its mid-point, the breeze becomes just a little softer, the air a little brighter, the ice shifts on the river, the road runs with tiny gullies of mud. Blood rises, souls stir. One can even imagine the unimaginable, a time when it was not always winter, a time that perhaps even may come again. It is the time, as Eliot says, of the "midwinter spring," "its own season/ sempiternal though sodden towards sun-down." It is the season that Ernest Lawson (1873-1939) knew in *Melting Snow.*

In many respects, Lawson's life was like his wintry landscapes, deep, cool, silent, but rich in subtle colors. Born in Nova Scotia to Archibald Lawson, a physician, and Anna Mitchell Lawson, he was the couple's second child and the only one of five to survive. When Ernest was ten, his parents moved to Kansas City, Missouri, leaving him behind. For the next five years he remained in the care of an aunt and uncle in Kingston, Ontario. Even though his uncle was at that time president of Queens University, Ernest remained unmoved by any scholarly as-pirations the family may have had for him, preferring instead to spend his time drawing. It was an occupation, his father said, fit only for drifters and otherwise lazy people. Nevertheless, when, in 1888, at age fifteen, Ernest joined his parents in Kansas City, he studied for a time at the Kansas City Art Institute with instructor Ella Holman (six years later, at age twenty-one, Lawson would marry the twenty-eight-year-old Miss Holman). Two years later, in 1890, Lawson went to Mexico City, where his

father had next gone to practice medicine, and worked as a draftsman for a firm of English engineers. He also studied at the San Carlos Art School in Mexico City. From there he went to New York City in 1891, where he studied with the American Impressionist painter of snow scenes John Twachtman and later, in Cos Cob, Con-necticut, with both him and J. Alden Weir. It was after studying with Twachtman and Weir that Lawson developed his definitive style.

> *. . . Lawson's life was like his wintry landscapes, deep, cool, silent, but rich in subtle colors.*

In 1893, at age twenty, Lawson went to Paris to study. Here he received a critique of his work from Sisley, whose style he greatly admired. Already bitter and disillusioned, but grateful perhaps for the opportunity to speak in English, Sisley looked first at the canvas and then at the young artist. His advice: "Put more paint on the canvas and less on yourself." Whether Lawson took Sisley's advice to heart is not known, but as he matured his paintings became known for his lavish, three-dimensional use of paint as he applied and shaped it with whatever means were at hand: brush, palette knife, even thumb. One critic jokingly suggested that he used a trowel. Another asked Lawson if he was planning to also use a hatchet and saw he had nearby. While in Paris, Lawson shared a studio with Somerset Maugham, who, as Émile Zola had earlier done in his novel *L'Oeuvre* with Cézanne, modeled the

artist in *Of Human Bondage,* Frederick Lawson, after Ernest Lawson, though loosely. Like Ernest, as a young student artist in Paris, Frederick had two paintings accepted at the Salon.

Returning briefly to the United States in 1894, the twenty-one-year-old Lawson married his former Kansas City instructor and the two returned to France. The couple's first child, Margaret, was born there in 1896. Back in the States once again in 1897, Ernest taught for a time in Columbus, Georgia, while Ella taught in Asheville, North Carolina. The couple had a second child that year, another daughter, Dorothy. Finally, in 1898, the family settled in the Washington Heights section of New York City. It was from there, in upper Manhattan, along the Hudson and Harlem rivers, that Lawson produced so many of the snowy landscapes that were his forte. In 1908, with this work continuing to gain recognition, Lawson exhibited in New York City with "The Eight," a breakaway group of painters headed by Robert Henri. The group later came to be known as the Ashcan School because the subjects they chose to paint— ash cans, drying laundry on a tenement porch, dirty streets—were considered ugly by the viewers. In 1913 Lawson was represented in the Armory Show. Mean-while, prizes and medals from around the country—St Louis, Philadelphia, San Fran-cisco, Washington, DC—began coming his way. But there were also family stresses, and Lawson began having problems with alcohol. The summer of 1920 was the last the Lawsons would spend together. Later, the younger daughter, Dorothy, died in Egypt while on a trip with her mother, and Mrs Lawson and Margaret settled in France. Lawson meanwhile taught in Kansas City and in Colorado Springs. New York City,

*Continued on p 214*

# JAMA®

The Journal of the American Medical Association

January 5, 1990

# MILTON AVERY

## The Checker Players

Milton Avery (1885-1965) came late to painting. Born in Sand Bank (later Altmar), a small town in Upstate New York between Watertown and Utica, to Milton Clark Avery, a tanner, and Esther March Avery, at age thirteen he moved with his parents and three older siblings to a small town near East Hartford, Connecticut. By now the household also included his sister's husband, and eventually it would include their five daughters as well. At age sixteen young Milton went to work as an assembler in a screw factory. Over the next few years he also worked as a lathe man and a mechanic. Sometime after his twentieth birthday, he responded to an advertisement that promised one could "Make money lettering," and he enrolled in a lettering class at the Connecticut League of Art Students. When the class was discontinued after only a month, Avery was persuaded to stay on in the league's life drawing class, where he would remain until he was into his thirties. Thus was discovered a talent that would continue to be developed over the next fifty years.

Meanwhile, Avery's father had died, as well as a brother and a brother-in-law, and the household was further increased by the addition of his sister-in-law and niece. Avery was responsible for a household of nine women and children. To support themselves, the family moved to more modest quarters in East Hartford, while Avery took a 6 PM to midnight shift as a file clerk in the claims department of an insurance company. Days he attended the School of the Art Society of Hartford. Over the next several years, in addition to studying and painting, he would work at a tire company and also as a construction worker in Hartford. Summers he began going to Gloucester, Massachusetts, to paint, where he met fellow artist

Sally Michel. Two years later, in 1926, the couple was married and settled in New York City. Milton was now in his forties, Sally in her twenties. It was agreed that Milton would paint full-time, while Sally would support the two of them by working as an illustrator, an arrangement that continued for the rest of their lives together. In 1927 Avery had his first New York City exhibition.

> *. . . other artists were concerned with content . . . Avery was concerned with process.*

Two years later his first work to enter a museum was bought by the Phillips Memorial Gallery in Washington, DC. About this time Avery also met Adolph Gottlieb and Mark Rothko, both of whose work he would influence. A daughter, March, who would figure prominently in Avery's work, was born in 1932. Summers were spent in Gloucester or in Vermont. There were also extended visits to the Gaspé Peninsula in Canada and to California and Mexico.

*The Checker Players* was painted in 1938, the year the Averys had been in Gaspé, and shows Sally and an artist friend, Vincent Spagna, deeply absorbed in their game. Homely, humorous, comfortable, it is typical of Avery's work in the 1930s. While other artists were concerned with content in their paintings, however, making rural landscapes or cityscapes or illustrating the social realism themes of the Depression years, Avery was concerned with process. Thus, he took whatever subjects were at hand—usually family and friends or, in Rothko's words, "whatever

world strayed through his studio"—and turned them into flat areas of color and shape, a process that caused him to be likened to Matisse and one that would also influence the later large color canvases of Rothko. To Avery the subject was not just a figure or an object in a landscape or against a background. It was a process of relationships—of positive and negative spaces interlocking, of interconnectedness between all parts—and of color harmonies wedded to those shapes. As Avery grew older, the shapes grew more abstract and the harmonies more subtle, but never did he go into pure abstraction. The colors and shapes were always related to a seen and felt object or circumstance. And what he saw most were family scenes, his wife Sally and his daughter March, and what he felt most was a gentleness toward all that is evident in all his works.

By 1948, when Avery was in his early sixties, his health had begun to deteriorate, and he suffered his first heart attack the following year. He continued to work and travel again for the next decade, however, until, in the winter of 1959, he needed daily medication for angina. In 1961 Avery had a second heart attack. Finally, in March 1964, he was forced to enter the hospital yet again, where he died ten months later, on January 3, 1965. He was seventy-nine years old.

*The Checker Players,* 1938, American. Oil on canvas. 68.6 × 91.4 cm. Courtesy of the Terra Museum of American Art, Chicago, Illinois; Terra Foundation for the Arts, Daniel J. Terra Collection; photograph courtesy of the Terra Museum of American Art. © 2001 Artists Rights Society (ARS), New York, New York.

# JAMA®

The Journal of the American Medical Association

January 12, 1990

# GEORGE WESLEY BELLOWS

## The Palisades

For George Wesley Bellows (1882-1925), the year 1909 was a banner year, long to be remembered. The twenty-seven-year-old painter and semiprofessional baseball player had been in New York City for five years, after saying good-bye to what he considered to be the stifling atmosphere of his home in Columbus, Ohio. Behind him he had left a three-fourths–completed degree at Ohio State, an invitation to play baseball with the Cincinnati Reds, and his devout parents (the Wesley in his name was for the founder of Methodism), George and Anna, aged eighty and seventy-one. He was their only child. In New York City, with money saved from playing baseball, he entered the New York School of Art, where, along with Edward Hopper and Rockwell Kent, he was a pupil of the American realist painter Robert Henri. Just two years later, in 1907, Bellows painted the first of the prizefighting pictures for which he is famed. The following year, though he did not himself exhibit, he was witness to Henri's "The Eight" exhibition, designed as a show of radical American art by a group of American realist painters, later dubbed the Ashcan School. But Bellows did win his first prize that year, for *North River*, exhibited at the National Academy of Design. Bellows' real success, however, would come the following year, 1909, when *North River* was bought by the Pennsylvania Academy of the Fine Arts for $250. More important than the price was the fact that this was Bellows' first painting to enter the collection of a major museum. And, to fill

his cup, Bellows was elected in April of that year to an associate membership in the National Academy of Design, the youngest painter ever to be so honored. Moreover, he was courting Emma Story, a former student at the New York Art School, who would eventually say "yes" to his proposal of marriage.

If Bellows exulted in his newly found freedoms in New York City, he exulted even more in those years in the outdoor beauty of

> *The color contrasts are harsh and even violent, but so is winter.*

its winters. He painted all of them: crusty snow along the city's riverbanks so white that the sky turned it blue, steaming snow in the wake of Manhattan's horse-clogged streets, even gray slush that seeped into pedestrians' galoshes. *The Palisades*, a companion to *North River*, was painted at this time and shows the New Jersey cliffs just barely tipped by the rays of the late afternoon sun. On the icy river a tugboat churns along while at the right midground a locomotive enters the picture, the underbelly of its steam catching the colors of the oncoming dusk. A man and a woman pause on the walk, while a lamppost stands sentinel behind them. The color contrasts

are harsh and even violent, but so is winter. Yet, a single barren tree, like that at the left, can have in its bark all the colors of summer—reds, yellows, greens, even blues. Like his other winter paintings of that time, *The Palisades* has all the sparkle, the crispness, the decisiveness of a well-executed double play in baseball. For Bellows during those years, life was joy, painting was joy, life was painting.

But the young, joyful, exuberant Bellows of those years had only sixteen more to live. He died, tragically, in 1925, at the age of forty-two, following surgery for a ruptured appendix. But in the meantime, he had married Emma, the couple had had two daughters, Jean and Anne, and he had completed some six hundred paintings on a variety of subjects and in many styles, including portraits, landscapes, cityscapes, seascapes, history, and various sports. Ironically, those for which he is most famous, the boxing paintings, numbered only six. Had Bellows been a shortstop, his career almost certainly would have been over at forty-two. But for a painter, which Bellows was, forty-two is when one is just getting started.

*The Palisades*, 1909, American. Oil on canvas. 76.2 × 96.5 cm. Courtesy of the Terra Museum of American Art, Chicago, Illinois; Terra Foundation for the Arts, Daniel J. Terra Collection; photograph courtesy of the Terra Museum of American Art.

# JAMA®

The Journal of the American Medical Association

January 19, 1990

# JAN VAN HUYSUM

## Vase of Flowers

When, in 1888, Vincent van Gogh made a painting of a vase of sunflowers, he was merely carrying on a tradition that had been begun by his Dutch forebears some three centuries before, in the late 1500s. Actually, as history tells it, the practice of flower painting dates back even earlier, to at least the fourth century BC, when Pausias, a follower of Apelles, the court painter to Alexander the Great, fell in love with Glycera, famed throughout the Peloponnese for her skill in arranging flowers. Despairing of ever attracting Glycera's attention on his personal merits, Pausias instead painted a bunch of flowers and sent the picture to her. Like the work of his master Apelles, who is said to have painted grapes so realistically that birds came to peck at the canvas, Pausias' flowers were so beautifully rendered that Glycera surrendered. Later, in the first century AD, in a somewhat less romantic but more practical use of flower painting, Dioscorides, army surgeon to Nero, included pictures of flowers in his materia medica. In medieval times flowers illuminated the borders of manuscripts, and still later gardens and various single blooms were used in paintings of the Madonna to signify virginity. But the first independent flower paintings, paintings in which the flowers themselves are the subject of the painting rather than a symbol or a specimen, came in the Netherlands in the late sixteenth century.

Throughout the seventeenth century, the Dutch took to flower paintings as they took to tulips. Newly independent of Spain, Protestant, bounded by a sea higher than some of their land, and a maritime power second to none, the Netherlands grew prosperous, and Dutch citizens began speculating in the various commodities carried by the Dutch trading companies. Principal among these was not gold or diamonds, or even tea, but flowers, seeds of which were brought from all over the world and bred in Dutch gardens. The most exotic was considered to be the tulip, brought from Turkey, and most highly prized of these was the rare red-and-white striped variety. A whole economy was built on the tulip. A single bulb could sell for 1,000 guilders. Indeed, so active did the tulip exchange become that when the bulb market collapsed in the 1630s, a whole country went into a

> *. . . not only a delight to the eye and a demonstration of the painter's virtuosity, but also a moral . . .*

recession. Yet the Dutch persisted in their love of flowers, and just as they covered their walls with paintings of what they loved—their landscape, their ancestors, their children, themselves at work, their churches, their kitchens and courtyards, their bawdy taverns, their moralistic emblems, their double-entendres of love and courtship—so did they also buy the "flower piece." Born toward the end of this golden century of Dutch painting was Jan van Huysum (1682-1749), both then and now considered to be one of the finest exponents of the flower piece. *Vase of Flowers* is typical of his finest work.

The facts of van Huysum's life are briefly told. Born in Amsterdam, he was the son of Justus van Huysum the Elder, a flower painter, and older brother to three other flower painters. All were taught by their father, and the three younger ones remained with him in his studio. Jan, however, who guarded his methods so jealously that he never took but a single pupil in his entire life, one Margareta Haverman, and her for only a brief period, worked independently. In 1704 he married Elisabeth Takens. Each summer he went to Haarlem to study new flower specimens. So conscientious was he in working from the real flower that once he delayed finishing a painting for an entire year because the yellow rose he needed to complete the painting was not yet in bloom. Van Huysum died in Amsterdam at age sixty-seven without ever divulging the secrets of his success. Today his methods, in particular how he prepared his pigments, remain a mystery.

At first glance *Vase of Flowers* is pleasant enough—a bouquet of flowers casually arranged in a terra-cotta bowl set on a marble ledge. But then the eye begins to see more. Individual flowers come forward: a tulip, a peony, a carnation, a rose, sweet peas, a lily. While some are full-blown, others are past their prime, overblown and drooping. A bee sits on the topmost flower, butterflies hover, an ant crawls on the petal of a peony, dewdrops glisten, a fly crawls on the urn. And, far from being a casual arrangement, the bouquet has a super-structure as intricate as that of a spider's web. Finally, not all the flowers pictured bloom at that same time. Considering the prosperous yet moralistic climate of that time, perhaps the painting was intended to be not only a delight to the eye and a demonstration of the painter's virtuosity, but also a moral: a reminder of the transience of life, which, as the psalmist says, is like a flower, springing up in the morning, fading in the evening. The fly recalls plague, or disease generally; the butterfly is a symbol of the resurrected

*Continued on p 214*

# JAMA®

The Journal of the American Medical Association

**February 2, 1990**

# BETSY GRAVES REYNEAU

## George Washington Carver, Scientist

To the young man from Diamond Grove, Missouri, son of slaves, orphaned in infancy, with little formal schooling, and now well beyond the age at which students usually studied for the baccalaureate degree, Simpson College in Indianola, Iowa, seemed the promised land. What caught the young man's eye was its catalogue, which noted that Science Hall had "an elegant art room immediately under the skylight." But once he was enrolled, getting permission to study art proved to be almost more difficult than getting into the college itself. Nevertheless, finally accepted into the art course on a two-week trial basis, he proved his talent so decisively that his teacher became an enthusiastic lifelong supporter. Two years later he became known statewide when four of his flower paintings were exhibited at a meeting of the Iowa Teachers' Association in Cedar Rapids. The following summer he won an Honorable Mention at the World's Columbian Exposition in Chicago for a lily painting. By now in Ames, Iowa, and a member of the 1894 graduating class of the Iowa State College of Agriculture and Mechanic Arts, he felt optimistic about his plans for the immediate future. In addition to his painting, he had demonstrated superior aptitude in botany, and he would stay on at Ames as an assistant botanist, meanwhile working on a master's degree in science. Moreover, because the two-year master's program was flexible, he intended to spend the second year in Chicago, where he would also study painting at the Academy of Arts. But events were to dictate otherwise.

As a result of his scientific lectures and bulletins, he was by now widely known in the field of agricultural science, and he was accordingly offered the Chair of Agriculture at Alcorn Agricultural and Mechanical College in Mississippi. While he hesitated before leaving Ames, which would mean he would leave an environment he loved as well as abandoning his plans to study art, a second request for his services came, this one from Alabama, where Booker T. Washington's Tuskegee Normal and Industrial Institute was now midway into

> *. . . his favorite flower,*
> *the amaryllis.*

its second decade. Though he still hoped that one day he could go to Paris to study art, this time there was no hesitation in accepting. In the fall of 1896, the thirty-two-year-old artist-turned-scientist left Ames to become the Tuskegee Institute's director of scientific agriculture. Thus began an association that would last for nearly half a century, until his death in 1943. Noted for the inventiveness and versatility of his mind, as well as for an almost uncanny way with soils and plants, he was to leave a mark as indelible as his plant dyes not only on agriculture, but also on areas ranging from commerce to economies to human relations. He was, of course, George Washington Carver.

Meanwhile, in Europe, in the late 1930s, a decision of another sort was shaping up for an American painter, Betsy Graves Reyneau (1888-1964). Now fifty, she had studied painting at the Boston Museum of Fine Arts as well as with Frank Duveneck, had married, had a daughter, Marie, and since 1925 had been working and studying in France, England, and Italy. Often she contributed work to the *London Bookman*, among them portraits of G. K. Chesterton, H. G. Wells, and W. B. Yeats. Thoroughly distressed by the rising fascism on the Continent, she returned to the United States at the outbreak of World War II, only to find similar conditions in her own country. Resolving to fight racial prejudice, as had her grandfather, a prominent abolitionist judge in Michigan, Reyneau began with the tools she knew: portrait painting. She would, she determined, combat negative racial stereotypes with a series of portraits of distinguished African Americans that would be exhibited throughout the country. *George Washington Carver, Scientist* was the first of these.

Dr Carver is shown as he was in late 1942, when he was in his late seventies. With him is his favorite flower, the amaryllis. No matter how many times he had had to move in boyhood and young manhood, the amaryllis bulbs were always carefully packed to accompany him. Here he is shown transferring pollen to the hybrid red-and-white variety that he had developed. Though Carver would be dead of pernicious anemia less than three months after he had sat for the painting, his figure is tall and strong. The soft back lighting emphasizes the strength, yet gentleness, evident in his hands and face, while the clear greens, blues, reds, browns, and whites give testimony to the simplicity, yet richness, of his character. Carver, who was notoriously reluctant to sit for portraits, liked this one and requested that it be included in a biography then being prepared by Rackham Holt. It appeared as the frontispiece when the book was published

*Continued on p 214*

# JAMA®

The Journal of the American Medical Association

**February 9, 1990**

# CHARLES FREDERIC ULRICH ⤳

## *The Village Print Shop*

After the Civil War, hundreds of Americans flocked to the art centers of Europe, there to study painting and sculpture. Most returned to the United States after their studies, and a few, notably Thomas Eakins, became famous. Others, such as James Abbott McNeill Whistler and Mary Cassatt, perhaps finding a more sympathetic reception for their works abroad or perhaps simply preferring the European lifestyle, became expatriates. Among the latter is the little-known American painter Charles Frederic Ulrich (1858-1908).

Born in New York City, he was the son of a photographer and painter. After studying at the National Academy of Design in New York City, Ulrich went to Munich, the art capital of Europe at the time, where he studied with Ludwig Loefftz during the late 1870s. Here he developed his strong academic style and gained an appreciation of the Old Masters. In 1883 he returned to the United States, and over the next couple of years he joined in several group exhibitions. In 1885, however, he was back in Europe. Over the next quarter of a century he would become one of the most peripatetic of the expatriates, living and working in Holland, Germany, Italy, France, and England. He died in Berlin, Germany, at the age of fifty. Ulrich is best known for his academically conceived and beautifully lighted genre scenes featuring new immigrants and the working poor. Among his finest is *The Village Print Shop*, which he painted in Holland shortly after arriving there from the United States. He was twenty-seven.

*The Village Print Shop* betrays the artist's academic orientation in its clear statement of the Golden Mean or Section (an ancient precept of harmonic theory that prescribes that a line should be divided in such a way that the smaller part is to the larger part as the larger part is to the whole). Ulrich accomplishes this by using the stovepipe as a major vertical. Thus, the printer, the printing press, the printer's stone (far right), and the stove, the "heavies" in the painting in terms of both actual weight and importance to the operation, occupy only the smaller part, or

> *. . . academically conceived and beautifully lighted genre scenes featuring new immigrants and the working poor.*

right third, of the painting, while the more replaceable people and objects—the assistant, the apprentice, or "printer's devil," the table with its assortment of pots, bottles, and packages—occupy the larger space but carry less weight and importance. Into this exquisitely balanced composition, which in its strong rectangularity itself echoes the shapes of a page of type, Ulrich sets up a tension with the leaning stove, a posture that is in turn reflected in that of the assistant, who, hand on hip, balances his weight on his left leg. The upright posture of the boy meanwhile establishes the major vertical in the left two thirds of the painting. Because *The Village Print Shop* was painted during Ulrich's stay in Holland just after he had left the United States, it is tempting to speculate that he was inspired by some of the seventeenth-century Dutch genre paintings in his handling of various textures. Certainly, he includes many: wood, metal, stone, glass, porcelain, ceramic, liquid, paper, cloth. And

his lighting has the same subtle quality of a Dutch "Little Master."

What social comment Ulrich's painting provoked a hundred years ago has not been recorded. But today such a workplace would bring speedy protests of child abuse based on child labor laws, citations for venting air pollutants directly into the atmosphere, and a summons for unsafe working conditions. Not only is the makeshift smokestack of the stove perilously close to the wooden rafters, but the open window suggests that ventilation may be poor. Most important, however, is the psychological tone of the painting. Confined in a relatively small area and performing a common task, the three figures yet remain separate from each other, with not even an attempt at communication. The printer is enclosed in his third of the painting, completely absorbed in his task. The other two figures, while occupying the same two-thirds section of the painting, stand facing away from each other, each isolated in his own world. The three could just as well be on separate planets. Though one may smile at the obsolete press and the crude working conditions that existed at the end of the nineteenth century, one is sobered by the realization that, for all the "high tech" at the end of the twentieth century, the major task is still undone: that of making the workplace safe and the work meaningful.

*The Village Print Shop*, 1885, American. Oil on wood panel. 58.4 × 58.4 cm. Courtesy of the Terra Museum of American Art, Chicago, Illinois; Terra Foundation for the Arts, Daniel J. Terra Collection; photograph courtesy of the Terra Museum of American Art.

# JAMA®

The Journal of the American Medical Association

February 16, 1990

# CELESTINE BACHELLER ❧

## *Crazy Quilt*

Like Emily Dickinson, whose contemporary she was, Celestine Bacheller (1839-1900) was a Massachusetts poet who became a national treasure. Both used the homely materials at hand to spin a magic that weaves its spell well beyond its maker's lifetime. But whereas Dickinson worked with the everyday words at her disposal, Bacheller worked with needle and thread and scraps of silk and velvet. With these and a repertoire of stitches every woman knew, she created *Crazy Quilt*, a piece of American folk art, the more charming because its panels speak of such simple themes: homes, women, men, gardens, bodies of water, boats, all scenes we presume Bacheller observed in the daily life around her.

Beyond the dates of her birth and death and the fact that she lived in what is now Lynn, Massachusetts, we know nothing about Celestine Bacheller. She remains nearly as anonymous as the nuns who

> *. . . what life was conceived in its warmth, whose coldness did it warm at death?*

stitched the vestments for medieval liturgies or the unnamed workers who wove the tapestries that hung in the halls of royalty. Nor do we know anything of the story of her quilt. From whose ball gowns did she collect her fabrics, and for whose trousseau did she stitch them together? Whose limbs did her poetry cover, what life was conceived in its warmth, whose coldness did it warm at death? To whom did it say in the darkness "Good night" and at the dawn "Good morning"? What child loved it?

Though Dickinson and Bacheller lived less than a hundred miles apart, it is unlikely that they ever met. Yet each a poet—a maker of beauty—they knew at least this in common: when a work of art is finished, it has only begun to live.

*Crazy Quilt*, mid-late nineteenth century, American. Silk, plush, pieced, appliquéd, and embroidered. 188.7 × 144.6 cm. Courtesy of the Museum of Fine Arts, Boston, Massachusetts; gift of Mr and Mrs Edward J. Healy in memory of Mrs Charles O'Malley.

# JAMA®

The Journal of the American Medical Association

February 23, 1990

# JOSEPH STELLA ❧

## *Telegraph Poles With Buildings*

Whether in his life or in his art, Joseph Stella (1877-1946) defies categorization. In each he was contradiction incarnate. Born in Muro Lucano, a small village near Naples, where the houses were stepped up the hillsides, he came to the United States at age eighteen and settled in the cramped and viewless Lower East Side of Manhattan. All he knew about his new country or its language was what he had learned from his two favorite American poets, Poe and Whitman. Selected by his family to study medicine (two of his four older brothers were already physicians, with the oldest, Antonio, a leader in the Italian American community in New York City; his patients included Enrico Caruso and Theodore Roosevelt), the young Stella tried, failed, switched to pharmacy, and then opted out of the medical field altogether. Supported by Antonio, he instead pursued the first love of his life, painting. He enrolled briefly at the Art Students League and later he became a student at the New York School of Art, whose director, William Merritt Chase, called him a second Manet.

In 1908 Stella was commissioned by a sociology periodical to draw the workers of the Pittsburgh steel mills. The combination of urban grime, the chaos of close living, and the dehumanizing working conditions was a scene he never forgot; industrial themes—factories, gas storage tanks, steel bridges, smokestacks, steel making—became one of his principal topics. But Joseph could not forget the natural beauty of his Neapolitan countryside or the Renaissance masters he so loved. The following year, 1909, aged thirty-two and still subsidized by Antonio, he returned to Europe to study. He went not as an expatriate, as was so common among artists in those days, but as a man with a divided heart who still lived with half of it in the Old World and half in the New. He tried desperately to heal his affections, but he remained always a man cut in two by ambivalence.

In 1914, Stella was back in the United States and painted his first major work, *Battle of Lights*, a visual cacophony of Coney Island. Immediately, he was cheered by the avant-garde of New York City. For Antonio, it was the last straw. Declaring his brother a failure, he cut off funds. Joseph, after much

> *Selected by his family to study medicine . . . Stella . . . opted out . . .*

desperation, finally found a job in a Brooklyn seminary, teaching Italian. Though he hated Brooklyn with its "snow that was blackened with coal," and he saw industrial America as a place of "iron fists and steel nerves," he also, now that he was supporting himself, no matter how marginally, felt for the first time that he was free to paint as he wanted. From this period came what is probably his best-known painting, *Brooklyn Bridge*, a commanding, though graceful, web of cables, roadways, cars, and subways that speaks of strength and speed. It was also during this period that he painted *Telegraph Poles With Buildings*. These six years, 1916 to 1922, have been called the most creative of his life.

*Telegraph Poles With Buildings*, with its centralized focus, strong verticals, and sharp color contrasts, is characteristic of Stella's mature style. In sharp opposition to scenes of his boyhood, where green hills were crisscrossed by grapevines, the America of

his manhood was to him a vast industrial empire, a country whose cities were strung together with wires. Across thousands of miles, from city to city, from factory to factory, from home to home, messages hummed along the wires. They moved in freedom, in the clear air of a blue sky. But below, where people had their houses, the undersides of the same sky were darkened with soot, the residue of a coal-stoked society, and living was as harsh as the red, blue, and green color contrasts. On the one hand freedom, on the other hand its price, was a contradiction that was to occupy Stella for most of his life.

By 1930, when he was in his early fifties, Stella had reached the apex of his career, being firmly established as an American modernist painter. But the country was in the Great Depression and not in the mood for Stella's art. Increasingly he turned to other subjects, passing from factories to flowers, emulating the simplicity and love of nature he had so long admired in his thirteenth-century fellow countryman, Francis of Assisi. Beginning in 1940, he developed persistent heart problems and also suffered a series of other health misfortunes. Forced to give up his studio, and finally bedridden, he did not, however, give up his painting. To the end, he remained true to the love of his heart and to his motto: *Nulla dies sine linea*. He died on November 5, 1946, of heart failure, aged sixty-nine.

*Telegraph Poles With Buildings*, 1917-1920, American. Oil on canvas. 91.4 × 76.2 cm. Courtesy of the Terra Museum of American Art, Chicago, Illinois; Terra Foundation for the Arts, Daniel J. Terra Collection; photograph courtesy of the Terra Museum of American Art.

# JAMA®

The Journal of the American Medical Association

March 2, 1990

# ERNEST LAWSON ❧

## Spring Thaw

It was the genius of Ernest Lawson (1873-1939) to see beauty where another might see only ugliness. In fact, wrote the collector and critic Duncan Phillips, if one were to go to the actual spot that had inspired a Lawson canvas, one would probably find it "a God-forsaken purlieu of starving cats, tin cans, and rubbish." Yet Lawson neither ignored the dreary and the squalid nor excluded them from his paintings—the dull day, the barren tree, the tumbledown shack, the abandoned rowboat. Rather, he transformed them into celebrations of color and light. "The power to see beautifully . . . is almost all that is worth bothering about," he wrote. "People in this age of hurry have their perceptions numbed so that they never really look at the world to see how fair it is."

*Spring Thaw* was painted around 1910, when Lawson was in his late thirties. It is characteristic of the many wintry motifs he chose as he roamed Upper Manhattan where the Hudson and Harlem (East) rivers joined. But where the cold and hurried passerby might have only an impression of dirty whiteness along a riverbank, Lawson

> . . . the time of the great womb-opening of the earth.

engaged all the colors of the spectrum in the service of seeing: yellow trees, green ice, blue shrubs, red branches, marbled sky, sapphire snow. Nor is his early spring landscape any longer locked motionless in its icy prison. Rather, the diagonals of the boats and the triangular juts of land suggest an energy that is already bursting its bonds. Ice floats past, the boats bob, melting snow trickles into the water. But most of all, to those who, like Lawson, would stop to listen as well as to look for a moment, a promise can be heard: "Arise. The winter is past, the rain is over and gone; the flowers appear in the land, the time of the singing of birds is come." It is spring, the time of the great womb-opening of the earth. Lawson, who refused to hurry on by, paused to look at the world. He saw that it was indeed beautiful.

*Spring Thaw*, c 1910, American. Oil on canvas. 63.5 × 76.2 cm. Courtesy of the Terra Museum of American Art, Chicago, Illinois; Terra Foundation for the Arts, Daniel J. Terra Collection; photograph courtesy of the Terra Museum of American Art.

# JAMA®

The Journal of the American Medical Association

**March 16, 1990**

# EDWARD WILLIS REDFIELD

## The Breaking of Winter

Impressionism, though birthed in France, was far from remaining exclusively French. Once mature, it traveled widely, carried by those who had returned to their native countries after studying in Paris in the last quarter of the nineteenth century. Sometimes quickly, sometimes more gradually, the style wedded itself to the culture of the new country and bore offspring not quite French, but not quite local either. Thus, there are discernible offshoots of Impressionism scattered throughout the world called British, Canadian, Australian, Russian, Spanish, Norwegian, Danish, Swedish, even Italian Impressionism. But French Impressionism established an especially strong progeny in the United States when it settled here in the late nineteenth century. American Impressionism remains the broad term, but once landed it scattered across the country, establishing distinctive colonies at Boston, Old Lyme, Cos Cob, New York, Indiana, and New Hope, Pennsylvania. Leader of the last-named group, also known as the Pennsylvania School of Landscape Painting, was Edward Willis Redfield (1869-1965).

Redfield was born in Bridgeville, Delaware, but shortly thereafter the family settled in Philadelphia, where the father sold fruit and flowers. When the boy was only seven, he had a drawing accepted for exhibition at the Centennial Exposition of 1876 in Philadelphia. Thereafter he took classes at the Spring Garden Institute and at the Franklin Institute in Philadelphia. At age eighteen, he entered the Pennsylvania Academy of the Fine Arts, where he and Robert Henri became friends. Two years later, with a promise of $50 a month support from his father, Redfield entered the Académie Julian in Paris with fellow student Henri. The following year he enrolled at the

École des Beaux-Arts, where he studied with the academicians Adolphe Bouguereau and Robert Fleury. A prodigious worker, he studied the model for up to eight hours a day, though his real interest lay with the work of Monet and Degas. In 1891, on a painting trip to Bois-le-Rois in the forest of Fontainebleau, he became fascinated with painting snow scenes, and one of them found acceptance at the Salon (his friend Henri's work meanwhile being rejected). Redfield also did a mural for the Hôtel

### . . . the sequel to an April day fooled by a sudden storm.

Deligant, where he was staying while in Fontainebleau. Late that year, after a summer in Venice, Redfield and Henri returned to the United States, where Redfield prepared for a one-man show in Boston (and Henri would become the founder of the Ashcan school). However, Redfield could not forget Fontainebleau, and in 1893 he returned to the Hôtel Deligant, where he married Élise, the innkeeper's daughter. After the couple returned to Pennsylvania, their first child of six, Elizabeth, was born. In 1898, the Redfields moved to Center Bridge, Pennsylvania, but when Elizabeth was killed there by a swinging barn door, the couple went back to France. They returned, however, and settled permanently in Center Bridge in 1900. It was there that Redfield began to specialize in the snow scenes that were to make him so famous, and it was also there that the New Hope School of American Impressionism was born. *The Breaking of Winter* (formerly called *River and Hills*) is characteristic of that work.

Since Redfield did not date his work, it is difficult to place *The Breaking of Winter* in context, but during the years 1900 to 1920, from about age thirty to age fifty, Redfield was at the height of his powers. It was also during this period that he consistently won awards, always one and sometimes up to three each year, making him, next to Sargent, winner of more honors than any other American painter. Redfield liked to work at what he called "one go." Thus, he made no preliminary sketches or watercolors of the scene that he could take back and finish at leisure in the warmth of his studio. Instead, he would anchor his easel to a tree, use lots of linseed oil to keep the viscosity of his paint workable, and protect his palette hand with a heavy glove. Under those conditions he could still finish a canvas the size of *The Breaking of Winter* in a single eight-hour period. Though he worked through the changing light of the day, he preferred the light of midday.

Snowy though it is, *The Breaking of Winter* is distinctly springlike, perhaps the sequel to an April day fooled by a sudden storm. And Impressionist though it is, *The Breaking of Winter* betrays Redfield's academic training. The vertical canvas is carefully divided into thirds, so that the trees both emphasize the verticality of the composition and form an open frame for the river and hills beyond. The light is, as Redfield preferred, that of full noonday, giving the trees, unlike those in a French Impressionist painting, edges hard as diamonds. The shapes of the scudding clouds cast their shadows against the bark of the trees, as well as across the foreground patches of snow and on the river. The shapes of the clouds also echo the shapes of the snow patches so that the composition is framed not only at its sides, but also at top and

*Continued on p 214*

# JAMA®

April 4, 1990

The Journal of the American Medical Association

# WILLIAM MATTHEW PRIOR

## Double Portrait of Mary Cary and Susan Elizabeth Johnson

**M**id–nineteenth-century America was the heyday of the itinerant entrepreneur, or, more simply, the peddler. An enterprising young man, with little capital investment, might earn a tidy income by hawking from a wagon, from horseback, or even on foot anything from fabrics and embroidery materials to patent medicines and diets of whole wheat flour or from healing to preaching to painting. Though some of the vendors were gifted and their products genuine, no special standards had to be met. When the market was sated, the seller simply hoisted his warehouse on his back or put it into his wagon and moved on to the next ready market. The more successful might establish a permanent base and from there radiate out to nearby villages and towns. Among the latter was painter William Matthew Prior (1806-1873), a "maker of likenesses."

Born in Bath, Maine, the second son of Sarah and Matthew Prior, a sea captain, as a child he reportedly made a chalk likeness of either his father or grandfather on a barn door that was greatly admired. The next record is of a portrait done when he was seventeen, which has not survived except in a fragment. For a time he apparently worked in the studio of Charles Codman, a portrait, landscape, marine, and sign painter in Portland. A self-portrait from 1825, when Prior was nineteen, shows evidence of some training in the academic style, but an advertisement he placed in the *Maine Inquirer* for June 5, 1827, just after his twenty-first birthday, describes him more modestly as a "fancy, sign, ornamental painter and decorator." Less than a year later, however, the same year he was married to Rosamond Clark Hamblin, he describes himself in the same newspaper as "Portrait painter, Wm. M. Prior," offering likenesses "at a rea-

sonable price," and promising "side views and profiles of children at reduced prices." His usual fees at the time ranged from $10 to $25, depending on the amount of detail his client wanted. In 1831, the year his second child was born, another notice, further adjusting his fees, appeared in the *Maine Inquirer*, in which he said, "Persons wishing for a flat picture can have a likeness without shade or shadow at 1/4 price."

> *"Portrait painter, Wm. M. Prior . . . side views and profiles of children at reduced prices."*

Apparently Prior could do one of these flat likenesses in about an hour, charging, according to one record, $2.92, and including frame and glass. Thus, like any other enterprising businessman, Prior hoped to raise his income by reducing his time per unit and increasing his volume. Most significant, however, is the fact that, although he could paint in the academic style, Prior chose to paint in the flat, abstract, nonacademic, so-called primitive or naive style. Thus, contrary to frequently held assumptions, the primitive style is not necessarily the result of the artist's inability to paint otherwise.

After his marriage, Prior joined his wife's brothers, who were also painters, in Portland. In 1841, the Prior-Hamblin painters, as they were called, moved to Boston, where Prior became one of the most influential painters of the area. Though listed in Boston business directories almost continuously for the next thirty years, Prior,

packing his stretched canvases in his wagon and often taking one or more of his children with him, continued to travel up and down the coast, reaching as far south as Baltimore. It was probably on such a trip in 1848 that he did, in his usual flat style, the *Double Portrait of Mary Cary and Susan Elizabeth Johnson*. Mary Cary, age five, and Susan Elizabeth, age three, whose interesting histories have survived, were the daughters of Joseph P. Johnson, a sail maker in Provincetown, who went on to become a state senator and a founder of the First National Bank of Provincetown, and his second wife, Susan Pierce Fitch Johnson, descendant of a *Mayflower* pilgrim. Mary Cary eventually became the mother-in-law of a New York physician named Arrowsmith, while Susan Elizabeth married a man who had sustained a permanent tracheostomy after being shot through the throat during the Civil War. He lived nearly fifty years with the tracheostomy and worked as a postmaster in Provincetown. A photograph of the two sisters holding the same pose and taken more than forty years later shows that Prior's portrait was indeed a likeness.

After 1839, when the daguerreotype was introduced from France, business for "likeness makers" such as Prior began to slack off. Enterprising as usual, he turned his talents to producing and selling likenesses of famous people who could not be photographed, such as George Washington. Using Gilbert Stuart's Athenaeum portrait as a model, Prior did innumerable copies on glass, which he then peddled in the Boston shipyards on workers' paydays. For a pair of George and Martha, he received up to $15. Toward the end of his life, Prior, whose second wife, Hannah Frances, was listed in the Boston Directory as a clairvoyant, began to paint posthumous portraits, claiming to

*Continued on p 214*

# JAMA®

The Journal of the American Medical Association

April 11, 1990

# REMBRANDT VAN RIJN

## St Bartholomew

In 1661, when he painted *St Bartholomew*, Rembrandt van Rijn (1606-1669) was fifty-five years old. Behind him were many triumphs, both in his birthplace of Leiden and in Amsterdam, where he had settled in 1631. There he had married Saskia, there his son Titus had been born, there he had been able to pay 13,000 florins for a huge house. There he had built an enviable art collection and had gifted Saskia with many pieces of fine jewelry. There he had also painted perhaps his best-known and most-discussed work, *The Night Watch*. But behind him was also tragedy and with him continuing sorrow. Before Titus, Saskia had borne three other children, all of whom had died in infancy, and, less than a year after Titus' birth, Saskia herself was dead. Rembrandt had been the object of a lawsuit by Titus' nurse for breach of promise. He had gone into bankruptcy and had watched the enforced sale of the great house, its contents, and his art collection. To protect future income, he had been forced to become an employee of Hendrickje, his common-law wife, and Titus. And he had witnessed the excommunication of Hendrickje from her church because of their living arrangements (although a daughter, Cornelia, born to them was permitted baptism). More tragedy lay ahead in the eight years left to Rembrandt before his own death at the age of sixty-three, namely, the death of Hendrickje in 1663 and that of his beloved Titus in 1668, less than a year after he had left his father to marry. But each decade also had brought new maturity, not only professionally, but psychologically as well, as chronicled in his many self-portraits. At the moment, in 1661, Rembrandt was at the height of his powers. Nor is there any evidence that they ever diminished. Instead, he continued to be original, breaking new ground and providing new insights into the human character, right up until his death in Amsterdam in 1669.

The *St Bartholomew* has been identified by various other titles over the years, including ones that identified the painting as a portrayal of Rembrandt's cook, his butcher, even an assassin. But now it is accepted that this was intended to be a painting, with a

*Just as it is the opposites, light and dark, that make a painting, so do they make a life.*

contemporary model, of the Apostle Bartholomew. This conclusion was reached partly because of Rembrandt's penchant for scriptural topics, partly because Rembrandt was known to be painting representations of several other apostles at the same time (in fact, he himself modeled for the Apostle Paul), and partly because of the knife, which was Bartholomew's attribute. (Legend has it that he died by being flayed alive.) The array of names the painting has had over the centuries is less important for any doubt it may cast, however, than for the fact that it is silent testimony to what is perhaps Rembrandt's greatest virtue: he painted human beings, not labels.

Just as it is the opposites, light and dark, that make a painting, so do they make a life. Perhaps Rembrandt's portraits still speak so powerfully after more than three centuries precisely because, just as neither all light nor all dark can make a painting, but rather how they are combined and shadowed, so it is that their combinations and contrasts form the patterns of a life. In life, as in art, it is chiaroscuro that reveals character. And by brushing the very souls of his sitters onto the canvas, Rembrandt thereby touches the souls of his viewers. For example, whatever the real name of the painting or occupation of the model, it does not matter. Emerging from the dark, the powerful head and hands—the square face with its low hairline, the skin wrinkled like an autumn apple, the large ears, the rheumy, fatigued eyes, the untrimmed mustache—become engraved in the viewer's own soul. Whether saint or not, this is not a man in his triumph, but a man in his doubt and in his fear. If death has become overcome, why, then, does he feel so chilled?

But a Rembrandt portrait is less for talking about than for looking at. In a Rembrandt can be found all the pain, hopes, fears, and doubts of the human struggle, crowned by the courage to continue. It is this courage, says the Czechoslovakian poet Miroslav Holub, that gives us the ability "to sort peas,/to cup water in our hands,/to seek the right screw/under the sofa/for hours." These are our "wings."

In one sense, every portrait by Rembrandt is a self-portrait. In another sense, each is a portrait of the viewer. But in the final, broadest sense, every Rembrandt portrait is a portrait of the entire human race and of the commonality that exists among all persons. In the final analysis, century, color, country, and gender have no relevance.

*St Bartholomew*, 1661, Dutch. Oil on canvas. 86.5 × 75.5 cm. Courtesy of the J. Paul Getty Museum, Los Angeles, California.

# JAMA®

April 18, 1990

The Journal of the American Medical Association

# EDGAR DEGAS

## Waiting: Dancer and Woman With Umbrella on a Bench (L'Attente)

Edgar Degas (1834-1917) was not an easy person to know. Self-described as a timid and fearful man, he was tortured throughout his life by self-doubt and bad temper. In a rare candid confession to a friend whom he had hurt, he explained that even though he knew his attitude toward art was correct, he felt badly equipped and weak, and that if he was harsh and brutal toward others, he was equally so toward himself. His behavior had been "born of my distrust in myself and my ill humor." He was disgusted, he continued, with everyone, but most of all with himself. And not the least painful of his feelings were those he had toward women: aversion and even revulsion. His misogyny has, in fact, become a legend. Yet, at the same time he is known today for his sympathetic portrayal of the women of his time—especially those of the working underclass in Paris: the laundresses, the café singers, the prostitutes, and, perhaps, most of all, the Opéra ballet students known as "rats."

Hilaire Germain Edgar de Gas was the eldest of five children born into a well-connected international banking family in Paris. His father had been born in Naples, his mother in New Orleans. In 1847, when Edgar was thirteen and the youngest child only two, his mother died. Other than that, his boyhood seemed the conventional one for a privileged youth of his time. He attended the Lycée, went to concerts and the Louvre with his father, and, as expected, entered law school at age nineteen. However, he also at the same time registered at the Louvre and at the Bibliothèque Nationale as a copyist. A year later, in what amounted to his adolescent rebellion, he moved out of the family home, gave up law, and enrolled at the École des Beaux-Arts, where he studied with Lamothe, a former pupil of

Ingres. Between 1856 and 1860, he made several trips to Italy, where, besides meeting his Italian forebears, he was especially captivated by the fifteenth-century Florentine masters. An avid student, he copied such masters as Raphael, Michelangelo, Botticelli, Mantegna, Filippino Lippi, and Leonardo. In 1862, settled in Paris and nearing thirty, he met Manet, through whom he would meet the Impressionists and become part of their exhibitions.

The two decades of his association with the Impressionists saw the greatest flowering of Degas' talent. Yet, his work was far removed from the almost literal rendering of

*They wait, but for what? . . .*
*Perhaps the waiting*
*is the story.*

light the Impressionists practiced. For one, Degas' eye problems, which began around his mid thirties, did not permit him to work out-of-doors; for another, he did not believe in spontaneity, inspiration, or even in artistic temperament, but rather in quiet study of the masters and reflection in the solitude of his studio; and, finally, he was not so much interested in the effects of light as in the arrest of movement. Moreover, as a disciple of Ingres, he believed that it was not landscape, but the human body that held the perfection of beauty. He preferred to work from memory rather than on the spot, believing that only thus would a picture contain what is essential, the unimportant having been forgotten. But the most telling difference between Degas and the Impressionists was in his use of line, advice he had

absorbed as a young man from Ingres. "Draw lines, many lines, from memory or from nature," the elderly master had said to him. "It is by this that you will become a good artist." Thus, while the Impressionists' contours are broken, Degas' are continuous. Often, he traced the contour over and over before filling it in.

In 1882, about the time he did *Waiting: Dancer and Women With Umbrella on a Bench (L'Attente)*, Degas was nearing fifty. The Impressionists were holding their seventh exhibition, but Degas, who had exhibited in all of the previous six, had had a falling out with the organizers and was refusing to exhibit in this one. He was growing increasingly cantankerous and reclusive. His eyesight was growing considerably worse, and there was evidence of macular damage in his heretofore good left eye. It is a "torment to draw," he wrote to the English painter Sickert, "when he could only see around the spot at which he was looking, and never the spot itself." With painting in oils becoming increasingly difficult, he had switched to pastels, and it is this medium he uses in *Waiting*. Also characteristic of this period are the artist's perspective and the composition. The figures are seen from above, as though the viewer is standing partway up a staircase. Perhaps that is the unexpected glimpse Degas had as he was climbing the stairs one day and happened to turn and see the two women.

The unorthodox perspective is combined with an equally unorthodox composition. Both figures are sequestered in the upper left triangle of the painting. Except for the opposing diagonals of the bench and the umbrella, the lower right triangle is almost completely empty. Degas gives few clues as to who the women are and what the

*Continued on p 215*

# JAMA®

April 25, 1990

The Journal of the American Medical Association

# MAURICE BRAZIL PRENDERGAST ⟿

## *Franklin Park, Boston*

Like fellow painter Ernest Lawson, Maurice Brazil Prendergast (1859-1924) was Canadian by birth but American by adoption. Both were members of "The Eight," the group of artists organized by Robert Henri who exhibited together in 1908 to protest the official policies of the National Academy of Design. But there the similarities end. Lawson's style was Impressionist and his palette was described as one of "crushed jewels"; Prendergast was an early—perhaps the first—American modernist, and his canvases were described as "explosions in a color factory."

Prendergast was born in St John's, Newfoundland, one of twins, the first children of Maurice Prendergast, the Irish owner of a trading post, and Mary Malvina Germaine Prendergast, born in Boston, of French Huguenot origin. A second set of twins was born the following year. In 1861, because of financial difficulties, the family moved to Boston's South End, where, in 1863, the couple's last child, Charles James, was born. Maurice and Charles, as the only children who survived to maturity (Maurice's twin, Lucy Catherine, died at age seventeen, while the other twins died at birth or in childhood) were destined to be very close, both becoming painters, traveling abroad together, and providing financial support to the other as needed. Maurice never married, while Charles married only after Maurice's death.

Though employed as a calligrapher and sketching constantly from boyhood on, Maurice had no formal art training until he was well into his thirties. With the help of Charles he spent four years in Europe in the early 1890s, where he studied at the Académie Julian. Nonetheless, he was all his life to remain largely self-taught, discovering for himself the emerging Cézanne and the early sixteenth-century Venetian painter Carpaccio, both of whom were to have a noticeable influence on his work. Other influences, though to a lesser extent, were the Nabis, Bonnard, Vuillard, and Whistler.

> *. . . the quintessential Sunday in the park.*

By the turn of the century Prendergast was exhibiting regularly and was beginning to establish a reputation beyond Boston, principally in New York City. However, in his midforties his hearing began to fail, and he temporarily curtailed his work while he adopted a regimen that prescribed regular sunbathing and sea bathing, regardless of temperature, from March to November of each year. All treatment failed, however, and by the time he was fifty, he was, like Goya, almost totally deaf. Nonetheless, his life resumed its regular rhythm of painting, travel abroad, and exhibiting. In 1914, with the war preventing further trips to Europe, Maurice moved to New York City with Charles but continued to spend summers in New England. With a major exhibition in New York City in 1915, serious collectors began acquiring his work. In 1923, he was awarded the Third William A. Clark Prize at the Corcoran Gallery's Ninth Biennial Exhibition in Washington, DC, but he was by then too ill to attend the ceremony. He died in New York City on February 1, 1924, aged sixty-four.

The watercolor *Franklin Park, Boston* is an example of Prendergast's early work, before he became internationally known. Already, however, can be seen the rhythmic movement of his line, the flat, abstract shapes, and the quickly applied puddles of color. And while the figures move in solemn procession around the park and the leaves flutter in the breeze, the squat building in the background anchors the scene firmly to the canvas. It is the quintessential Sunday in the park.

Most telling about Prendergast and his work is perhaps the fact that, unlike most of the members of "The Eight," he has never been accused of showing the seamier side, the "realist" side, of life, of painting "ugliness." Rather, his watercolors are more like a May garden—freshly blooming colors and shapes, all put there for no more purpose than the sheer delight of the eye.

*Franklin Park, Boston*, American, 1895-1897. Watercolor and graphite on paper. 43.8 × 31.8 cm. Courtesy of the Terra Museum of American Art, Chicago, Illinois; Terra Foundation for the Arts, Daniel J. Terra Collection; photograph courtesy of the Terra Museum of American Art.

# JAMA®

May 2, 1990

The Journal of the American Medical Association

# JULIUS L. STEWART

## The Baptism

In the last third of the nineteenth century, it was almost an imperative that any young American aspiring to be a painter or sculptor should study for several years in one of the art centers of Europe. Of the hundreds who did so, most returned home, there to apply their European-honed skills to the American experience. Two of the most successful in making the transition were Winslow Homer and Thomas Eakins. But some, notably Mary Cassatt, James Whistler, and John Singer Sargent, for one reason or another preferred to stay on and make a permanent home abroad, Whistler and Sargent in London, Cassatt in Paris. To this latter group, expatriate American painters, belongs a fellow Philadelphian of Cassatt, Julius LeBlanc Stewart (1855-1919).

Stewart was one of eight sons and three daughters of William H. Stewart, a wealthy owner of Cuban sugar plantations, and Ellen Price Morgan. At the end of the Civil War, when Julius was ten, the family moved from Philadelphia to Paris, where the father became a respected collector and patron of contemporary art. He specialized in the work of Spanish painters, and, because of his fluency in that language, his home became a center for Spanish painters living in Paris. Two of them, Eduardo Zamcois and Raimundo de Madrazo, became the young Julius' teachers. In 1873, at age eighteen, Julius entered the studio of Gérome in Paris, another master who was to be not only teacher, but friend as well. Success came early and easily to Stewart. He received his first popular and critical acclaim at the Salon of 1883, where he had entered a painting of Paris' elite at afternoon tea. From then on, while his fellow American painters might be in the streets or fields looking to the urban poor and the peasant to idealize in paintings for the people back home, Stewart went about painting the rich at their pastimes, including their yachting parties, their balls, and their hunts. But Stewart also knew how to idealize his subject to suit the popular taste. Said one critic of his work in 1889: "He never paints a woman who appears to be of lower rank than that of baroness, and all his young girls look like daughters of duchesses." Nor did Stewart lack for entrée to these elite circles. Himself wealthy and accomplished—he was a patron of the Paris Opéra and an amateur pianist—he was also known to his friends as "a genial host, a sought-after dinner guest, and an ardent sportsman," loving "beasts, birds—and automobiles."

> *. . . the new mother was accorded invalid status for a prolonged period.*

The Baptism, painted in 1892, when Stewart was thirty-seven, might be considered representative of his work at that time. In a richly appointed drawing room, family, old and young—grandparents, mother, father, sisters, in-laws, children—gather to witness the initiation of its newest member into its circle. But, despite the pious demeanor of the women, the scene is more of a grand social event than a religious event, with the children either bored or bug-eyed with curiosity and two of the men taking advantage of the gathering for a discussion of business of some sort. Further, although it is the baby who is the putative subject of the painting, Stewart gives pride of place to the women, especially to the new mother. At a time when maternity was not much discussed in genteel company, Stewart has managed to make it the real subject of the painting. It is generally accepted that this is a family portrait—at one time thought to be of the Vanderbilts—albeit with the individual likenesses idealized to conform to late nineteenth-century standards of beauty. Despite wide exhibition, however, the identity of the family has never been discovered. Compositionally, the work is faintly evocative of Velázquez' *Las Meninas* with its mirror and draped doorway in the background and figures grouped along the right side. Stewart could easily have studied Velázquez, if not in Madrid, then certainly through his Spanish instructors. In its finish the work is like that of the academics who taught him, while the lightness of the palette is a reminder of the Impressionists. But most interesting, perhaps, is Stewart's unwitting historical footnote to the obstetric philosophy of the day, in which the new mother was accorded invalid status for a prolonged period.

In the 1890s, Stewart gradually shifted his focus from large social gatherings of the fashionably elite to paintings of the female nude out-of-doors, a form of art that found more tolerance in Paris than in the United States. Nonetheless, although he continued to live in Paris, he was popular and active in art organizations in the United States. In France he continued to have successes at the Salon and was made a chevalier of the Legion of Honor. He also received major honors in Berlin, Munich, and Brussels. At the outbreak of World War I, Stewart, almost sixty, enlisted in the Red Cross ambulance corps, but an emotional breakdown forced him to resign, and he spent most of the war years in the United States. He died in Paris on January 5, 1919, aged sixty-three. His work by that time was

*Continued on p 215*

# JAMA®

The Journal of the American Medical Association

May 9, 1990

# HORACE PIPPIN

## *Barracks*

As a boy of seven in Goshen, New York, he was reprimanded both in school and at home for drawing pictures of the words at the end of his spelling lesson. At age ten, in response to a newspaper ad, he sent a drawing to an outfit in Chicago and, much to his delight, won a prize: "crayon pencils of six different colors, a box of cold water paint and two brushes," as he later recalled it. He also made his first sale, at a Sunday school social: six biblical scenes, each painted on a fringed muslin doily he had made. But a month later he had to face the irate buyer when the watercolor paints came out in the wash. At age fourteen he drew his employer, who then offered to send him to art school. But his mother, who worked as a domestic servant, was by that time ill, and the boy left school to support her. At fifteen he worked in a coal yard, a feed store, and finally as a hotel porter, where he remained for seven years. His mother died when he was twenty-three and he moved to Paterson, New Jersey, where he worked for a furniture storage firm. In 1916, now twenty-eight, he learned to be a molder for the American Brakeshoe Company, but the following year he enlisted in the US Army, became an infantryman in the fifteenth New York regiment, and arrived in France just after Christmas, 1917. Becoming part of the 369th regiment under French command, he spent the summer and autumn under German fire and recorded his experiences in pencil and crayon sketches. More than twenty years later, he would recall the deaths around him as matter-of-factly as he wrote of the rain that fell constantly, of the "men shoulder to shoulder in trenches, the artillery hub to hub on the road," and of the French lieutenant beside him in a shell hole who stood stock-still for a full ten seconds after

being shot in the head, and then slid slowly to the ground, his helmet still in place.

Then his own sketches stopped. He himself had been hit in the right shoulder, and his arm was paralyzed. Sent home by hospital ship, he received the French Croix de Guerre (only in 1945 did he receive the Purple Heart for his World War I service) and was discharged in May 1919, aged thirty-one, his right arm useless. Living on a small disability pension, he married a widow with a young son. They moved to West Chester, Pennsylvania, and she supplemented the pension by taking in laundry, while he

*. . . each one is numbered, classified, sorted, and pigeonholed into his regulation space . . .*

himself delivered it. Ten years after his discharge, still regretting sketches he had lost in France, he began laboriously making burnt wood pictures, balancing a "white-hot poker" on his knee with the right hand, while with his left he moved a wood panel around its tip. But the war pictures remained on his mind, and in 1930, by placing a small brush in his right fingers and supporting and guiding his wrist with his left hand, he completed his first oil painting: *The Ending of the War Starting Home*. It had taken him three years and probably one hundred coats of paint. After that, he made other paintings of the life around him and remembered scenes such as Saturday night baths and Sunday morning breakfasts, until, in 1937, he was, as he put it, "discovered by Dr Christian Brinton," president of the West

Chester Country Art Association, and given a one-man show. After that came an almost instant rise to fame, exhibits in museums throughout the country, and sales almost faster than he could complete a work. A master of color, a genius of design, an eloquent communicator, he is acknowledged today as one of the greatest of the American primitive painters. He is Horace Pippin (1888-1946).

Pippin's war paintings, which are considered to be among the greatest ever done in the genre—he could see design in the nails in a fence, pattern and meaning in a tumble of barbed wire fence—number only five, but they are among his first as well as his last. *Barracks*, a remembered scene of World War I, was his last and was painted only at the end of World War II. It is typical that Pippin chose to remember war not as a spectacular scene of battle, but rather as a scene of subdued color—browns, grays, khakis—and subdued activity—preparing for sleep—a scene so commonplace that one almost gives it no second thought. Yet there is something compelling that pulls one back. Perhaps it is the center post that so nearly divides the painting into halves. Or perhaps it is the three evenly spaced horizontal planks that further divide each half into quarters. Or the two vertical figures who, though awake, yet ignore the viewer, or the horizontal ones who try to sleep or to read. Or the humps at the top. We are told that this is the soldier's life, where each one is numbered, classified, sorted, and pigeonholed into his regulation space, like so many documents in a drawer. Or stacks of coffins in which they could well travel home; or neatly spaced tiers of graves such as one can find in France. But wait, says Pippin, these men are not government issue; they are real, flesh and blood. They

*Continued on p 215*

# JAMA®

The Journal of the American Medical Association

May 23/30, 1990

# CHARLES COURTNEY CURRAN ⟿

## *Summer Clouds*

To the American Impressionist painter Charles Courtney Curran (1861-1942), the late nineteenth/early twentieth–century world seems to have been drenched in perpetual sunlight, its air washed continually by soft breezes, and its fragrant landscapes peopled by long-limbed young women who not only were bursting with good health, but whose sole purpose seemed to be to outshine nature itself. Turn-of-the-century taste considered the type to be the ideal of "the American beauty." It has been immortalized in a genre of painting that art historian Linda Nochlin calls the "American iconography of leisure." Often appearing in a white dress, the woman represents the nonutilitarian aspects of life, its "finer" aspects, art itself, and, by inference, leisure. Usually alone, she is playing the piano, draped across a sofa, resting, or gazing at her image in the mirror. No narrative or story line is given or even intended; rather, the figure is simply another object in a still life dedicated to beauty.

Born in Hartford, Kentucky, Curran was raised in Norwalk, Ohio. His first art study was at the Cincinnati School of Design, but in 1879, at age eighteen, he moved to New York City, where he studied at the National Academy of Design and at the Art Students League. In 1889, at age twenty-eight, he, like most other American art students of the time, went to Paris, where he studied for two years at the Académie Julian. In 1890 he won an Honorable Mention at the Salon for a work that the French Impressionist collector Ernest Hoschede called "delicious." Returning to the United States, he won the Second and Third Hallgarten Prizes at the National Academy of Design and was made a full

> *. . . the figure is simply another object in a still life . . .*

academician in 1904. About that time he also became an active member of Cragsmoor, an artists' colony in Ulster County, New York, near Ellenville. There, in the Shawangunk Mountains, with their broad sweeps of valley and peaks and constantly changing light, he developed his now familiar theme of women on mountaintops.

*Summer Clouds* was painted in 1917, just after the United States had entered World War I. By June, troops were already landing in France. Thus, although the three young women in white could represent muses of the fine arts, or even ancient goddesses defending Trojans or Greeks, they could also be twentieth-century American women looking anxiously into the gathering clouds of Europe. Loyalty, strength, and stability are suggested by the right-angled triangle the three figures describe, with the platform of rock, reinforced by the stick, as the base. The figure in yellow (probably the artist's daughter, Emily) stands outside the group, in color as well as place, giving a needed asymmetry and also suggesting that, while goddesses may indeed contemplate and arrange the affairs of both men and gods from atop their pedestals, it is mortal women of flesh and blood who carry on the necessary tasks of daily living.

Cragsmoor, with its prosperous artists, leisurely lifestyle, teas, card parties, musicals, and theatricals, continued to flourish for about a decade after World War I, but then, with the advent of the Great Depression, went into decline. Curran, however, who had built a house there, stayed on. He died in Cragsmoor in 1942, long after it had ceased to be fashionable. He was eighty-one.

*Summer Clouds*, 1917, American. Oil on canvas. 127 × 101.6 cm. Collection of Carl and Gail Icahn.

# JAMA®

The Journal of the American Medical Association

**June 6, 1990**

# GEORGE CALEB BINGHAM ❧

## The Jolly Flatboatmen

To the poet T. S. Eliot, it was "a strong brown god—sullen, untamed and intractable." To the writer Mark Twain, it was a rite of passage from adolescence to manhood. But to the American genre painter George Caleb Bingham (1811-1879), the Mississippi River was a mirror of American frontier life as it existed in the mid nineteenth century. Echoing the popular song "Jolly, Jolly Raftsman's the Life for Me," Bingham's boatmen dance and sing their way down the Missouri and Mississippi rivers, high-spirited, boisterous, and free of any but the most immediate cares, such as getting the jug filled and keeping on hand an adequate supply of tobacco. To Easterners, already overtaken by civilization, Bingham's robust river paintings were a romantic reminder of a way of life they could only imagine and one that, even as it was recorded, was disappearing as fast as the river mists. The railroad was opening the West to even the most delicate traveler, and steam was overtaking the Mississippi flatboats.

Bingham was born in Augusta County, Virginia, to Henry Vest and Mary Amend Bingham. At age eight the boy moved with his family to Franklin, Missouri. There, until his death just four years later, George Caleb's father owned a tavern, was a partner in a tobacco factory, and served as a county and circuit court judge. At age sixteen George was apprenticed to a cabinetmaker who was also a Methodist minister. Under the minister's tutelage he studied religion, preached, and read law, acquiring that knowledge and those skills that would stand him in good stead in his later career in politics. His early career, however, began at age twenty-one, when he became an itinerant painter of signs and portraits. An attack of smallpox in 1835, when he was twenty-four, left him bald and obliged to

wear a hairpiece for the rest of his life. In 1836 he married Sarah Elizabeth Hutchison, and the couple's first child was born the following year. In 1838 Bingham went east, where he studied at the Pennsylvania Academy of the Fine Arts.

Thereafter his life became a busy round of travel between Missouri and the East, where he both exhibited and worked for extended periods. He also entered politics,

> *. . . a way of life . . .*
> *disappearing*
> *as fast as the river mists.*

where campaigning for and later serving in public office would occupy a sizable portion of his time and energy. In 1848, when his artistic reputation was nearing its zenith and his political career as a member of the Missouri legislature was finally taking off, Sarah Elizabeth died, and Bingham married Eliza Thomas of Columbia, Missouri, the following year. His genre paintings of life on and around the Mississippi and Missouri rivers had in the meantime become well known, and now he turned his brush to the second genre topic for which he is known: electioneering. Again, he was successful, especially in the East, where people were avid for anything having to do with the American "West." Between 1856 and 1860 Bingham made two trips to Europe, where he studied and worked at Düsseldorf, Germany; for all practical purposes, the period of his great American genre paintings was over, and the rest of his work, much of which was unfortunately lost to fire after his death, concentrated on portraits, usually of important political figures. In 1876, with himself now in his midsixties, Eliza became

mentally ill and died shortly thereafter in an asylum. Appointed professor of art at the University of Missouri, Bingham married Martha Livingston Lykins of Kansas City. The following summer, in July 1879, he himself died there suddenly of "cholera morbus." He was sixty-eight.

*The Jolly Flatboatmen* was painted in 1878, the year before Bingham died, and is one of three versions he did of this subject. The first, which is very similar to this last, was completed in 1848, when Bingham was thirty-seven and at the height of his powers. The principal differences between the two versions are an overall simplification in the latter, with the number of figures being reduced from eight to seven and the flatboat itself being made nearly a silhouette. In addition, some of the models have changed since the first version. But the geometry bears the Bingham signature: the sharp outcrops of the bank, the flatboat coming squarely at us, the paddles set at right angles, the horizontal crate with its vertical slats set squarely atop the boat. The figures are piled into an obvious triangle, with the red kerchief at the apex, but six of them form a circle around the dancer, making the triangle a cone. Moreover, the seven figures are arranged in three rows of three each, with the dancer a part of every row. The foot of the figure sprawled on his back marks the geometric center of the painting and points at the apical kerchief. It is the end of a day on the river, and the men make merry. The only discomfited one is a turkey, perhaps intended for dinner, which pokes its scrawny neck through the slats of the crate to see what all the stomping on its roof is about.

Between the first and last versions of *The Jolly Flatboatmen*, a generation elapsed. The boatmen grew old, and so did Bingham. A

*Continued on p 216*

# JAMA®

## The Journal of the American Medical Association

**June 13, 1990**

# EDWARD HENRY POTTHAST

## Ring Around the Rosy

Like his slightly older contemporaries and countrymen Winslow Homer and Mary Cassatt, the American Impressionist Edward Henry Potthast (1857-1927) is remembered today chiefly for his paintings of childhood. Bright and sunny, they recall the French Impressionist stroke of Cassatt, while in their beach settings and the children's happy absorption in games they recall the sturdy youth of Homer. Interestingly, among those whose legacy to art was children, none of the three had ever had children of their own. In fact, none had ever married.

Potthast was born in Cincinnati, Ohio, the second son of Bernadine Scheiffers, a milliner and clerk, and Henry Ignatz Potthast, a German cabinetmaker and chair maker. Young "Eddie's" talent appeared early, and by age thirteen he was a student at the McMicken School of Design in Cincinnati. Apprenticed at sixteen to a lithography firm, he attended art classes six nights a week for a total of twelve hours a week in addition to his full-time employment. By 1882, when he was twenty-five, he had saved enough money to spend the next three years studying in Munich, an art center for American students and in particular for those from Cincinnati. Returning home in 1885, he resumed his work for the lithography firm, but also enrolled in life classes held evenings at the Art Academy of Cincinnati. By the late 1880s he was back in Europe, this time for six years, where he studied again in Munich and, most important for his future direction, in Paris. It was here that he came across the bright palette and choppy strokes of Impressionism, which was to cause a marked departure in his work from the dark tones of the Munich school.

Back again in Cincinnati, Potthast was still too cautious and unsure of himself to attempt a full-time art career and thus returned once again to the financial security of the lithography firm. Finally, however, in about 1896, just before he would turn forty, he made the commitment to a full-time painting career and moved to New York City. Even so, he hung on for a number of years as a freelance lithographer for *Scribner's* and *Century* magazines. Although he never dated his work, it was after his move to New York that he began the sparkling beach scenes that

> *. . . each is an equal and neccessary part of the whole.*

would become his signature. Rising early, this land-locked Midwesterner would travel from his elegant and well-appointed studio near Central Park to Coney Island, where, dressed in business suit and vest, he would set up his panels and paint box and capture the images of children enjoying the freedom of sun, sand, and sea. Summers he traveled the New England coast as far as Maine, again, drawn to the ocean. Though always reticent about his work, Potthast was one of five American artists chosen in 1910 by the Santa Fe Railroad to paint the Grand Canyon. Nevertheless, he still left instructions to his heirs to destroy at his death all work that they found "unfinished or inferior." As one historian of Potthast's work has remarked, one hopes that their judgments were not too harsh. Potthast died, suddenly, of a heart attack on March 9, 1927. He had just returned to his studio after attending a luncheon at the National Academy and was planning to spend the afternoon working. He was sixty-nine.

*Ring Around the Rosy* is typical of the small seashore panels Potthast was so fond of. With his bright, prismatic colors he conveys a visual impression so vivid that it carries the other senses along in its wake. One can hear the surf, the invisible gulls, the delighted shrieks of the children. One can feel the mist and the breeze and the sand shifting under one's feet. And one instinctively shades one's eyes before looking out to the horizon. Whatever strife or unhappiness or pain existed either in Potthast's life or in the rest of the world, it is momentarily forgotten. In contrast to Homer's boys, who play competitive, hierarchical games of survival like *Snap the Whip*, Potthast's girls are more like Gauguin's girls shown in *Breton Girls Dancing, Pont-Aven*, who move in a circle where each is an equal and necessary part of the whole. It is a rainbow world, the greens, yellows, oranges, and reds of the dancers' hairbows and skirts set against the violets, indigos, and blues of the sea and sky.

It is ironic that a spinster and two lifelong bachelors should have left such memorable pictures of childhood. To each it had a special character. To Cassatt it was a time of tenderness and soberness, and to Homer it was a rough-and-tumble generation of post–Civil War boys. But to Potthast it was a world of eternal sunshine and limitless oceans and one's first experience of sheer joy at being alive among them.

*Ring Around the Rosy*, not dated, American. Oil on panel. 30.5 × 40.6 cm. Courtesy of the Terra Museum of American Art, Chicago, Illinois; Terra Foundation for the Arts, Daniel J. Terra Collection; photograph courtesy of the Terra Museum of American Art.

The Journal of the American Medical Association

June 20, 1990

# JEAN BAPTISTE GREUZE

## *The Laundress (La Blanchisseuse)*

When Jean Baptiste Greuze (1725-1805) was born in Tournus, a small town in Burgundy midway between Dijon and Lyons, the great "Sun King" Louis XIV had been dead only ten years. But already, in that decade, French taste and French society had changed dramatically. The court, with all its nobles, pretenders, and just plain hangers-on, had moved itself from the opulent but stifling formality of Versailles to Paris, where courtiers enjoyed their freedom in smaller and more casual, but perhaps even more elegant, apartments. Interior decoration turned to the delicate rococo and inspired a style of painting that would combine easily with it on the walls of the smaller rooms. The Salon, which had held exhibitions of Academy paintings at irregular intervals, was now closed and would not reopen for another twelve years, but when it did reopen in 1737 it became an annual meeting place for aristocracy and commoners alike and a forum for critics and moralists such as Diderot. Meanwhile, the ideas that would culminate in the Social Contract were still fermenting in the mind of Rousseau, but first, in 1750, in Dijon, not far from where Greuze was born, he tried to answer the question of whether the restoration of the sciences and arts had tended to purify morals. Knowledge, Rousseau concluded, depends on the existence of "our vices," and thus the arts and sciences are inherently dangerous.

All of this, however, seemed of little consequence when Greuze was born in the provinces, far from Paris, the sixth of nine children of a tiler and his wife. Little else in known of the boy's early life except that until he was twenty his father refused to recognize an artistic talent that was obvious to everyone else. Finally, in 1745, he was permitted to go to Lyons, where he studied with Grandon, soon to become official painter to that city. In 1750, at age twenty-five, Greuze went to Paris, and within five years had scored a major success at the Salon with a pointedly moral scene of a rustic father explaining the Bible to his family. There followed six years of travel in Italy, where he refined his technique but remained unaffected by the grand, large-scale works. Instead, he leaned to the small, intimate genre scenes of the Dutch and Flemish painters of the seventeenth century, scenes

> *. . . scenes that painted a moral as broad as a barn door . . .*

that pointed a moral as broad as a barn door and/or had sly (and sometimes not so sly) sexual overtones. It was on his return from Rome that he had his greatest success, with an anecdotal painting, *The Village Betrothed*, again a rustic scene. It was at the same Salon, in 1761, that he also showed *The Laundress (La Blanchisseuse)*.

Rich in its Rousseauistic theme of the virtues of poverty, the painting nevertheless departs from it when Greuze gives the young laundress, who is perhaps resuming an interrupted task, a bold and saucy look. Certain of her power, she returns the viewer's gaze steadily and without embarrassment, almost daring a reaction. Poor though she may be, and a servant, she is nevertheless the one in charge. The diagonal thrust of the upper body gives a dynamic sense to a composition that is otherwise stable and classic.

Shapes and objects, such as the laundry bowl and the upturned pail atop the chest and the ewer and the long-handled cup, echo each other. The warm colors and the careful delineation of textures, from plaster and brick to pewter and muslin, evidence Greuze's Dutch leanings. But it is the facial expression of the young laundress, which Greuze has so skillfully caught, that raises the painting from just another highly competent work to one of interest. In her face is the whole story.

Despite his early and sudden popularity, Greuze fell from grace almost as fast. At first championed by Diderot, he later became the object of the critic's scorn. He was publicly humiliated by the Academy, perhaps in retaliation for his overweening pride and relentless self-promotion as much as anything, when its members judged his large history painting, necessary to membership in the Academy, as worthy of membership, but only in the much lesser regarded genre category, not in the full membership category. Cuckolded as well as swindled by his wife, a pretty Parisian bookseller who had once served as his model and who, he said, had tricked him into marriage, he was penniless by the time of the Revolution and never recovered. When, nearing eighty, he died in Paris on March 21, 1805, this man, once the lion of the Salon, had only a handful of people at his funeral. But a week later a letter from Tournus addressed to him was received at his address in Paris. His birthplace, said the letter, wishing to honor a great man, had renamed one of its streets rue Greuze. The officials hoped that he would be pleased and would visit them.

In the skies of the Enlightenment Greuze was a brilliant but short-lived meteor, quickly burning out in the atmosphere of public taste,

*Continued on p 216*

The Journal of the American Medical Association

July 11, 1990

# JEAN FRANÇOIS MILLET ❧

## *Man With a Hoe*

In his review of the Paris Salon of 1861, the art critic and historian Théophile Thoré called for art to return from portrayals of the ideal to portrayals of the real, from an art that was "affected" to an art that was "natural." "Art is sick in France," wrote Thoré, and does not wish to be cured. It "does not like these country doctors who come with solid recipes and unshakeable health," doctors whose taste, he said, is different from that of "the charming artists who paint with pink in the midst of boudoirs." Who were these "doctors" who would heal French art? One, Thoré said, was the political radical and father of French Realism, Gustave Courbet. The other was Jean François Millet (1814-1875), a peasant from Normandy, then living and painting "among the boulders of Fontainebleau."

Millet was born into a peasant family in Gruchy, a small hamlet near Cherbourg. A precocious child, he studied the Latin classics (in adult life Millet could and did quote from not only Virgil, but from La Fontaine, Burns, Milton, Dante, Shakespeare, Theocritus, and the Bible as well) and art, using the family Bible as the source of his drawings. In 1833, when he was nineteen, his family sent him to Cherbourg to study painting with Mouchel and Langlois, former students of David and Gros. At age twenty-three he won a town scholarship to study at the École des Beaux-Arts in Paris with Paul Delaroche. Delaroche, however, found him "impossible" and without talent, and after two years Millet went to the Académie Suisse, where he could work with less supervision. The following year he began to support himself, though just barely, by painting portraits. In 1841, after a year of such work, he married Pauline Ono. The years 1843 to 1846 are considered his greatest portrait period.

When Pauline died in 1844, after just three years of marriage, Millet returned to Cherbourg, where he married Catherine Lemaire. On his return to Paris shortly thereafter, his portrait commissions dropped off, and he turned to religious and mythological subjects, as well as to genre and nudes (which are today considered to be among his greatest works).

The Revolution of 1848 affected Millet profoundly. Turning from his earlier Neoclassical style to the naturalism, now

> " . . . I see the halos of dandelions, and the sun, also . . . the steaming horses . . . a man, all worn out . . . "

called Realism, introduced by Courbet, he made his first attempt at the new style with *The Winnower*. It had a great success at the Salon of that year. The peasant, the "common man" of the Revolution, was shown shaking his winnowing basket while a breath of air comes through to separate the wheat from the chaff. It was for sentiments such as these that Millet was subsequently accused of being a socialist, a label that dogged him the rest of his life despite his many protestations to the contrary. *The Winnower* was followed in 1850, 1857, and 1859 by *The Sower, The Gleaners*, and *The Angelus*, all likewise huge successes at the Salons of those years. Not all reviews were complimentary, however. Baudelaire, for one, found *The Angelus* "pretentious and melancholy," a "disastrous element" that ruined all

that was good in the picture. Nonetheless, it was after these works that Millet's paintings found a steady market. (But, as with Grant Wood's *American Gothic*, reproductions of these works became so familiar in the fifty years after Millet's death that they eventually became caricatures of themselves. Today, even when looked at, they are seldom seen. The *Gleaners*, in fact, was recently parodied on a *New Yorker* cover [June 18, 1990] in conjunction with Seurat's *A Sunday on the Grande-Jatte*.)

*Man With a Hoe* created a sensation at the Salon of 1863 (the same year that Manet was causing a sensation at the spin-off Salon des Refuses with *Déjeuner sur l'Herbe*). The bourgeoisie considered Millet's painting inflammatory, radical, and "socialist." In the press *Man With a Hoe* was renamed "*Dumoulard*," after a peasant who had recently been accused of murdering his employer's family. In a letter to his friend, Alfred Sensier, shortly thereafter, Millet tried to defend himself: "Is it impossible to admit that one can have some sort of idea in seeing a man devoted to gaining his bread by the sweat of his brow?" he asked. "Some tell me that I deny the charms of the country. I find much more than charms—I find infinite glories. . . . I see the halos of dandelions, and the sun, also, which spreads out beyond the world its glory in the clouds. But I see as well, in the plain, the steaming horses at work, and in a rocky place a man, all worn out, whose 'han!' [grunting sound] has been heard since morning, and who tries to straighten himself a moment and breathe. The drama is surrounded by beauty. . . . This 'cry of the ground' was heard long ago. . . . I have never seen anything but fields since I was born, I try to say as best I can what I saw and felt when I was at work." Millet was a realist, seeing nature

*Continued on p 216*

# JAMA®

The Journal of the American Medical Association

July 18, 1990

# ROBERT SPEAR DUNNING ⟿

## *Harvest of Cherries*

**U**ntil the Dutch arranged a crust of bread, a goblet of wine, and some fruit on a linen cloth, took brush and canvas, and recreated them for posterity, still life painting as we know it today did not exist. In their unique perception of light shining on the humble objects of everyday existence, the Dutch not only managed to bring heaven to earth but also raised matter to the level of a sacramental. Even so, still life painting remained low in the hierarchy of subjects worthy of artistic expression for another two hundred years, until well into the nineteenth century.

It was the same for American painting. While numerous members of the Peale family, most notably the women, had excelled at still life painting in the early to mid-1800s, it was considered just that: an occupation fit only for women. Only with the immense popularity of the works of William Harnett and John Peto in the late nineteenth century did still life begin to acquire a greater critical acclaim in America. Even so, Harnett and Peto captured the public eye more by witchery than by their artistic merits. With their trompe l'oeil technique, many an unsuspecting viewer could be deceived into trying to brush away an immovable fly or straighten a crooked sign. But Harnett and Peto were far from the only still life painters working at the time, and trompe l'oeil was far from the only style that caught the public attention. In Fall River, Massachusetts, a whole other school of still life painting had developed, headed by Robert Spear Dunning (1829-1905). Fall River would become an important center of American still life painting, with its small but influential group of students working well into the twentieth century.

Dunning was born in Brunswick, Maine, the son of a marine engineer. (He was reportedly also descended from the Earl of Ashburton.) When the boy was five, the family moved to Fall River. Little is recorded about Dunning's early interests, except that he attended local public schools and worked in a textile mill and on coastal vessels in and around Fall River. At age fifteen he began serious art study with James Roberts in Tiverton, Rhode Island. In 1849, at age twenty, Dunning moved to New York City, where he studied with Daniel Huntington. His early works were portraits and genre scenes. Returning to Fall River in 1852 (where he would live for the rest of his life), Dunning continued to paint, adding landscapes to

*. . . a tale the more tantalizing because its actors are temporarily off stage.*

repertoire and taking part in a number of exhibitions. About 1865, in his midthirties by now, he began the still life painting for which he is chiefly remembered, though his principal means of support continued to come from his portraits of Fall River's leading citizens. In 1869 Dunning married Mehitable Hill, and in 1870, with a colleague, he founded the Fall River Evening Drawing School, destined to become an important center of American still life painting. Dunning died at his summer home in Westport Harbor, Massachusetts, on August 12, 1905, aged seventy-six, active to the end.

*Harvest of Cherries* is one of Dunning's earliest still lifes, painted when he was thirty-seven. Later, more typical still lifes would show fruit, meticulously painted honeycombs, and silver or gilt objects on a highly polished

and ornately carved table indoors, all the various reflecting surfaces designed to show off the virtuosity of the painter. In *Harvest of Cherries*, however, whether unwittingly or no, since he did not travel in England, Dunning adopts the Pre-Raphaelite style that had burst upon English painting in 1850, placing his objects in a nature setting rather than on a tabletop, painting in extreme detail, and using bright, vivid colors. And also—again whether knowingly or not—Dunning accedes to London critic Ruskin's dictum that every painting must have a moral—in Ruskin's case, the necessity for art to show the superiority of nature and agriculture over cities and industrialization. Each cherry, veined to bursting, is perfectly rendered, without variation in size, color, or any other quality, and represents nature in her ideal state. On the other hand, the hat, which is rendered with equal care, nonetheless has the slightest break in the circle of its brim, as if to suggest, with Ruskin, that man-made items are inevitably flawed, while nature grows only more perfect with time. In his handling of textures Dunning borrows from the Dutch. The satin ribbon, the straw of the bonnet (which differs from that of the honeycombed basket and the more carelessly handled man's hat), the peeling cherry bark, the flattened grass, each has it own unmistakable tactile quality. Though the color is the same, no one, for example, could mistake the stiff cherry stems for the yielding blades of grass. More subtle—and perhaps an American touch—is the hinted-at narrative: the casual juxtaposition of the demure basket, the bold hat, and the graceful bonnet suggests a tale the more tantalizing because its actors are temporarily off stage.

But whatever the Dutch, English, or the Americans may have brought to Dunning's painting, the most intriguing aspect,

*Continued on p 216*

# JAMA

## The Journal of the American Medical Association

**August 8, 1990**

# JOHN GEORGE BROWN ⟿

## *The Cider Mill*

One of the most popular—and highly paid—American painters of a century and more ago, more popular even than his contemporaries Thomas Eakins and Winslow Homer, was the English immigrant John George ("J. G.") Brown (1831-1913). But whereas today Eakins and Homer endure, Brown's freshness has grown as stale as last week's television commercial. Ironically, it was this very ability to appeal to the taste of the post–Civil War culture—a culture that embraced paintings with the surefire mix of children, everyday events, and a strong moral underpinning just as enthusiastically as it responded to magic or patent medicine shows—that has caused Brown's work to be devalued. After its long and bitter war and the assassination of its leader, the nation was shaken and needed a strong tonic of the commonplace, trivialized but laced with hope. J. G. provided the intoxication.

Born in Durham, England, on November 11, 1831, Brown was apprenticed from age fourteen to twenty-one to a glass cutter in Newcastle. During the latter years of this period he studied painting evenings at the Newcastle School of Design with William Bell Scott. At twenty-one he went to Edinburgh, where he worked at the Holyrood Glass Factory, at the same time studying painting evenings with Robert Bell Scott. Brown then spent three months in London and immigrated to the United States, arriving on his twenty-second birthday. At first he worked at the Flint Glass Company in Brooklyn, but two years later he married Mary Owen, his employer's daughter, and began his full-time career as a painter, living with his wife's parents and supporting himself by painting portraits. From 1857 to 1859 he was enrolled at the

National Academy of Design in New York City and exhibited there almost every year from 1858 until his death more than fifty years later. In 1861, the same year the couple's first child, a daughter, was born, he became a founding member of the Brooklyn Art Association and was elected an associate

> " . . . I teach my pupils to see—that is all."

member of the National Academy of Design; he was elected a full member two years later, at age thirty-two. A second daughter was born the following year, and Brown also became a naturalized citizen. While his career moved forward, however, his personal life became one of grief; his wife died in 1867, leaving him with two daughters under age six. Four years later he married his wife's eighteen-year-old sister, Emma Augusta, and the couple eventually had three sons and two daughters.

Meanwhile, Brown had found his métier, and he began to specialize in paintings of street urchins, ragamuffins, bootblacks, newsboys, and young, unsuspecting smokers: poor but honest boys, who though presently impoverished would one day by thrift and hard work be wealthy. It was a story America thrived on: J. G. Brown was doing Horatio Alger in color. Less often, as with most painters of the time, did Brown paint girls, but when he did, they, too, obeyed the canons of Victorian behavior and Yankee idealism. Never boisterous, always decorous, apple-checked, and brimming with health, they promised a fecund future. The message

was simple and biblical: the men would be wealthy, the women fruitful.

*The Cider Mill*, painted in 1880, when he was nearing fifty, is Brown's vision of this abundance: ripened corn in the background, apples so plentiful and heavy they fall to the ground, the turning trees in luxuriant autumn color, the barreled cider fermenting for winter. But while nature in her profusion may be casual, the girls are not. As if on command they all raise their apples simultaneously and bite. Meanwhile, life goes on as a rooster preens himself beneath a platform. Brown has been called one of the finest figure painters of his time, and *The Cider Mill* is no exception. Most striking, however, is his use of dappled sunlight to suggest the autumn thinning of the trees. In doing so, he invokes and unites the colors of the apples themselves: yellow corn, red dresses, green leaves. Brown's canvas has itself become an autumn apple.

In remarks published in 1879, shortly before he painted *The Cider Mill*, Brown said to the writer G. W. Sheldon, "Art should express contemporaneous truth, which will be of interest to posterity. I want people a hundred years from now to know how the children that I paint looked. . . . I paint what I see, and in my own way. . . . I teach my pupils to see—that is all."

Brown died of pneumonia on February 8, 1913, in New York City, where he had had his studio in the Tenth Street Studio Building since 1860. He was eighty-two.

*The Cider Mill*, 1880, American. Oil on canvas. 76.2 × 61.0 cm. Courtesy of the Terra Museum of American Art, Chicago, Illinois; Terra Foundation for the Arts, Daniel J. Terra Collection; photograph courtesy of the Terra Museum of American Art.

The Journal of the American Medical Association

August 22/29, 1990

# EDWARD HICKS 〜

## *The Cornell Farm*

**B**y trade a carriage maker and sign painter, by vocation a Quaker minister, by avocation a painter: these were the contradictions that warred in the soul of Edward Hicks (1780-1849). These were the wolves and lambs, the leopards and kids, the bears and cows, the lions and oxen that Hicks had to reconcile and teach to live together. A portrait of Hicks painted by his cousin Thomas Hicks in 1838, when Edward was fifty-eight, showed that such peace was not coming easily. Wide-eyed, square-jawed, his spectacles pushed wearily above a furrowed forehead, he looks directly at the viewer from a colonial-style high-back chair. In his left hand he grasps his palette firmly while in his right his loaded brush pauses, but only briefly. Before him is a canvas on an easel with a bushy lion and a sleek leopard just visible in the right lower corner. At his right is a large book of Scripture, opened to the prophecies of Isaiah. The portrait commemorates one of the some sixty versions Edward Hicks painted of *A Peaceable Kingdom*, the work for which he is chiefly known today. Taken in turn, each *Kingdom* can be read to relate to many of the events Hicks was experiencing in both his inner and outer life. Here, in his cousin's portrait, he is yet far from being reconciled with these events. His body still, his eyes alert and fiery, he is ready to spring at the slightest stimulus.

Hicks was born in Bucks County, Pennsylvania, on April 4, 1780, the son of British aristocracy greatly impoverished by the American Revolutionary War. When the child was eighteen months old, his mother died (he would later describe her as "the very reverse of a perfect woman," an example of "pride and idleness"), and his father, now that the British were defeated and his own fortune irrevocably lost,

deserted the boy. He was taken by Elizabeth Twinning, a devout Quaker and close friend of the boy's mother, into her own family, where she and her husband raised him as one of their own on the couple's prosperous Bucks County farm. At thirteen, Edward was apprenticed to a coach maker, whose completion of each coach, he later noted, was traditionally celebrated with "three or four gallons." His life of "lechery and debauchery" ended when, after a severe illness, he joined the Society of Friends in

> "*. . . Painted by E. Hicks in the 69th year of his age.*"

1803, aged twenty-three. The same year he also married Sarah Worstall, like his foster mother a devout Quaker. The couple eventually had five children. Sensing a call to the ministry, and after being accepted by the Friends, he became an itinerant preacher, traveling as far as Upper New York State and Canada, supporting his family meanwhile as best he could by painting street and tavern signs. In 1827, he was forced to take sides in a schism within the Friends led by his cousin Elias Hicks. It was during the events leading up to his agonizing decision to join with Elias that Edward, now forty, began painting the first of what would become his long series of *Peaceable Kingdoms*, each a mirror of the conflict within and without. Even more incongruous was the fact that this minister within an imageless tradition painted at all, a conflict he could never resolve until the end of his life, when he decided to leave all to "the mercy and forgiveness of God," who would understand that he had done that of which he was

capable, even if it was to be "nothing but a poor old worthless insignificant painter."

*The Cornell Farm*, painted in the autumn of 1848, less than a year before he would die, is one of the few nonreligious or nonpatriotic paintings Hicks did. Indeed, it appears that he may even have done it on commission, for its inscription reads, "An Indian summer view of the Farm & Stock of James C. Cornell of Northampton Bucks County Pennsylvania. That took the Premium in the Agricultural Society; october the 12th, 1848. Painted by E. Hicks in the 69th year of his age." In it Hicks has at last found his peace. The lines are clear, some dividing the land neatly into separate segments, others dissolving into infinity, others furrowing the earth in promises of another year. The trees, thinned for the oncoming winter, are tall and straight, the houses spacious and secure, the barns ample, anchors on the land. A woman's figure is framed solidly in a doorway as she watches her husband's brothers arrive to admire his stock and congratulate him on his abundance. But it is the domesticated animals, tamed and put to men's use, that are the focus of the painting. Larger than life, they stretch across the entire lower frame of the painting, with James Cornell's prize bull occupying pride of place. Meanwhile, over the autumn landscape drowse the hazy remnants of summer, its existence now only a smoky memory.

Some three months before he painted *The Cornell Farm*, in July 1848, Hicks, who had been ill for some time, thought he was going to die, probably that very summer. Considering any effort to prolong his life "foolish self-righteousness" and fearing that later his mind would be clouded by opium or other medications, he wrote that surely he would "triumph over death, hell and the

*Continued on p 216*

The Journal of the American Medical Association

September 12, 1990

# CHARLES FREDERICK NAEGELE

## September Forenoon

Traditionally, it is the time when the old meets the new, when night and day become briefly equal, when the sun's angle is just a little sharper, when the dying warmth causes the earth to flame in a last protest against the coming cold. Summer's regrets bore like a worm in an apple, autumn's resolutions are as energizing as cider. It is the time for storing one's abundance, looking after supplies, and getting out the woolens. It is the time for checking the children's shoe needs and whether they have their lunch money. It is the end of the year, it is the beginning of the year. It is, as Charles Frederick Naegele (1857-1944) suggests, *September Forenoon*.

Naegele was born in Knoxville, Tennessee, but the boy moved with his family to Memphis when he was three. There, in his teens, he was apprenticed to a carver of tombstones, but he also painted signs. Coming by chance to the attention of Colonel Charles Myles Collier, a marine painter in Memphis, the youth was sent to New York City to study with William Sartain and William Merritt Chase, where he eventually opened his own studio, doing mainly portraits and numismatic designs. Naegele was also the originator of a plan whereby local communities could build an art collection at a nominal fee.

*September Forenoon* is a departure from Naegele's usual subject matter and shows the influence of Chase's American Impressionist

*Summer's regrets bore like a worm in an apple . . .*

style. Vividly evocative of a particular time of year in its play of light and dark on the moving leaves, the sharp ground contrasts, and the full light in the distance, the painting is also intriguing in its composition. Three trees (one with three apples remaining on it) form a triangle, which is broadly repeated on the ground by the russet carpet of fallen apples and leaves. The interlocking branches of the tree on the left form an interesting geometric shape, while the more graceful, leafy branches form an arch that opens on a conversation between two women. The older one kneels at her gardening, the younger is dressed for a special occasion. The sense of mystery is heightened by a kind of brooding atmosphere, at once drowsy with the hum of insects and sharp with the smell of apples, a day that will not come again.

During his lifetime Naegele was the winner of many medals, and his work *Mother Love* was added to the collection of the National Gallery of Art in Washington, DC. It remains probably his most famous painting. Naegele remained in New York City until the late 1920s, when he gave up his studio and moved to Marietta, Georgia. He died there on January 27, 1944, aged eighty-six.

*September Forenoon*, c 1910, American. Oil on canvas. 67.3 × 71.1 cm. Courtesy of the Lauren Rogers Museum of Art, Laurel, Mississippi.

# JAMA®

**September 19, 1990**

The Journal of the American Medical Association

# NANCY HILD ✦

## *Let's Quit Smoking*

Like the eighteenth-century French painter Élisabeth Vigée-Lebrun, contemporary Chicago artist Nancy Hild (1948-   ) often poses as her own model. Like Rembrandt, she will assume different roles for her self-portraits, even donning a costume if the role dictates it. And like the twentieth-century Mexican painter Frida Kahlo, she will often portray herself in a dual (sometimes even multiple) role. She favors whimsy, invention, the unexpected, the juxtaposition of images in an ambiguity that catches the viewer off guard, forced, however unwillingly, to reexamine ideas and issues long thought decided. Many of her themes are feminist, many of her titles, such as one for a painting showing her scolding her female dog, point to visual puns. Evident throughout her work is a gentle, caring humor that, in letting us see ourselves as others may see us, succeeds, paradoxically, in letting us see ourselves as we really are and to not only accept, but also to love that reality.

Hild was born in Ohio, the second of two children. At age five she lost her brother, three years older than herself, to a brain tumor. She cannot remember a time in childhood when she didn't draw. In 1970, at age twenty-two, she received a bachelor of fine arts degree from Indiana University, Bloomington, and six years later a master of fine arts from the same institution. Between 1970 and 1976 she also studied at the University of Missouri in Kansas City and at the Kansas City Art Institute. Beginning in 1975, Hild has had numerous group and individual exhibitions throughout the Midwest and

> *. . . a microcosm of the painful macrocosm of ambivalence that is the human condition.*

also at Pima College, Tucson, Arizona, where she served as guest artist in 1983. She is the winner of numerous awards, including the Municipal Art League Prize given by the Art Institute of Chicago in 1981. In 1990 she won an arts assistance grant from the Department of Cultural Affairs of the City of Chicago and a regional visual arts fellowship from the National Endowment for the Arts. Her work hangs in private collections and in the collection of Standard Oil Indiana, where it may be seen at the

Standard Oil Building, Chicago. She is a member of the Artemisia Gallery in Chicago, where her work frequently appears.

*Let's Quit Smoking* is an eloquent portrayal of one of the chief health problems of the twentieth century, initially recognized among men, now known as a major cause of death among women as well. Wordless, the painting speaks volumes. Soundless, the inner dialogue of the two characters, one pro quitting, one con (or at least skeptical), is only too audible. Now that the rational will has decided the addiction must be broken, one hears only too clearly the arguments, rationalizations, bargaining, and pleas for time from its antagonist. *Let's Quit Smoking* portrays the threshold to every smoker's purgatory: painful, but, one hopes, only for a time, with a permanent reward to follow. It is also a microcosm of the painful macrocosm of ambivalence that is the human condition. It is a universal reality that one enters by studying the particular, in the case of Hild, like Vigée-Lebrun, Rembrandt, and Kahlo, the self.

*Let's Quit Smoking,* 1989, American. Oil on canvas. 91.4 × 121.9 cm. Courtesy of the artist.

# JAMA®

The Journal of the American Medical Association

**September 26, 1990**

# BRUCE CRANE ⟡

## October Day

If spring was made for the poet, then surely autumn belongs to the painter. And of the autumn months it is October that begs most eloquently for the artist who can gather up the shards of its shattered sunlight and fashion them into a golden tree. Such an artist was the American Tonalist Bruce Crane (1857-1937), now nearly forgotten, but in the early years of this century famed for his seasonal landscapes.

Crane was born in New York City in October 1857, the son of an amateur artist who began his son's art training early. When the boy was seventeen the family moved to Elizabeth, New Jersey, where Bruce was employed as a draftsman in an architectural firm, developing skills that no doubt contributed to his later work. It was not until a summer trip to the Adirondacks, however, that painting really took fire in the young man's soul and he began serious study. His first teacher, after his father, became the then-famous Tonalist Alexander Helwig Wyant. Crane was twenty, Wyant forty-one. Although Crane's formal study with Wyant was not long, the two remained friends until Wyant's death fifteen years later. Presumably, Wyant's influence continued, even after his death.

Initially, Crane painted scenes of the Catskills, Adirondacks, and eastern Long Island, but in 1878 he began a series of trips abroad, concentrating on Paris and its surrounding towns. The most important of these trips was probably his third, in 1882, when, working at Grez-sur-Loing, near Barbizon, he came under the influence of the French landscape painter Jean Charles Cazin. Cazin was an advocate of "memory painting," a method whereby the visual memory was trained so that the artist would be able later to record "solar, lunar, and atmospheric effects"—in short, nature's "fugitive beauty." Later, Crane would write that he studied and sketched out-of-doors to "fill the memory with facts," but that once back in his studio, he relied on his memory, not his sketches, to recall the most

> *. . . that threshold where nature flames up one last time before it fades.*

outstanding impressions. Based on the influences of Wyant and Cazin, and leavened by his association with other American artists abroad, by age twenty-seven Crane had found his métier: twilight and autumn scenes, noted for their mood and atmospheric effects. *October Day* is representative of these works.

In *October Day* Crane distills the essences of all his many remembered October days into one ideal moment of one ideal day. The tiny particulars have become a grand universal, a thousand years have become a single day and a single day a thousand years. In his role as artist, it is Crane's genius to suggest that something the viewer has never seen has yet been experienced a thousand times before and will be experienced a thousand times again. It is a day that will tremble forever on that threshold where nature flames up one last time before it fades. To be aware of such fugitive beauty is to be at the same time pained by the passing of time, Crane tells the viewer. What is red and gold today is brown and shriveled tomorrow. It is the dying leaves, after all, that must form the compost from which the spring will be born. But not yet, says *October Day*. This day must have its glory.

Always a modest man, Crane, though popular and the consistent winner of many prizes, never achieved the acclaim of some of his contemporaries. His own life flamed up briefly in a much publicized divorce and remarriage, but then settled back into a satisfying and productive routine of work. He became a popular member of the Old Lyme (Connecticut) art colony after the turn of the century, but was forced to forgo his annual visits there after he broke both hips in a fall in 1935. He died at his home in Bronxville in 1937, aged eighty. Meanwhile, Crane's autumns remain, their skies threatening, but never erupting, their stately trees blushing perhaps at their future nakedness, but remaining always luxuriantly draped, and a tiny house, nestled in the crook of a hill, promising warmth and safety until the poet can sing again.

*October Day*, c 1915, American. Oil on canvas. 33.0 × 43.2 cm. Courtesy of the Lauren Rogers Museum of Art, Laurel, Mississippi; gift of Nina Eastman Rogers.

The Journal of the American Medical Association

October 3, 1990

# ARSHILE GORKY ⌒

## *Organization*

One way to conceal oneself is to confuse others. Armenian-born, American painter Arshile Gorky (1904-1948) was a master of this sort of camouflage, disguising himself in a personal history whose facts shifted to suit circumstances, trying on the painting styles of his predecessors like discarded clothes he hoped would fit, even plagiarizing, paragraph for paragraph, intimate letters and poetry published by others that he then sent to his lover as his own. In the ultimate twist he even adopted a pseudonym that was already the pseudonym of another. Yet one fact stands clear of the confusion: Arshile Gorky was a great painter. He was also very vulnerable and needed his protective covering.

Arshile Gorky was born Vosdanig Manoog Adoian in a village near Lake Van in Turkish Armenia, the third child and only son of Sedrag and Shushanig Adoian. When he was four years old his father, in order to escape Turkish conscription, fled to America, leaving behind Vosdanig, his mother, and three sisters. They were later resettled in Erivan after a forced march of some 125 miles. The two older girls managed to get to the United States, but Vosdanig and his younger sister remained behind. With the family subsisting only marginally, the mother became progressively weaker and finally died of starvation in her son's arms in the spring of 1919. Vosdanig was fifteen. A year later, the two children, helped by friends, reached the United States. They stayed briefly with their father in Providence, Rhode Island, and then moved to Watertown, Massachusetts, to live with a sister.

The next several years are lacking in the details of Vosdanig's life except for the fact that he apparently continued the drawing he had begun as a child. In 1925, aged twenty,

he arrived in New York City and there began the great fabrication of his life. Adopting Gorky, after Maxim Gorky, the pseudonym of the Russian fiction writer Alexey Maximovich Peshkov, as his surname, he added Arshile after the Homeric hero Achilles. Although stressing that Gorky meant "bitter," he yet never bothered to put straight people who wrote that he and Maxim were cousins. Indeed, he reinforced the misconception by dropping remarks about his "famous cousin, Maxim, in Venice." Hard hit by the Depression, Gorky nonetheless had his first exhibition, at the Museum of Modern Art, in 1930. Four years later he had his first one-

> *"Eyes . . . the prime communication between the artist and those who view his work."*

man show in Philadelphia, and the following year he found work as an artist in the Works Progress Administration Federal Art Project, receiving assignment in the coveted mural division. His major works of this period were the Aviation Murals for the Newark Airport. Of the ten panels, all have been lost or destroyed except two. It was during this period, 1933 through 1936, that Gorky painted *Organization*. He was also, during this period, completing work on his most famous figure painting, *The Artist and His Mother*, a work he had begun nearly a decade before.

Although Gorky thrived on confusing people, it was an organized confusion, not chaos. *Organization*, for example, though perplexing at first glance, has clearly an

organizing principle. At the center of the painting is an *organic* form in relation to which all the other, geometric, forms and lines are arranged. Circles, rectangles, and triangles of all sizes are deftly balanced both by shape and by color and are reinforced with a web of straight lines that either connect at a nodal point, end in a circular cul-de-sac, or form the boundaries of a color. What the organizing shape is, one can only speculate. It could be a remembered dog from his childhood or it could be the palette, skewed to be sure, that was the focus of his life. Off to the right, in rust and gray, is what looks like a portion of a woman's dress, a dress that figured prominently in his memory. He once recalled how he would, as a child, bury his face in his mother's apron while she told him stories that "keep unravelling pictures in my memory." Most intriguing, however, is the pair of ellipses that look down on the scene from the upper left like the eyes of the mask he so effectively wore. Or they could be the eyes Gorky featured in his portrait *The Artist and His Mother*, eyes he called Armenian eyes. "Eyes," he said, are "the prime communication between the artist and those who view his work." And again, "The eyes of the Armenian speak before the lips move and long after they ceased to."

In 1939 Gorky did the murals for the Aviation Building at the New York World's Fair. Appropriately enough, he also organized a course in camouflage painting at the start of World War II. In September 1941 he married Agnes Magruder, and by 1945 the couple had two daughters, Maro and Natasha. Such an idyll, however, could not last long for one whose first name was Achilles and whose last name meant "bitter." If his early life had been charged with tragedy, his later was more so. In January

*Continued on p 216*

# JAMA®

The Journal of the American Medical Association

October 17, 1990

# DANIEL GARBER ❧

## *Fisherman's Hut*

Among the American Impressionists working with Edward Redfield around New Hope, Pennsylvania, was Daniel Garber (1880-1958). Born in Indiana, at age seventeen he was already studying with Frank Duveneck at the Cincinnati Art Academy. Two years later he moved to Philadelphia, where he studied at the Pennsylvania Academy of the Fine Arts under Thomas Anshutz, who had taken Thomas Eakins' place as teacher of painting. From 1905 to 1907 Garber toured Europe on a traveling scholarship, and in 1909, at age twenty-nine, he was appointed to the faculty of the Pennsylvania Academy of the Fine Arts. Four years later he was elected to the National Academy of Design.

Like Eakins, Anshutz stressed the anatomy of the human body to his pupils, an influence evident in the work of Garber. Garber was more permanently influenced, however, by the American Impressionist

*. . . delicate effusions of color, blending in subtle harmonies.*

J. Alden Weir, who had been visiting instructor in painting at the academy when Garber was a student. Thus, Garber's work falls into two distinct categories: figure paintings and rural landscapes, principally of the Delaware Valley north of Philadelphia. His figure paintings are bathed in full sunlight, his landscapes are delicate effusions of color, blending in subtle harmonies. Of these latter, *Fisherman's Hut*, painted when he was sixty, evokes his finest work.

Winner of numerous awards and prizes, Garber's work has only recently come to be more widely appreciated. He died in Lumberville, Pennsylvania, in 1958.

*Fisherman's Hut*, c 1940, American. Oil on canvas. 127.6 × 153.0 cm. Courtesy of the Terra Museum of American Art, Chicago, Illinois; Terra Foundation for the Arts, Daniel J. Terra Collection; photograph courtesy of the Terra Museum of American Art.

# JAMA®

The Journal of the American Medical Association

October 24/31, 1990

# CAMILLE PISSARRO

## Landscape in the Vicinity of Louveciennes (Autumn)

By the autumn of 1869, things were going smoothly for thirty-nine-year-old Camille Pissarro (1830-1903). Although still not financially independent and although his marriage had still not been regularized, he and Julie were the parents of two children and they had recently settled in Louveciennes, a middle-class suburb on the road to Versailles from which he could easily commute to Paris. There he visited his mother Rachel regularly and there he was also part of the group of young, innovative painters who gathered around Manet at the Café Guerbois. In their noisy discussions the group, including not only Manet and Pissarro, but also Degas, Bazille, Guillemet, Fantin-Latour, Monet, Renoir, Cézanne, Zola, and others, debated the demerits of academic painting, new theories of their own, the government's attitude toward painting, the Salon's refusals of their work, photography, Japanese prints, and anything else that came across the path they so passionately pursued. A good ten years older than the rest of the group and with several acceptances at the Salon to his credit, Pissarro was recognized as the patriarch of the group.

Born in St Thomas in the Danish West Indies to a Sephardic shopkeeper of Portuguese descent, as a boy Camille was sent, as was customary, to Paris to be educated. Returning home at age seventeen, he joined his older brother and father in the family business but could not quench the desire to be an artist that had been born in Paris. Finally, in 1852, aged twenty-two, he and a friend ran off to Caracas, determined to be painters. Despite appeals from his family to return home, he pursued his career, finally arriving in Paris in 1855, just in time to be intoxicated by the hundreds of paintings at the large Exposition Universelle.

He knew he had chosen rightly. Moreover, father and son reached a compromise of sorts when Camille agreed to enroll for training in the officially sponsored École des Beaux-Arts in return for a parental subsidy. Later, Camille's mother and father would move to suburban Paris, where the father kept a lively interest in his son's work. Camille would assert his independence even more boldly, however, when he took Julie, his mother's maid, as his common law wife. They married, finally, some ten years and

> *The colors are the humble, honest colors of earth . . .*

three children later, in London in 1870. *Landscape in the Vicinity of Louveciennes (Autumn)* was painted shortly before this, when they had just moved to Louveciennes.

In a sense this painting is transitional in Pissarro's work. It bears the marks of its classical heritage and it suggests its eventual progeny. Meanwhile, it is stamped indelibly by Pissarro's own personal characteristics: gentleness, honesty, humility, sincerity. Pissarro observes the classical Golden Mean, placing his light-colored houses in approximately the right third of the painting. But he bisects the painting, almost exactly, with a tall, slender tree. The weight on the right is balanced by a large tree placed in the left foreground. Roof diagonals on the right guide the eye to the figures of the boy and girl in the foreground, while roof diagonals on the left lead to a tiny, almost unnoticed figure in the left midground. Parallel rows of vines add contrast. The colors are the humble, honest colors of earth: browns, greens, blues. But

most interesting is the brush stroke, which announces the coming birth of Impressionism: commas and short, quick strokes, each representing light seen in a different aspect of being.

Pissarro's idyll of 1869 did not continue long. Less than a year later Camille and Julie and their children were forced to flee to Brittany when Prussian troops surrounded Paris during the Franco-Prussian War. There their third child, a daughter, was born but died at age three months of an intestinal infection. And, in a loss, the full extent of which will probably never be appreciated, soldiers destroyed all but forty of the works Pissarro had done during the previous fifteen years and had left stored at Louveciennes. Included were also some works Monet had left with Pissarro for safekeeping.

If it can be said that the war of 1870 was Pissarro's winter, then the following year, 1871, was its inevitable spring. Now in London, Camille and Julie were married and a son was born. Most decisive for the world of painting, however, was the chance meeting of Monet and Pissarro in London, where, both refugees, they gave birth to what would eventually be named Impressionism. Since that time no one has been able to look at anything in the same way again.

*Landscape in the Vicinity of Louveciennes (Autumn),* 1870, French. Oil on canvas. 89 × 116 cm. Courtesy of the J. Paul Getty Museum, Los Angeles, California.

# JAMA®

## The Journal of the American Medical Association

**November 7, 1990**

# JOHN SLOAN ❧

## The Wake of the Ferry II

Fed up with the overly sweet, saccharine concoctions of American academic painting at the turn of the century—the largely Impressionist-style works that reminded at least one novelist of confectioner's sugar sprinkled over tea cakes—and frustrated by their attempts to have their works exhibited in the official "Establishment" shows of the National Academy of Design, a group of eight artists led by Robert Henri held their own, nonjuried show at the Macbeth Gallery in New York City from February 3 to 15, 1908. It was a watershed for American art, changing its direction from Impressionism to realism, though not without resistance. Known variously as "The Eight," the Black Gang or the Revolutionary Gang, and later as the Ashcan School (because they painted trash, the critics said), the group included, besides Henri, George Luks, William Glackens, Everett Shinn, Maurice Prendergast, Ernest Lawson, Arthur B. Davies, and, perhaps most prominently, John Sloan (1871-1951).

Sloan was born in Lock Haven, Pennsylvania, to parents of Irish, Scottish, and English descent and had Revolutionary War forebears. When the boy was five, the family moved to Philadelphia, where the father ran a small stationer's business. When the business failed in the Depression of 1886, young Sloan, aged sixteen, abandoned hopes of being a dentist—or a "doctor, lawyer, or preacher"—and went to work in a bookseller's and print dealer's shop. There, with the help of a book, he taught himself to etch, doing freelance calendars, advertisements, and novelties. At age twenty-one, he joined the staff of the *Philadelphia Inquirer* as an artist-reporter and also entered the Pennsylvania Academy of the Fine Arts, where he studied under Thomas

Anschutz, former assistant to Thomas Eakins, and also met Henri. In 1895 he moved over to the *Philadelphia Press* for which he would do word charade puzzles until 1910.

Only in 1897, at the relatively advanced age of twenty-six, did Sloan begin to consider painting as a serious career. Shortly thereafter he met Anna Marie (Dolly) Wall, whom he married in 1901. In 1904 the couple moved to New York City, by then the mecca for artists. Benefiting from his reporter's eye, made keener no doubt by his

> *. . . any day that is sunless, blustery, unfriendly, and raw . . .*

work at the *Inquirer* and *Press*, Sloan did a series of etchings of city life as he witnessed it when he roamed New York's streets every day. The result is a vibrant record of the common people at common activities: sleeping on rooftops, wrestling in a one-room tenement, turning out the light in a bedroom. Such subject matter was considered vulgar and beneath "art," but Sloan had a precedent in the work of not only Henri, but Frans Hals and Édouard Manet as well, all of whom influenced him. Meanwhile he was also painting similar scenes, garnered each day from the streets of New York and stored in his memory until he could set them on canvas in his studio. One of his frequent—and favorite—routes took him across the Hudson River on the Jersey City ferry. *The Wake of the Ferry II* was inspired by one of these crossings.

Whenever Sloan painted a picture,

recalled his second wife, Helen, "it was of a place or neighborhood he had studied for a long time. And then he waited for some human incident to give him the idea or final concept for a picture." He was able "to take this kind of visual experience, to reform it in his memory, finding the composition that would tell what he wanted to say." Thus, while *The Wake of the Ferry II* was suggested by a single event, yet as a true artist Sloan has made it the many. In this case the date is March 19, 1907, and the lone woman is Mary Perkins, a fellow painter whom Sloan was starting on her return to Philadelphia from New York. On the other hand, the painting could be of any day that is sunless, blustery, unfriendly, and raw, and Mary Perkins can be any person who has ever traveled alone, had fears, yearnings, regrets, desires, hopes, or been lonely, battered, or dwarfed by life's happenings. It is the genius of Sloan that while he makes a painting of largely empty space that is even further emphasized by the interior frame of the ferryboat's structure, places the figure to the side, and even makes it anonymous, he nonetheless makes the figure the subject of the painting. She travels to the future, but looks to the past, her life compressed into a posture. All that has ever happened to her to that point of intersection of past and future fills the space of the canvas as the life of a patient to the point of the present illness fills the consulting room.

*The Wake of the Ferry II*, as its title indicates, is not the version begun on that March day in 1907. That version was damaged a month later, when, in a row with Dolly, he threw a rocking chair through it, and was not repaired until many years later. In the meantime he began and completed this second version, slightly altered from the first. The story of the painting also has a

*Continued on p 217*

# JAMA®

### The Journal of the American Medical Association

**November 14, 1990**

# BENJAMIN MESSICK

## *Main Street Café Society #5*

The year was 1938. The place was Main Street, USA. The number of unemployed stood at nine million, the same as at the beginning of the decade, down from the decade's peak, to be sure, but up from the previous year's total by two million. It was estimated that this amounted to one in five workers unemployed. The term "recession" had recently been coined to account for an economic situation less catastrophic than the Great Depression, but a serious downswing nonetheless. Overseas the news was worse. Hitler went into Austria and Czechoslovakia, demanded that Jews carry identity cards, and staged "Crystal Night" in Berlin. China, Japan, and Spain were ravaged by war. Back at home again, the House Un-American Activities Committee was formed, and corporate taxes were eased to, so it was said, stimulate the economy. But there were some glimmers of light. The minimum wage was set at forty cents an hour, up from as little as ten and twenty-five cents an hour earlier in the decade. Grass began to grow officially in the Dust Bowl again, the *Queen Mary* crossed the Atlantic in under four days, and the *Queen Elizabeth* was launched on her maiden voyage. Eddie Rickenbacker bought Eastern Airlines for $3.5 million. Pearl Buck won the Nobel Prize for Literature, and Marian Anderson was awarded an honorary degree from Harvard. In Pasadena on New Year's Day, it was California over Alabama, thirteen to zero, the Black Hawks took the Stanley Cup, the Cardinals traded Dizzy Dean to the Cubs, Lawrin with Acaro aboard won the Kentucky Derby, and Joe Louis returned a knockout to Max Schmeling at two minutes, four seconds into the first round of his defense of his heavyweight title. Finally, on the last Saturday of November, Army beat Navy, less than a month after the Martians, with a little help from Orson Welles, had invaded planet Earth. It was, as has been said, "the best of times and the worst of times." It was the time of *Main Street Café Society #5* by California artist Benjamin Newton (Ben) Messick (1901-1981).

Born on January 9, 1901, in a log cabin in Stafford, Missouri, Ben was the son of a deeply religious housewife and a part-time prospector–general storekeeper in the Ozarks. Little has been recorded of his

> *The term "recession" had recently been coined . . .*

boyhood, and he next comes to attention as a student at the Chouinard Art School (later California Institute of the Arts, Valencia), established in Los Angeles in 1921 by Nelbert Chouinard, who had studied in Munich. Messick also studied at the Los Angeles School of Art and Design. While working at his painting he supported himself as a department store designer, as a mural artist for the Treasury Section of the Works Progress Administration, and as a sketch artist for the Disney and MGM studios. From 1943 to 1951 he was a very popular teacher of life drawing at Chouinard and also taught at the San Diego School of Arts and Crafts. Classified most often as a Social Realist painter, Messick has also been called an American Daumier, and his work has been compared with that of fellow Missourian Thomas Hart Benton. Messick's subjects were most often the downtrodden, the poor, prostitutes, and circus performers, people he was able to portray with such warmth and compassion that we are sure we have met them before. He is known for his paintings of clowns, especially of Emmett Kelly. He loved the circus for its invitation to step into the big top and live for an hour or so in another reality.

Messick's key to his works is his color, as demonstrated in *Main Street Café Society #5*. First, however, he worked his way methodically through several other steps. Initially he worked with just the idea itself, letting it evolve with the help of a series of sketches done in the field. Often he would return again and again to a place or scene that had especially struck him. In his sketches he looked for rhythm of spacing and the development of a satisfying composition. He could, for example, make subtle use of the jamb of a door frame or the post of a chair back to separate his picture space into thirds and contain his figures. Next came anatomic studies and drawings of details and gestures, garnered with such an eye that a personality could be picked up in the angle of a hat or a life story told in the way a head is shaped, a shoulder is rounded, or a thumb is cocked. Next, all this material was assimilated into a master cartoon, which was then transferred to the canvas. Finally came the choice of palette in an overall color tone that would suggest the psychological mood of the painting. If the emotional mood of the finished painting was not what he was after, he would redo the entire picture in another color key, keeping at it until he was satisfied.

That Messick has been successful in *Main Street Café Society #5* is evident. The dull yellows and browns evoke the sepia tones of the Sunday rotogravure photographs and the monotonous sameness of the décor of the cheap cafeterias of the times. But lest the viewer be left with a sense of hopelessness for these people of the Depression, Messick, as is noted in the Los Angeles

*Continued on p 217*

The Journal of the American Medical Association

November 21, 1990

# J. FRANCIS MURPHY

## *November Sunset*

The typical work by American Tonalist J. Francis Murphy (1853-1921)—if ever the work of any artist may be called typical—is a small canvas showing a wet, marshy terrain, often with pools of standing water, under a cloudy, heavily impastoed sky. The year is at autumn, the day is at sunset. The mood is brooding, somber, reflective. The sky is done in opalescent tones of gray, green, and pink, the terrain in weary greens and warm browns. To the left foreground stands a clump of trees done in the style that only Murphy could master, to the right midground another, secondary clump of trees and shrubs. His titles set the tone of his theme: *Opal Sunset, Twilight in Venice, A Cloudy Afternoon, A Gray Morning, After the Frosts, April Weather, Sundown, November Sunset*. But formula or not, both the public and the critics approved. His work the subject of what almost became a cult among collectors, at age fifty Murphy saw one of his autumn paintings enter the Corcoran Gallery of Art in Washington, DC; before he died he saw one of his paintings bring a record $15,600 at auction. Besides the Corcoran, he has works in the Buffalo Fine Arts Academy, the National Gallery of Art, the Art Institute of Chicago, and the Metropolitan Museum of Art.

Murphy was born to Irish immigrant parents in Oswego, New York, on December 11, 1853. When the boy was in his teens the family moved to Chicago, where young Francis worked as a stage and scene painter.

> *The year is at autumn, the day is at sunset.*

Largely self-taught, he did, however, take some classes at the Chicago Academy of Design (now The Art Institute of Chicago). His first paintings date from age seventeen. A sketching trip to the Adirondack Mountains at age twenty-one, where he met Winslow Homer, seems to have been decisive, for shortly thereafter he moved to New York City, where he worked as a magazine illustrator and greeting card artist. Ten years later, now married to a painter, Murphy went with his wife to France, where he saw the works of the Barbizon school, no doubt absorbing an influence that would later earn him the name of "the American Corot." Murphy's greatest successes came when he was in his late fifties and early sixties. He continued painting until about six months before his death in New York on January 29, 1921, at the age of sixty-seven.

In a critical assessment of Murphy's work written shortly after his death, art historian Royal Cortissoz asks, "Was he, in his turn, a man of genius?" "Hardly," is the answer. "He had, at the most, a modest spark of the divine fire." On the other hand, perhaps only a modest spark is all it takes to light up a November day and give a warm glow to an entire winter. Or so it seems to have been for the last seventy-five years or so.

*November Sunset*, c 1890, American. Oil on canvas. 27.9 × 33.6 cm. Courtesy of the Lauren Rogers Museum of Art, Laurel, Mississippi.

The Journal of the American Medical Association

November 28, 1990

# ANONYMOUS ⌒

## *Cat and Kittens*

Among the painters working in the United States in the mid to last quarter of the nineteenth century—Eakins, Homer, Hunt, La Farge, among others—none was as productive as the ubiquitous artist called by the name of Anonymous. Wandering the byways with canvas and paints strapped to his (or her) back, or secluded in a sunny front parlor, she or he left a body of work that, while hardly fashionable at the time, not infrequently showed evidence of considerable talent. This work, variously called naive, primitive, or folk art because of its often very awkward solutions to technical problems such as lighting and perspective, nonetheless suggests that its makers were sometimes well trained and even quite sophisticated in other aspects of art such as color, composition, or design. Indeed, in what would seem to be a twist of poetic justice, folk art is greatly sought after today simply because of its design qualities, which suggest modern abstraction. Moreover, not only does the work convey an immediacy and a charm that are hard to resist, but it also provides an access that abstract art often does not give.

*Cat and Kittens*, painted somewhere around the time of the nation's centennial, is the work of one such anonymous folk painter. What the artist's name is, we have no clue. On the other hand, the cozy domesticity of the scene—the kittens themselves, the vigilant mother cat, the cared-for, delicate lace curtain, the elaborate wall decoration, the yarn on the lid of what is possibly a sewing basket left on a table beside a window—suggests that the artist could have been a woman. Perhaps it had been her custom to sit and knit in the window light with the cat purring in the sun at her feet. But then came the disruptive kittens, and needlecraft turned to paint craft. Moreover, the careful and exact rendering of detail—the shading on the individual strands in the ball of yarn, the light on the cat's whiskers, the velvet of the ears, the attentive delineation of wicker—suggests an

> *. . . none was as productive as the ubiquitous artist called by the name of Anonymous.*

eye that could have been trained in botanical painting, a popular subject for refined young women of the time. But man or woman, the painter, like the well-trained physician of the day, was someone who had the eye of the scientist and the hand of the artist.

Cats recall more associations than they have lives, among them the fireside or the hearth, majesty, freedom, self-reliance, patience, independence, cleanliness, virility—all qualities the century-old nation was seeking to renew. But cats are also inscrutable, mysterious, bewitching, and instant connoisseurs of the best chair in any room. They were known in ancient Egypt, in Rome, and in Pompeii. They are mentioned in Scripture and in Shakespeare. Thomas Gray lamented his favorite cat, who drowned in a bowl of goldfishes. "Not all that glisters may be gold," he moralized. Cowper's cat always slept in the partially open top drawer of a chest "lined with linen of the softest kind." Samuel Johnson's cat, Hodge, ate only the finest oysters, which Dr Johnson went out to buy himself, lest his servants, burdened with extra work, came to dislike the cat. Matthew Arnold likened his cat to the Emperor Tiberius, or perhaps it was the other way around, while Christopher Smart named his cat Jeoffry and then considered him in a lengthy poem. "For he can creep," concluded Smart. But it is to T. S. Eliot that belongs the most accurate insight into the nature of cats: there is no point in naming a cat, says Eliot, for he answers to no name, or, at best, only to one that he alone knows. He, too, for all practical purposes, prefers to remain anonymous.

The latter part of the nineteenth century in America had no scarcity of well-known painters. Even longer was the list of lesser lights. But by far the greatest number were those anonymous folk artists whose work continues to charm us, but who, like Eliot's cat, answer to a name only they know. But that makes them not less artists, and, perhaps, even more artists, for they had no artificially imposed standards or reputations to duplicate. They were free to answer their inner voice.

*Cat and Kittens*, c 1872/1883, American. Oil on millboard. 30.0 × 34.9 cm. Courtesy of the National Gallery of Art, Washington; DC; gift of Edgar William and Bernice Chrysler Garbisch.

# JAMA®

December 5, 1990

The Journal of the American Medical Association

# ANNA MARY ROBERTSON (GRANDMA) MOSES

## *The Daughter's Homecoming*

Her colors are as fresh and inspiring as a new box of Crayolas on the first day of school, her themes are as familiar as home itself, and her fame is the rival of that of any twentieth-century American painter. She was untrained and did not start painting in earnest until she was well into her seventies. Her first "exhibit" consisted of a few pictures displayed in the window of Thomas' Drugstore in Hoosick Falls, New York. Within the year, three of her paintings were being exhibited in the Museum of Modern Art in New York City. At age eighty-six, postcard-size reproductions of her paintings began decorating the fireplace mantles across the country as Americans began exchanging them as Christmas cards. But that was only the beginning. When she died on December 13, 1961, in the midst of the season she had helped to brighten, she had completed more than 1,600 paintings, fifty yarn pictures, and eighty-five tiles. She was 101 years old. She is the American folk artist Anna Mary Robertson Moses (1860-1961), America's "Grandma Moses."

Anna Mary Robertson was born on September 7, 1860, the third of ten children of Mary Shannahan and Russell King Robertson, farmers in Greenwich, New York. Beginning at age twelve, and continuing for the next fifteen years, she worked on neighboring farms as a live-in hired girl. In 1887, at age twenty-seven, she married Thomas Salmon Moses, also a hired hand on one of the farms. The couple moved to their own farm in Staunton, Virginia, where they eventually had ten children, five of whom died in infancy. Anna Mary was not as initially optimistic as her husband about farming opportunities in the post–Civil War

South, however, and kept enough money on hand to get back to New York State if necessary. She also bought a cow, from which she made and sold butter, and when she loaned her husband money out of her earnings, she made sure she charged interest. In 1905, the couple did finally move back to New York, purchasing a farm in Eagle Bridge and becoming dairy farmers. Both of Anna Mary's

> *. . . to take the commonplaces of daily life . . . and give them back their sense of wonder.*

parents died in 1909, and her husband died in 1927, leaving her a sixty-seven-year-old widow. Five years later she lost her daughter, and soon after that, while in her seventies, she began painting in earnest. At age ninety-two she was persuaded to write her autobiography, entitled *My Life's History*. September 7, 1960, was celebrated in New York State as Grandma Moses Day to commemorate her one hundredth birthday. A similar commemoration was made the following year as well. She was already ill, however, and died in Hoosick Falls in December, beloved of and mourned by millions.

*The Daughter's Homecoming* was painted in Grandma Moses' "midcareer," when she was eighty-seven. It is characteristic of her work of that time in its wealth of detail condensed into a relatively small space against a more spacious background of house, hills, and trees. The relationships so clearly drawn in so little space are perhaps autobiographical,

but they are also generic for relationships of nineteenth-century rural America: The well-gowned daughter steps like a princess from her coach, assisted proudly by her obviously prosperous husband, the grandfather boosts the baby to his shoulder, the little girl rushes to give the grandmother a present, a servant stands in the doorway beckoning them to enter into the warmth and good smells within, a turkey hangs ready for dinner, the dog wags his welcome. A trunk on the ground suggests that the journey was long and the stay will not be short. Most interesting, however, are perhaps the implications of relationship in Grandma Moses' choice of title. Regardless of a woman's marital and maternal status, to her parents she remains always a daughter, and home is not where she now lives, but where she started from. Thus it has been, and thus it will always be, says Grandma Moses.

Perhaps the unique aspect of Anna Mary Robertson Moses' life is that it is not only her work that continues to charm and inspire Americans today, but her longevity as well. But not mere longevity. Hers was a life that, in spite of unusual personal losses, she picked up long after many other people have given up. As one critic has noted, she became the American generic for any elder—indeed, any person—who fulfills a long-delayed ambition. But, in justice, she did more than just live a long time and paint. What she did was to take the commonplaces of daily life, things we rarely look at because they are so homely, and give them back their sense of wonder. Relationships, she says, are the mystery of human life.

And how does Anna Mary Robertson Moses herself look at this extraordinary life?

Continued on p 217

# JAMA®

The Journal of the American Medical Association

**December 12, 1990**

# JEHAN GEORGES VIBERT ∽

## *The Marvelous Sauce*

When, in 1895, *Century* magazine asked the immensely popular fifty-five-year-old French painter Jehan Georges Vibert (1840-1902) to write an autobiographical sketch for one of its upcoming issues, he replied in a whimsical mode, submitting an imaginary dialogue between himself and his conscience. He asked his conscience whether it were better for him to err on the side of modesty or of vanity in stating his accomplishments, or whether in either case he might come off sounding just plain ridiculous, and it replied by recalling to him some of his considerable accomplishments that were outside the field of painting: for one, that he had written songs and plays that were performed in the Comédie Français, as well as two books; for another, that, like Molière, he was a talented actor; that he was his own architect, and even, like Louis XVI, worked in iron and, like St Joseph, in wood; and finally, that, in decorating his house he had distinguished himself as an upholsterer, something not even Molière, the son of an upholsterer, had done. But to head the list of such accomplishments, his conscience recalled the one Vibert most visibly enjoyed: his creative cookery. "You hope to use the opportunity now offered you," chided his conscience, "to let your new readers—that is to say, half the world—know that, being an excellent cook, you have invented and prepared sauces that make your compatriots lick their fingers." Vibert did not demur. And that he may have enjoyed his own sauces even more than did his compatriots is documented more than amply in a photograph made of him while he was still in his thirties. But besides his cooking, writing, acting, building, and crafts, Vibert also painted. A contemporary writer called him "one of the most familiar names in America of all the French world of artists." A more recent critic named him "the most successful of the 19th-century narrative painters."

Vibert was born in Paris on September 30, 1840, on his maternal side the grandson of the then well-known engraver Jazet and on the paternal side that of a horticulturist who developed a red rose that he named for his grandson, the Georges Vibert. From the one he received his facility for the incisive line, from the other his love of color, especially the color red. He had been "dedicated to red from his cradle," he wrote. After early art lessons from grandfather Jazet, Vibert decided to be a painter rather than an engraver because painting permitted him the use of more colors. Accordingly, at age

> *. . . while Vibert's wit may be pungent as garlic, it is as delicate as the sauce it flavors.*

sixteen, young Georges entered the École des Beaux-Arts, where he studied with the miniaturist and porcelain painter Felix Joseph Barrias, himself a follower of Meissonier. Vibert made his début in the Salon of 1863, at only age twenty-three, and won medals in the Salons of 1864, 1867, and 1868. In 1878 he won a third-class medal at the Universal Exposition and in 1882, at age forty-two, he was made a Chevalier of the Legion of Honor. In keeping with the scientific temper of the time, Vibert studied the chemistry of colors and prepared all those he used, as well as his own varnishes. He was also an accomplished watercolorist and one of the founders of the French Watercolor Society.

He took part in the siege of Paris in the war of 1870 and was wounded. He died at age sixty-two in Paris, having been, in the words of a contemporary, a "stout, full, merry" gentleman, "shrewd and sensible," an indefatigable worker who equally loved his play hours.

Besides his sauces, Vibert was best known for his humorous, mildly satirical paintings of French clerics, usually princes of the church, whose pomposity, like his own, he loved to puncture. For example, in one such painting, *The Marvelous Sauce*, it is not difficult to decide whether the portly prelate eats to live or lives to eat. He knows his pleasures. Moreover, the cardinal obviously, like Vibert, knows his sauces, whereas the skinny cook can only look at the miraculous sauce with an expression as perplexed as must have been on the face of the wine steward at Cana. And while Vibert's wit may be pungent as garlic, it is as delicate as the sauce it flavors. By pointing out the foibles of others, he is actually poking good-natured fun at his own frailties—indeed, at the weaknesses of all humankind—in a way that does not threaten.

It has been suggested that Vibert's subject matter "overpowered" his technique. One can become so engrossed in the humorous narrative of the painting that one overlooks Vibert's considerable draftsmanship and his subtle harmonies of color. For example: the perfect counterbalance between the figures of the stout cardinal and the thin cook and between the scarlet vertical bulk of the cardinal and the horizontal black squat shape of the stove; the repetition of the round copper pans on the far wall against the repetition of the square copper tiles on the right wall above the stove; the repetition of the French tricolor in the cook's and cardinal's clothes in the crest on the side of the

*Continued on p 217*

# JAMA®

The Journal of the American Medical Association

December 19, 1990

# REMBRANDT VAN RIJN ❧

## *An Old Man in Military Costume*

Unlike the Saint Bartholomew, which Rembrandt (1606-1669) painted toward the end of his life, when he was at the height of his powers, *An Old Man in Military Costume* was painted some thirty years earlier, when he was at the beginning of his career. A former pupil of Jacob Lastman, Holland's most prestigious history painter, Rembrandt was living in Leiden, where he had been born a quarter of a century earlier to a miller and the well to do daughter of a baker, the eighth of their nine children. At age seven his parents sent him to Latin school, indicating perhaps that they had aspirations for him beyond those of becoming a tradesman of the town. At age fourteen, Rembrandt entered the university in Leiden, but he did not stay long. Asserting his desire to become a painter, he apprenticed himself for three years to a Leiden painter of whom we know little, Jacob van Swanenburgh, and later to Lastman in Amsterdam, with whom he studied for only six months but who was to have the decisive influence on Rembrandt's work. At age eighteen Rembrandt declared himself to be a master painter and set out doing history paintings and portraits. *An Old Man in Military Costume* was completed in about 1631, just before Rembrandt left Leiden for Amsterdam. He was twenty-five and, though admired for his work, was not considered particularly outstanding.

*An Old Man in Military Costume* has been known in the past by other titles, including simply *An Officer*, and was at one time also thought to be a portrait of Rembrandt's elderly father. In his *Rembrandt*, Horst Gerson notes that a modern signature covers the remnants of an old one and that x-rays

### *. . . it is the man's face alone that carries the painting . . .*

show that there was originally another head on the canvas, to the right of the present head. However, as in all Rembrandt paintings, the identity of the sitter matters less than what the sitter, with Rembrandt as author, has to tell us. Moreover, the techniques he uses to tell his story, though subtle, have artistic qualities second to none. For example, in texture compare the soft plume of the hat with the silkiness of the gentleman's beard, or contrast the heavy, warm cloth of the tunic against the smooth, cold metal of the breastplate. In color, the man's skin and the gold band on the hat are similar, but the textures are clearly different. In shape, the hat reverses the breastplate, while the twist of the plume reverses the twist of the man's body. But artistic devices aside, it is the man's face alone that carries

the painting: the rheumy eyes, the large ears, the red-tipped nose, the carefully tended beard, the intent look, the furrow between the eyes that marks the center of the painting, the light and shadow that lie across his face like the joys and sorrows that must alternate in his life. Who is this man? What is his work? Does he have family? Wife? Children? Is he happy? What does he most want? What does he most regret? What would he do differently if given the chance? Does he look back from the end of a year or from the end of a life? What does he see in the future? Is his life over, or is it only beginning?

Rembrandt did not remain in Leiden long. In 1631, about the time he finished *An Old Man in Military Costume,* Rembrandt moved to Amsterdam, where his fame and success, not unmarked with sorrow, however, would grow until he died there in 1669. His legacy, meanwhile, is one that time can only burnish, like gold.

*An Old Man in Military Costume,* c 1630-1631, Dutch. Oil on wood. 66.0 × 50.8 cm. Courtesy of the J. Paul Getty Museum, Los Angeles, California.

# JAMA®

The Journal of the American Medical Association

December 26, 1990

*continued from p 2*

## GEORGE WESLEY BELLOWS

along the sidewalks, bent against the wind, hands holding hats or skirts. Others wait at the intersection, patiently standing in slush. A policeman tries valiantly to unscramble the mess and the street cleaner is busy behind the horses. In the background, standing side to side and looking on like innocent bystanders, are the city's fledgling skyscrapers, their shoulders squeezed in tight as if they must occupy as little space as possible. But they are allowed to make up in height what they lack in width.

Finally, one begins to discern that in all this seeming chaos there is, after all, an order: There are rhythms of light and dark, there are color cadences; most interesting is the composition. Diagonals, which impart motion to a painting, are virtually absent, except for small, broken ones in the bent figures of the pedestrians. The major lines are horizontals and verticals, which themselves form a rectangle in the upper left quarter of the painting, which is then joined to the right half of the painting by the elevated train. Bellows has used a static design to show that this bustling, dynamic city is temporarily—at least on its surface—at a standstill. Foot power, in this case, is more effective than horsepower. And, for all the apparent chaos, there is an order to be seen when the perspective is proper. Bellows' commentary on the scene is perhaps summed up in the figure of the young man who sits atop what look like bundles of newspapers on a delivery cart: in a pose of good-natured resignation, he says there is nothing one can do but wait. Sometimes, waiting is itself action.

Many painters are into their fifties and beyond when they do their finest work. We shall, unfortunately, never know what George Bellows' full potential was. He died unexpectedly on January 8, 1925, of a burst appendix. He was forty-two years old.

*New York,* 1911, American. Oil on canvas. 106 × 152 cm. Courtesy of the National Gallery of Art, Washington, DC; collection of Mr and Mrs Paul Mellon.

*continued from p 4*

## ÉDOUARD MANET

its way. Thus, Manet's painting of the girl and the woman in their different costumes may be seen as suggesting the stations of a woman's fertility, from its beginning in puberty to its waning in maturity. For the child gazing at the steam, it is a time of spring and innocence, where everything is as yet unknown, but where all is possible, where hopes and dreams and loyalties change as rapidly as vaporizing steam. For the woman reading the book, it is a time of knowledge and reaping, where she begins to see what has been sown and to understand where she has been. Finally, this possibility that Manet saw the girl and the woman as one is strengthened when it is noted that both of them wear the same black circlet, the one at the throat, the other in the hair.

Unsettled and uncertain as he was before he began a painting and again after it was hung, Manet was, according to his friend Mallarmé, a happy man during the actual painting. Then, he threw himself into his work in a frenzy, as though he had never painted before, amazed and astonished continually at the original ideas and discoveries that seemed to descend on him as he worked. Manet was, wrote Mallarmé some years later, "a lesson that one must risk oneself entire and anew each time" one engages in a creative act. That Manet did his entire life, often with disastrous response, but as Degas said after his death, he was "the greatest of us all."

*The Railway,* 1873, French. Oil on canvas. 99.3 × 114.5 cm. Courtesy of the National Gallery of Art, Washington, DC; gift of Horace Havemeyer in memory of his mother, Louisine W. Havemeyer.

*continued from p 6*

## EDVARD MUNCH

on the other hand, though partly outlined in green, are very much alive. Facing in opposite directions, they represent opposing desires of Munch's soul. He is drawn to the woman of passion, to the murdering woman, but at the same time he is also drawn to the quiet beauty of the sea and the land where he lives, for the orange amoeba shape duplicates the undulating shoreline of his home in Norway. (It also reverses itself in Munch's hairline.) It, too, is bordered by green, but less insistently. One could go on to note the empty plate, the bottle and the glass, and the missing silverware, but it is perhaps enough to note the figure of Munch himself. He sits passively, his hands useless, but the harsh contrast of the red tie and dark green suit betrays the violence and rage he feels within. The posture and the impotence are defenses to ensure that he will not take violent action on what he feels.

As in all groundbreaking work, Munch's viewers only gradually came to understand what he was saying. While faulting his technique, one critic acknowledged that what Munch paints are "the most subtle visions of the soul. The intensity of the psyche is the main subject, and this might well be the intensity of suffering." For himself, Munch said near the end of his life, "My art is really a voluntary confession and an attempt to explain to myself my relationship with life—it is, therefore, actually a sort of egoism, but I am constantly hoping that through this I can help others to achieve clarity." Rembrandt excepted, seldom has a painter been so honest in his self-analysis or so eloquent in expressing it. Munch has indeed achieved his goal.

*Self-portrait With Bottle of Wine,* 1906, Norwegian. Oil on canvas. 28.3 × 25.7 cm. Courtesy of the Munch-Museet, Oslo, Norway; © 2001, The Munch Museum/The Munch-Ellingsen Group/Artists Rights Society (ARS), New York, New York.

continued from p 8

## CHRISTIAN KROGH

Engelhart, also a painter, in 1888; they had a son, Per, who followed in his parents' footsteps.

*Sovende barn (Sleeping Child)*, 1883-1884, Norwegian. Oil on board. 50 × 39 cm. Courtesy of The Nasjonalgalleriet, Oslo, Norway.

continued from p 14

## DOMENICO VENEZIANO

In his portrayal of the monks and the physicians, it is possible that Domenico is contrasting the Age of Reason with the Age of Faith. Or, perhaps Domenico is more subtle and wishes the viewer to look harder at his composition. For example, if a line is extended upward along the widow's right arm and another is extended upward through Zenobius' folded hands, they will meet to form a near-perfect triangle that has the fallen man as its base. No matter what the bystanders are doing, says Domenico, Zenobius and the mother are wholly united in a common desire, the restoration of the son's life.

Domenico died in 1461, reported (falsely, as it turned out to be) by Vasari to have been murdered by his friend Castagno out of envy over Domenico's ability to use color. The story of the murder persisted until the late nineteenth century, when it was discovered that Castagno could not have killed Domenico, since he himself had been carried off by the plague some four years before the death of his friend. As for Domenico, he did indeed do "marvelous things."

*A Miracle of St Zenobius*, c 1442-1448, Italian. Wood. 28.6 × 32.5 cm. Courtesy of The Fitzwilliam Museum, Cambridge, England.

## PAUL GAUGUIN

gracefully, gravely, solemn as postulants in procession, their intricate headdresses like still-folded wings. With their clogs they mark the silent rhythms of a fruitful earth. To the right, a small dog looks away, his attention diverted to something apparently more compelling than the dance. In the background is a village, with three towers and three poplar trees.

What thought or mood Gauguin wanted to suggest with these symbols can only be guessed at. A statement he would make some ten years later concerning his Tahitian masterpiece, *Where Do We Come From? What Are We? Where Are We Going?* could perhaps serve the Pont-Aven work as well: "[I sought to] express the harmony between human life and that of animals and plants in compositions in which I allowed the deep voice of the earth to play an important part." As for what van Gogh thought of the painting when he saw it in Arles, we have his letter to his brother Theo. Generous as he usually was when speaking of others' work, he did not seem especially impressed with it. He liked it, he wrote to Theo, but it was well it had been sold, as Gauguin had others, more recent, that were "thirty times better."

The last word, and the most telling as it has turned out, must be left to Gauguin himself. Near the end of his stay in Pont-Aven, shortly after completing the painting, Gauguin wrote, again to his former banking associate, "I know very well that I shall be *less and less* understood. . . . For the masses I will be an enigma, for some I will be a poet, and sooner or later that which is good will take its rightful place. . . . Come what may, I tell you that I shall eventually do *first class things*; I know it and we shall see. You know that in questions of art I am always right in the end."

*Breton Girls Dancing, Pont-Aven*, 1888, French. Oil on canvas. 73.0 × 92.7 cm. Courtesy of the National Gallery of Art, Washington, DC; collection of Mr and Mrs Paul Mellon.

continued from p 20

## DAVID TENIERS THE YOUNGER

in Teniers' paintings. He could represent a kind of signature or trademark, or, more in keeping with the *vanitas* theme, he could be the artist who, putting his eye on his neighbor with all his frailties, his infirmities, and his foibles, sees not only his neighbor, but, finally, himself, as humble as a drop of water, as magnificent as a god.

*The Surgeon*, c 1670s, Flemish. Oil on canvas. 59.7 × 73.7 cm. Courtesy of the Chrysler Museum of Art, Norfolk, Virginia; gift of Walter P. Chrysler, Jr.

continued from p 26

## AUGUSTE RENOIR

water lilies commissioned by Clemenceau, then prime minister of France, as a gift to the nation.

*Claude Monet*, 1872, French. Oil on canvas. 65.1 × 49.4 cm. Courtesy of the National Gallery of Art, Washington, DC; collection of Mr and Mrs Paul Mellon.

continued from p 28

## HENRI MATISSE

away from the center. Matisse has not found, after all, the harmony and balance one had at first supposed. But then, at last, it is there: in the very center of the painting, just above the lip of the vase, is a deep purple anemone, the source and the destination of the two purple lines. One's sense of balance is restored with a feeling not unlike that which Matisse must have had when he knew a painting was just right—that it was, indeed, finished. The "center has held," after all.

After *The Anemones*, which came at the midpoint of his career, Matisse was to work for another thirty years, even though an intestinal disorder and surgery at the age of seventy-two left him confined to his home and finally to his bed for the last twelve of those years. To the very last day he sculpted, made large sketches, and designed stained glass windows, chapel walls, and even sacerdotal vestments for a local convent. It was in these last years that he happened on to the paper cutouts for which he is perhaps best remembered today. "Sculpting in pure color" is what he called it as he cut forms out of colored paper. Matisse had reached at last the simplicity he sought: pure color and pure shape. Nothing less.

*The Anemones*, 1924, French. Oil on canvas. 73 × 92 cm. Courtesy of the Museum of Fine Arts, Bern, Switzerland; © Succession Matisse, Paris, France.

continued from p 32

## AUDREY FLACK

pretzel shape, for example, forms a second handle on the beer stein), and glass, liquid, ice, cellophane, metal, and ceramic each reflect off the other. The painting has about it a quality of trompe l'oeil, like those paintings by the nineteenth-century Americans William Harnett and John Peto (one can barely resist reaching for the cigarette and knocking its ash off before it falls and burns the table), but there is also something of the Baroque about its entanglements, like a centuries-old Spanish

altarpiece. The objects themselves seem to float just off the surface, as though the viewer is playing poker in the cabin of a spaceship, and they also drift in and out of focus, as though they are seen through a haze of cigarette and cigar smoke.

Flack was born in New York City and received her art training at Cooper Union and Yale University, where she studied with Josef Albers. She also attended the Institute of Fine Arts of New York University and received an honorary doctorate from Cooper Union in 1977. Since 1959, her work has been shown in numerous exhibitions, both solo and group, in this and other countries. Her work hangs in many major museums.

*Royal Flush*, 1973, American. Oil over acrylic on canvas. 177.8 × 243.8 cm. Courtesy of the Louis K. Meisel Gallery, New York, New York; private collection.

continued from p 34

## PIETER DE MOLIJN

something of the sea. Later in his life, de Molijn would turn from these sandy dune scenes to scenes of forests, mountains, winter, hunting, and even scenes of a highway robbery and plundering soldiers.

During their golden age, the Dutch truly lived among an "embarrassment of riches." Certainly, they also lived among "an embarrassment of painters"; besides de Molijn, there were Rembrandt, Dirk and Frans Hals, Salomon van Ruysdael and his nephew Jacob van Ruisdael, Seghers, Saenredam, Steen, Vermeer, van Goyen, Cuyp, Terborch, Kalf, and Pieter Claesz, to mention only a small fraction. It is an image almost too rich for the mind to accept. Though the golden age of Dutch painting began to fade after only two generations, lasting barely to the end of the seventeenth century, its rays have managed to reach across hundreds of years to warm almost the whole of the twentieth century. We, too, live among an embarrassment of riches.

*Landscape With Open Gate*, c 1630, Dutch. Oil on wood. 33.6 × 47.9 cm. Courtesy of the National Gallery of Art, Washington, DC; Ailsa Mellon Bruce Fund; gift of Arthur K. and Susan H. Wheelock.

continued from p 38

## JOHN MARIN

and he loved to play the *Inventions*, perhaps because they answered his own ambidexterity. He also painted with both hands, one answering the other as he "played around with paint." But just as music measures time for the ears, so, art critic Frederick Wight reminds us, does a Marin painting reveal itself only gradually to the eye, in time.

Near the end of one of his summers in Maine, Marin, who in his later years called himself "the Ancient Marin *er*," wrote, "The wind has changed. Now the west wind blows. Just as I was getting used to the wind that was, I have the wind that is . . . The summer is a thing of the past—all summers I have known are things of the past. Autumn is here—Enjoy it."

Marin died at his home on October 2, 1953, just shy of his eighty-third birthday. The storm had blown itself out. The sea was calm. The goal was not the possession, but the seeking. The paintings, as William Carlos Williams, another Rutherford native, reminds us, remain.

*Grey Sea*, 1938, American. Oil on canvas. 55.9 × 71.1 × 1.9 cm. Courtesy of the National Gallery of Art, Washington, DC; gift of Mr and Mrs John Marin, Jr.

continued from p 40

## PETER PAUL RUBENS

Like his paintings, Rubens was larger than life. He was rich, he was famous. He was a nobleman welcome at all the courts of Europe. He was a painter, and 350 years after his death he is still admired as the greatest of the Northern Baroque painters. He was also a well-known diplomat whose efforts contributed to the future peace of Westphalia. But to his first child, who was as beautiful as her name, none of this was of the essence. To Clara Serena, for her twelve short years, he was clearly and simply "Father."

*Portrait of Clara Serena Rubens,* c 1616, Flemish. Oil on canvas, mounted on wood. 33.0 × 25.3 cm. Collection of the Prince of Liechtenstein.

continued from p 44

# PIETRO LONGHI

both were "painters of morals," but whereas Hogarth's satire could be savage, Longhi was far more gentle. Most times he was content merely to hint at the moral, leaving it to the viewer to tease it out (the viewer meanwhile having his or her own senses delighted by Longhi's colors and shapes).

Longhi did not live to see the final disintegration of Venetian society. He died in 1785, aged eighty-three, during the reign of the next-to-last doge.

*The Faint*, c 1744, Italian. Oil on canvas. 48.9 × 61.0 cm. Courtesy of the National Gallery of Art, Washington, DC; Samuel H. Kress Collection.

continued from p 46

# JEAN-BAPTISTE-SIMÉON CHARDIN

portraiture. At the Salon of 1775, he exhibited two self-portraits and a portrait of his second wife, today considered to be among his finest works for their psychological insight.

Chardin died in Paris in 1779, aged eighty. He left more than a thousand paintings.

*The Attentive Nurse*, probably 1738, French. Oil on canvas. 46.2 × 37.0 cm. Courtesy of the National Galley of Art, Washington, DC; Samuel H. Kress Collection.

continued from p 48

# ALBRECHT DÜRER

separate hairs of a rabbit's coat. Yet, though the strokes in the painting are meticulous, the spirit of the sitter has not been stifled. Calmly, he looks to the future.

In addition to his travels, his studies, his diplomatic work, his painting, and his engraving, Dürer was also a prolific writer. He has left scrupulously kept expense accounts, diaries of travels, and treatises on such topics as measurement and

fortifications for a town. His *Proportions of the Human Body*, published posthumously, has been judged as important to its day as Luther's translation of the Bible. However, with the beginning of the Reformation and the death of Maximilian in 1519, Dürer's fortunes began to decline, though he still continued to work. Ironically, the strange self-portrait that Dürer had done to mark the midpoint of the millennium would soon come also to mark the midpoint of his life. Dürer died suddenly in 1528, in Nuremberg, aged fifty-seven.

*Portrait of a Clergyman,* 1516, German. Oil on parchment attached to fabric. 43 × 33 cm. Courtesy of the National Gallery of Art, Washington, DC; Samuel H. Kress Collection.

continued from p 52

# WASSILY KANDINSKY

Kandinsky, he is certainly the most well known of the group. He was also one of the founders of the Blaue Reiter group, active before World War I, and he taught at the Bauhaus in Germany between the two world wars. Kandinsky settled in France in 1933, where he died, at Neuilly-sur-Seine, in 1944, aged seventy-eight.

*Improvisation 31 (Sea Battle)*, 1913, Russian. Oil on linen. 145.1 × 119.7 cm. Courtesy of the National Gallery of Art, Washington, DC; Ailsa Mellon Bruce Fund; © 2001 Artists Rights Society (ARS), New York, New York/ADAGP, Paris, France.

continued from p 54

# RENÉ MAGRITTE

August 15, 1967, in Brussels. He was sixty-eight.

*La Trahison des Images (Ceci n'est pas une pipe)*, 1928/1929, Belgian. Oil on canvas. 64.6 × 94.1 cm. Courtesy of the Los Angeles County Museum of Art, Los Angeles, California; purchased with funds provided by the Mr and Mrs William Preston Harrison Fund Collection. © 2001 C. Hersovici, Brussels, Belgium/Artists Rights Society (ARS), New York, New York.

continued from p 64

# THEODORE WORES

The following year he began another California series, this time of Bay Area ocean beach flora, from Lake Merced to the Golden Gate. He also visited the Canadian Rockies and the American Southwest; he became interested in North American Indian culture and did yet another series of exotic paintings, joining those of Japan, Hawaii, and Spain. More and more Wores concentrated on California, however; in 1926 he and Carolyn established a studio-home in Saratoga. For the next dozen years, he captured on canvas the wild flowers of the northern California coast—the blue and yellow bush lupine, the golden poppy, and the scarlet Indian paintbrush—and the fragile blossoms of Santa Clara County—plum, almond, peach, cherry, and pear—that reminded him so of his Japanese years. But, sadly, as Wores knew they would, the flowering orchards fell to "development." It was as though humankind was determined to expel itself from the garden all over again. In 1939, with his eyesight failing, Wores closed his Saratoga studio and he and his wife returned to San Francisco. He died the same year, on September 11, aged eighty.

*Honolulu Garden*, 1902, American. Oil on canvas. 40.5 × 30.5 cm. Collection of Ben and Jess Shenson, MD.

continued from p 66

# FRANCISCO JOSÉ DE GOYA Y LUCIENTES

on the subject. From the deeply cleft chin in need of a shave to the heavy-lidded eyes, dull with fatigue, this Sureda is a man of action, a man of deeds, a man who has no time to sit for a portrait. His cheeks, the tip of his nose, and his ear are rosy, as though he has just come in from the cold and is hastily snatching a few moments between appointments to "sit." Untidy, casual, confident, self-assured, hinting of arrogance, touching the world's weariness, dynamic, energetic, defiant, and at the same time pensive—these were all attributes of Goya as well. This is the face of the new Spain. It is the face of Goya's hope.

After his portrait of Don Sureda, Goya painted for another twenty years and his work reached even greater heights. One of the drawings from 1826, when he was eighty, is perhaps the epitaph the biographers are seeking. The drawing shows an old man, bent, crippled, and hobbling on two canes, one in each hand. The title, in Goya's own words, is *Aun Aprendo* ("I am still learning").

*Bartholomé Sureda y Miserol*, 1803/1804, Spanish. Oil on canvas. 119.7 × 79.4 cm. Courtesy of the National Gallery of Art, Washington, DC; collection of Mr and Mrs P. H. B. Frelinghuysen in memory of her father and mother, Mr and Mrs H. O. Havemeyer.

continued from p 68

## HANS HOLBEIN THE YOUNGER

Holbein presented his portrait of Edward VI to Henry on New Year's Day, 1539. In exchange he received a gold cup as a token of the king's affection. Although he remained in royal favor, less than five years after he had completed Edward's portrait, Holbein too was dead. At forty-six, he had succumbed to the plague during an epidemic in London.

*Edward VI as a Child*, probably 1538, German. Oil on panel. 57 × 44 cm. Courtesy of the National Gallery of Art, Washington, DC; Andrew W. Mellon Collection.

continued from p 72

## ROGIER VAN DER WEYDEN

The lady is undoubtedly noble, but that is as far as one can go. As to the type of portrait, it is the hands that identify this as an independent, secular portrait and not a devotional portrait, such as would be part of a religious diptych, for example. If this were in fact a portrait of a donor of an altarpiece, the lady's hands would be held upright in prayer with fingers extended, not entwined, and the hands would not rest, as they do, on the edge of the frame. It has also been suggested that *Portrait of a Lady* is part of a double portrait of husband and wife, but no husband's portrait has ever been found.

Perhaps *Portrait of a Lady* is best considered as an icon placed by Rogier at the crossroads of fifteenth-century art: part of her beckons to the Gothic, which is the realm of the spiritual and the ideal, and part of her points the road to the Renaissance, which is human and flawed. Meanwhile, Rogier, in fashioning this icon, has, like the medieval alchemist before him, combined the most ordinary elements, but, unlike that magician, he has succeeded in transforming them. Nameless though the lady be, ageless is her beauty.

*Portrait of a Lady*, c 1460, early Netherlandish. Oil on panel, painted surface. 37 × 27 cm. Courtesy of the National Gallery of Art, Washington, DC; Andrew W. Mellon Collection.

continued from p 74

## DIEGO RODRÍGUEZ DE SILVA VELÁZQUEZ

between the two royal parties was to take place. In June, exhausted after three months of preparations and festivities, Velázquez returned to Madrid. At the end of July, while working with the king one morning, he became ill with what the royal physicians diagnosed as "tertian fever." Despite their efforts, Velázquez died a week later, on August 6, aged sixty-one. His wife followed in less than a week. Philip's grief was profound. In his own hand, he added to a memo announcing the vacancy for the position of court painter: "Quedo adbatido" ["I am utterly crushed"].

*The Needlewoman*, c 1640/1650, Spanish. Oil on canvas. 74 × 60 cm. Courtesy of the National Gallery of Art, Washington, DC; Andrew W. Mellon Collection.

continued from p 78

## GILBERT CHARLES STUART

paint Washington only three times from life, in 1795 and 1796, Washington's portrait became somewhat of an obsession with him and for the next thirty years he continued to make replicas of these three paintings. The last of the three, "the unfinished," when compared with portraits made by numerous other painters, has been the cause of many disputes over how accurate a likeness it was. Nevertheless, that is the image generations of American schoolchildren carry as the father of their country. Indeed, it is probably the single image that has made the name Gilbert Stuart known to these same generations of American schoolchildren.

*Catherine Bras(s) Yates (Mrs Richard Yates)*, 1793/1794, American. Oil on canvas. 77 × 63 cm. Courtesy of the National Gallery of Art, Washington, DC; Andrew W. Mellon Collection.

continued from p 80

## JOHN SINGER SARGENT

with the red of the drape above him contrasting with the green of the hood across his shoulders, provides an effective counterbalance, both in composition and in color. The books on the table (one of which, according to Welch, was an early edition of Petrarch, from Sargent's own library) symbolize the broad knowledge of the men, not only in science, but also in the humanities. The quill in Osler's hand calls attention to his considerable literary output, and perhaps even to his textbook of medicine.

For his entire life Sargent's joy was in working, and indefatigable he was. Usually recalled chiefly as a portraitist, he had done more than six hundred by the time he died.

But he did some 2,500 other paintings as well, from watercolors to Impressionist works, World War I paintings, and murals for the city of Boston. He died in his sleep on April 15, 1925, at his London studio, aged sixty-nine, apparently of heart failure. The evening before he had been guest of honor at a farewell party prior to his planned departure for the United States in three days' time. Lying open beside him was Voltaire's *Dictionnaire philosophique*.

*The Four Doctors*, 1906, American. Oil on canvas. 327.7 × 276.9 cm. Courtesy of The Alan Mason Chesney Medical Archives of the Johns Hopkins Medical Institutions, Baltimore, Maryland.

---

continued from p 84

# ANTHONY VAN DYCK

monarch, van Dyck was, as the nineteenth-century painter and historian Eugène Fromentin reminds us, "a Prince of Wales dying as soon as the throne was empty, who was not to reign." On the other hand, van Dyck did create a portrait tradition that was to be felt right up to the beginning of the nineteenth century, especially in the work of the English portraitists Reynolds, Gainsborough, and Lawrence.

*Isabella Brant*, 1621, Flemish. Oil on canvas. 153 × 120 cm. Courtesy of the National Gallery of Art, Washington, DC; Andrew W. Mellon Collection.

---

continued from p 86

# MARJORIE ACKER PHILLIPS

in 1951. Whether DiMaggio hit a home run, stayed inside the park, or even struck out is left to memory. To give the score would, after all, be to end the possibilities. Instead, she leaves us at the moment of highest potential, when anything and everything, even dreams, are still possible. In the meantime, it is Marjorie Phillips who has hit a home run—with the bases loaded.

*Night Baseball*, 1951, American. Oil on canvas. 61.5 × 91.4 cm. Courtesy of The Phillips Collection, Washington, DC.

---

continued from p 88

# LUCAS CRANACH THE ELDER

at the threshold of adolescence. At one moment she is ready to join in a game and at the next she is reluctant and shy and wishes to be alone. At one moment she is a private person, at the next fully conscious of her special duties as a princess. Cranach has managed to reconcile these contradictory aspects of her personality. In doing so, he succeeds in giving us a princess who, while the identity of her name may today be in doubt, is nevertheless quite sure in her own mind of who she is. The daughter of her times, she is yet unmistakably herself.

*A Princess of Saxony*, c 1517, German. Oil on panel. 43.4 × 34.3 cm. Courtesy of the National Gallery of Art, Washington, DC; Ralph and Mary Booth Collection.

---

continued from p 92

# MARIE-LOUISE-ÉLISABETH VIGÉE-LEBRUN

resettled permanently in Paris, continuing to paint. During her exile, her husband, who had remained in France during the Revolution, had divorced her to protect his own citizenship. Without his drain on her earnings, she was able to keep her second fortune. Her mother also had died while she was in exile, in 1800. In 1819 she lost her only child, Julie, and in 1820 her only sibling, her brother Etienne. In 1835, at age eighty, she published her memoirs, a recollection of some of the history she had witnessed and an interesting companion to her portraits. She died in Paris at age eighty-seven, following a stroke that had left her helpless for the last year of her life.

Two hundred years later Vigée-Lebrun is still both praised and criticized, again, not only for her painting, but for her personal attitudes as well. Her fellow countrywoman, Simone de Beauvoir, complained in 1949 that women in the arts and letters "very often continue to be torn between their narcissism and an inferiority complex. . . . Mme Vigée-Lebrun never wearied of

putting her smiling maternity on her canvases." (It should perhaps be noted that, in the same context, de Beauvoir had equally harsh words to offer about women physicians: "Most women doctors, for example, have too much or too little of the air of authority. If they act naturally, they fail to take control, for their life as a whole disposes them rather to seduce than to command.") But the art critic John Russell sees things differently, calling Vigée-Lebrun a "paragon of painters." Most fitting, perhaps, is, however, his graceful summation of her work: "Her best portraits," he says, "look like spring flowers with the dew still on them."

*Portrait of Marie-Gabrielle de Gramont, Duchesse de Caderousse*, 1784, French. Oil on oak panel. 105 × 76 cm. Courtesy of Nelson-Atkins Museum of Art, Kansas City, Missouri; purchase: Nelson Trust through exchange of the bequest of Helen F. Spencer and the generosity of Mrs George C. Reuland through the W. J. Brace Charitable Trust, Mrs Herbert O. Peet, Mary Barton Stripp Kemper, and Rufus Crosby Kemper, Jr, in memory of Mary Jane Barton Stripp and Enid Jackson Kemper, and Mrs Rex L. Siveley.

---

continued from p 94

# PIET MONDRIAN

simple, it becomes a labyrinth of relationships. While giving the impression of many squares and right angles, there is actually only one complete square and only two lines that intersect at all. Appearing symmetrical, there is actually no center to the painting. And even what looks at first glance like a black triangle anchored firmly at the bottom turns out to be missing a corner. Lines that appear to be uniform turn out to be irregular, both in length and in thickness. But it is this very irregularity, this slightly tipsy austerity of Mondrian, that prevents the painting from looking like just another box of floor tiles. In his careful placement of the colors and precise measurement of the lines, Mondrian creates a tension. He sets up an interplay of forces that invites the viewer to interact with the painting, to enter into the relationships that are set up. In Mondrian's words, there is not mere balance among the lines and colors of his paintings, for that would make the painting static, but rather there is a dynamic equilibrium.

Mondrian worked in Paris until 1938, when, because of the threatening war, he moved to London. Again, however, the war uprooted him and in 1940 he settled in New York City. A painter's painter, known and respected in Paris and London, but not exactly overwhelmed with publicity in either place, Mondrian was embraced by New York. He replied in kind, entering into yet another phase of his work, his finest and his final, his paintings with syncopated bands of color, the well-known *Broadway Boogie-Woogie* and, left unfinished at his death, the *Victory Boogie-Woogie*. If the absolute or the divine had eluded him throughout his life, Mondrian had at least managed to capture the rhythms of the twentieth century. No longer did he paint the stately equilibrations of the diamonds and squares of the Old World; now he painted the vital, thrusting beat of the New. The black lines were gone. Color was its own boundary. Writing to a friend at the end of his life, Mondrian reached his final statement about line and color: "Only now do I realize that my works in black and white with little planes of color were simply drawings in oil. In drawing, lines are the main means of expression; in painting, planes of color are. For, in a painting, the lines are absorbed by the planes of color; but the edges of these planes are still equivalent to lines."

The boogie-woogie paintings were Mondrian's last. Always one to discourage visitors, at the end of January 1944 he lay ill in his studio for two days before friends looked in on him. Despite immediate hospitalization, he died on February 1, 1944, of pneumonia.

*Tableau No. IV: Lozenge Composition With Red, Gray, Blue, Yellow, and Black*, c 1924/1925, Dutch. Oil on canvas on hardboard. 142.8 × 142.3 cm diagonal. Courtesy of the National Gallery of Art, Washington, DC; gift of Herbert and Nannette Rothschild. © 2001 Artists Rights Society (ARS), New York, New York/Beeldrecht, Amsterdam.

*continued from p 100*

## BARTOLOMÉ ESTEBAN MURILLO

Murillo's religious works have been familiar to generations of parochial schoolchildren through reproductions on holy cards passed out as prizes in grammar school competitions. And if today those images are too sweet for modern taste, *Two Women at a Window* presents another Murillo eminently worthy of fresh consideration, a lesser light than some of his contemporaries, perhaps, but only for the brilliance in which he lived.

*Two Women at a Window*, c 1655/1660, Spanish. Oil on canvas. 125.1 × 104.5 cm. Courtesy of the National Gallery of Art, Washington, DC; Widener Collection.

*continued from p 102*

## GRANT WOOD

automobile and city strangers. There is the intrusion of the mass-produced, industrial product into the handcrafted agrarian society, and there is the collision of urban values with rural values. But even more to the point, the painting seems almost to prophesy collisions then building in Wood's personal life. For example, the year of the painting saw him, who, at age forty-four, had lived with his mother all of his life, marry for the first time. His bride was Sara Sherman Maxon, a striking, white-haired grandmother of forty-nine years. It saw him move from Cedar Rapids, where he had lived since the age of ten, to Iowa City. And it saw the death of his seventy-seven-year-old mother, shortly after he had brought her from Cedar Rapids to live with him and Sara. Nor would the marriage long survive. Three years later the couple separated, and in 1939 they were divorced. But that was not to be the end. Never good at financial accountings, Wood also came into collision with the Internal Revenue Service after he failed to pay income taxes over a three-year period. After that the skies cleared briefly,

but in 1941 Wood began to feel increasingly ill. In December he was admitted to the hospital in Iowa City, where he died of inoperable liver cancer on February 12, 1942, hours short of his fifty-first birthday. Yet Wood's mission had been completed. It had taken him thirty-five years to realize that Iowa's countryside was just as poetic as that of fifteenth-century Bruges or Brussels; he immortalized it in just fifteen.

*Death on the Ridge Road*, 1935, American. Oil on Masonite. 99.0 × 116.8 cm. Courtesy of Williams College Museum of Art, Williamstown, Massachusetts; © estate of Grant Wood/licensed by VAGA, New York, New York.

*continued from p 104*

## MICHELANGELO MERISI DA CARAVAGGIO

expensively dressed youngster, not even old enough to shave, intently studies his cards as he decides on a play. A slightly older youth, his faint mustache proclaiming his worldly status, openly cheats according to the privileged information he is receiving from the older man, one who obviously has successfully lived by his wits. It is a scene that must have been known firsthand to Caravaggio, if those who claim he could not paint from imagination are to be believed. In that respect the scene has little subtlety. On the other hand, if one considers the older man and the youth to be in the relationship of master and apprentice in the art of cheating, then one might also see Caravaggio as the youth and his Milanese master Peterzano as the older man teaching him another art of deception: painting. To the young Caravaggio, who could paint so facilely and so realistically, it must have seemed indeed that he was duping the innocent. Like the cardsharps, Caravaggio was a hustler in the art of illusion.

After Caravaggio's death one of his biographers grudgingly praised him for his color and his realism, but in the next breath took it back: "Many of the best elements of art were not in him . . . neither invention, nor decorum, nor design, nor any knowledge of the science of painting." Closer to the mark, perhaps, was his death announcement: "In painting not equal to a painter, but to nature itself."

*The Cardsharps (I Bari)*, c 1594, Italian. Oil on canvas. 94.2 × 130.9 cm. Courtesy of the Kimbell Art Museum, Fort Worth, Texas.

continued from p 108

# FERDINAND HODLER

to suffer from recurrent pulmonary edema. He died in 1918, aged sixty-five, painting from his sickroom right up until the end. Besides his many paintings on love and death, despair and hope, he left more than one hundred self-portraits, a number approached only by Rembrandt. Conversant with death as he was from his earliest years, his was a life thoroughly examined.

*The Disillusioned One*, 1892, Swiss. Oil on canvas. 56.2 × 45.1 cm. Courtesy of the Los Angeles County Museum of Art, Los Angeles, California.

continued from p 110

# JEAN ÉTIENNE LIOTARD

Liotard died in Geneva at age eighty-six, leaving some four hundred pastels and oils, 250 drawings, and several dozen miniatures.

*Portrait of Maria Frederike van Reede-Athlone at Seven Years of Age*, 1755/1756, Swiss. Pastel on vellum. 53 × 43 cm. Courtesy of the J. Paul Getty Museum, Los Angeles, California.

continued from p 114

# JAMES SIDNEY ENSOR

day put down his brushes. Having found the colors, he no longer has anything he wishes to say.

*Skeletons Warming Themselves*, 1889, Belgian. Oil on canvas. 74.8 × 60.0 cm. Courtesy of the Kimbell Art Museum, Fort Worth, Texas.

continued from p 118

# THOMAS EAKINS

detractors, he also had a few loyal friends. In 1902, as he was nearing sixty, he was elected to the National Academy of Design. He presented the finished version of *The Wrestlers* to the academy as his diploma picture. But controversy had taken its toll. While he continued to produce outstanding portraits of some of Philadelphia's most prominent citizens, among them many in the medical, scientific, and religious communities, by 1911 his health had begun to fail. For more than a year he produced nothing, and then, in 1913 and 1914, he painted two portraits but needed the assistance of his wife. Even so, one remained unfinished. Increasingly blind and infirm, he now began to reap some of the public acclaim denied him earlier, but it came at a time when he no longer cared about public opinion. He died on June 25, 1916, shortly after his election as an honorary member of the Art Club of Philadelphia.

*The Wrestlers*, 1899, American. Oil on canvas. 40.6 × 50.8 cm. Courtesy of the Los Angeles County Museum of Art, Los Angeles, California; Mr and Mrs William Preston Harrison Collection.

continued from p 124

# ALFRED SISLEY

impression is the life-giving factor, and only this impression can free that of the spectator."

For the forty-year-old Sisley in the autumn of 1878, the spot he fell in love with was a road in Veneux-Nadon on the morning of its first snow of the season. Through a gauze of moisture the viewer follows the diagonal line of a lane to a low horizon where the snow-laden sky seamlessly joins the newly covered ground. Barren except for a few brown leaves still stubbornly clinging to its branches, a tree leans into the scene at the right in another diagonal. To its left a rough fence cuts a third diagonal, its purpose being to keep in or keep out, one does not know. A small enclave of houses huddles within its

triangular boundaries. Finally, bent figures brace themselves against the storm. To the passerby the first snow is cold and wet, much too early, and a forerunner of the dark and colder winter to come. But to Sisley, the poet and dreamer, it is a duet of light between earth and sky, echoes of each being found in the other, and a harbinger of hope. For the leaves that lie beneath the snow are but the compost of spring.

When, in the autumn of his life, financial problems and continued rejection of his work covered Sisley like a blanket of cold and wet snow, and when, grown surly and suspicious in his illness, he clung to life as a dried-up leaf clings to a tree, still he managed to discover his joy again whenever he painted. And just as he had once, from his own largess, generously given financial aid to his friends when they were in need, so it is joy he now gives and continues to give to each of his viewers, though he has been dead nearly a century.

*First Snow at Veneux-Nadon (Premiere Neige à Veneux-Nadon)*, 1878, French. Oil on canvas. 50 × 65 cm. In private collection.

continued from p 130

# ALBERT BESNARD

touch that could mark them as a painting by Manet or Cézanne is marked. Nonetheless, many are, by Besnard's own definition, masterpieces, "the fruit of profound and continuous observation," as he noted in a 1913 speech in Chicago. Like Cézanne, he realized that nature reveals herself ultimately only to those who are willing to wait.

*The First Morning (Albert and Charlotte Dubray Besnard With Their Son, Robert)*, 1881, French. Oil on panel. 55.9 × 39.0 cm. Courtesy of the Los Angeles County Museum of Art, Los Angeles, California; museum purchase with Balch Fund.

continued from p 132

## ERNEST LAWSON

however, remained his base until 1936, when, discouraged and ill with rheumatoid arthritis, he moved to Coral Gables, Florida. He was found dead on the beach in Miami on December 18, 1939, aged sixty-six, under circumstances that have never been fully explained.

Like Sisley, Lawson in late life became disillusioned with his profession. Yet, like Sisley, he retained his joy in the beauty of a landscape. His close friend, the American painter Guy Pené du Bois, wrote in the *New York Herald Tribune* two days after Lawson's death, "He was innocent and simple . . . a lover of nature who knew the language of his art so well that he could render all the richness he saw in her and all the joy she made him feel." As another painter had put it years before when trying to describe Lawson's color, he had "a palette of crushed jewels." Or, as Eliot would have said, he painted "sapphires in the mud."

*Melting Snow,* c 1919, American. Oil on canvas. 66.0 × 91.4 cm. Courtesy of the Terra Museum of American Art, Chicago, Illinois; Terra Foundation for the Arts, Daniel J. Terra Collection; photograph courtesy of the Terra Museum of American Art.

continued from p 138

## JAN VAN HUYSUM

body. Some painters emphasized this point by including a caterpillar that symbolized the body before its transformation. And, as the Aphrodite- and Adonis-like figures on the vase suggest, not even love lasts. Though Aphrodite, the goddess of love and beauty, loved the beautiful Adonis, a mortal, she could not prevent a wild boar from killing him. So she loved instead the beautiful red anemones that grew anew each spring wherever a drop of his blood had soaked the earth. But for all that, life begins again, as the speckled bird's eggs nested at the side of the bouquet suggest. The painting is nature herself in all her profusion: blooming, decaying, and giving birth, all at the same time.

Flower paintings remain popular today. Sometimes, however, the demand for one or another of them reminds one of the seventeenth-century tulipomania. Van Gogh's sunflowers, for example, recently fetched $39.9 million on the market. Yet, for all the speculation, perhaps the most memorable aspect of flower painting is its happy marriage of science and art.

*Vase of Flowers,* 1722, Dutch. Oil on panel. 79.5 × 61 cm. Courtesy of the J. Paul Getty Museum, Los Angeles, California.

contnued from p 140

## BETSY GRAVES REYNEAU

shortly after his death. In May 1944 the painting was presented to the Smithsonian Institution in Washington, DC, and is the first portrait of an African American to be part of the permanent collection of the National Portrait Gallery. Reyneau, in the meantime, painted some thirty-five other portraits of distinguished African Americans before she died in October 1964 following a myocardial infarction. She was seventy-six.

*George Washington Carver, Scientist,* 1942, American. Oil on canvas. 112.4 × 88.9 cm. Courtesy of the National Portrait Gallery, Smithsonian Institution, Washington, DC; transfer from the National Museum of American Art; gift of the George Washington Carver Memorial Committee to the Smithsonian Institution.

continued from p 150

## EDWARD WILLIS REDFIELD

bottom. Within the frame the eye is then led willingly from the green boats in the foreground to the blue water in the midground to the purple hills in the distance.

After 1920, though Redfield continued painting and exhibiting, his art changed little. When his wife died in 1947, he burned, in a fit of despair, 1,000 of the 1,200 paintings he then had in his possession. In 1953, at age eighty-three, he

stopped painting. His talent could not be silenced, however. He took to hooking rugs from bits of old clothing, painting chests, and making reproductions of early American furniture. Like Cézanne and Lawson before him, Redfield also fell victim to the pen of a novelist: Cézanne to that of Émile Zola in *L'Oeuvre*, Lawson to that of Somerset Maugham in *Of Human Bondage*, and Redfield to that of Edmund Schiddel in *The Devil in Bucks County*. And like Cézanne, whom Zola portrayed as a failed artist, Redfield was deeply wounded. He was portrayed not only as failed in his art, but as failed in his marriage as well, having, as the novel said, entered into a liaison with another woman. They were pure fictions, both.

Though in decline and largely forgotten during the last thirty years of his long life—he died in 1965 at the age of ninety-six —Redfield is today considered one of the country's most important landscape painters and its leading painter of snow scenes. Unwittingly, Schiddel pays him perhaps the truest tribute: "His life was there," he says of his fictional character, " . . . in the veridian springtimes, the chrome yellow summers, the crimson autumns, and the blood red sunsets and the zinc-white snows of winters." Truly, those are the seasons of a man's life.

*The Breaking of Winter*, not dated, American. Oil on canvas. 142.6 × 127.6 cm. Collection of Jim's Antiques and Fine Art Gallery, Lambertville, New Jersey.

continued from p 152

## WILLIAM MATTHEW PRIOR

produce likenesses "by spirit effect" of persons who had died more than fifty years earlier. Prior himself died on January 21, 1873, aged sixty-six. In a recent assessment of his work, critic Nina Fletcher Little noted that Prior "was an able and varied craftsman," who could perform with great competence when occasion demanded, but that "his flat likenesses are perhaps more interesting as examples of a conscious effort to give the public what it wanted at a price it was willing to pay, than for their inherent merit."

Although the demand for portraits in the primitive style declined after the mid-nineteenth century, in the midtwentieth century it took on a whole new life. Much sought after by collectors and the subject of much research by art historians, the flat planes and decorative symmetry of the primitive style continue to influence much of contemporary art. And, not the least, to the viewer the style is pleasing because it is unpretentious, nonthreatening, and a source of immediate and enduring charm. It is tempting to wonder what of today will be collected tomorrow.

*Double Portrait of Mary Cary and Susan Elizabeth Johnson*, c 1848, American. Oil on board, mounted on panel. 41.9 × 59.7 cm. Courtesy of the Terra Museum of American Art, Chicago, Illinois; Terra Foundation for the Arts, Daniel J. Terra Collection; photograph courtesy of the Terra Museum of American Art.

continued from p 156

# EDGAR DEGAS

relationship between them is. That one is a dancer is obvious, but the identity of the other is left in doubt. Is she a shop girl, a mourner, a former dancer—or all three? That the women are together is probable since they sit close together on an otherwise empty bench, but are they mother and daughter, sisters, friends, colleagues? And what are their thoughts and their feelings? They are together, but far apart. One is absorbed, totally, in massaging an ankle; the other is staring at an empty place on the floor. They wait, but for what? Degas does not say. Perhaps the waiting is the story.

For all purposes, Degas' professional life ceased in 1905. He was seventy-one. He stopped working altogether in 1912 when the house he had lived in for twenty-five years was condemned to the demolition crew. Almost totally blind, he could be seen groping his way around the city of Paris, being led across the street by a gendarme. A clerk, thinking him a beggar, once offered him a package of cigarettes. Time and time again, he returned to the scene of his former house to stare, sightless, at the empty space. He died finally in 1917, an old man, nearly forgotten, as anonymous, but at the same time as immortal, as the nameless laundresses, café singers, prostitutes, and Opéra rats of his masterpieces.

*Waiting: Dancer and Woman With Umbrella on a Bench (L'Attente)*, c 1882, French. Pastel on paper. 48.2 × 61 cm. Courtesy of the J. Paul Getty Museum and the Norton Simon Foundation, Los Angeles, California.

continued from p 160

# JULIUS L. STEWART

judged to be outdated, like "what we used to send to Europe in years gone by." Today, however, it might be considered to be more like the work of another expatriate, the novelist Henry James. Richly detailed, superbly crafted, exquisitely nuanced, it is an intimate glimpse into a way of life experienced by few.

*The Baptism*, 1892, American. Oil on canvas. 201.3 × 397.5 cm. Courtesy of the Los Angeles County Museum of Art, Los Angeles, California; purchased with funds provided by the Museum Acquisition Fund, Mr and Mrs William Preston Harrison Collection, Mr and Mrs J. Douglas Pardee, Jo Ann and Julian Ganz, Jr, Mr and Mrs Charles C. Shoemaker, Mr and Mrs William D. Witherspoon, Mr and Mrs Thomas H. Crawford, and other donors.

continued from p 162

# HORACE PIPPIN

give form to the blankets, they cause the mattress to sag into the bunk below, they cast shadows on the wall. And within the drab exterior, there burns a brilliant red flame.

Pippin's message is that, even in close-living groups, perhaps more so even, war destroys communication, sacrifices community. Individualities are suppressed, identities are based on function, and each member is expendable as needed. This is not the horror of the battlefield, but what is perhaps an even greater terror: war's tedium, its utter banality, its systematic regimentation, its ultimate dehumanization. Stacked away on their shelves, its soldiers hang on to their sanity by isolating themselves in the trivia of routine: sleeping, reading, washing, mending. No song here, no stories, none of the happy camaraderie of fable. Pippin's painting is a memorial of the men who must go to war and whose lives, like candles, burn brightly for a brief space and then are as easily extinguished. It is interesting in this context to realize that Pippin used the identical burning candle in paintings about two other figures who also died in the cause of freedom, those of John Brown and Abraham Lincoln. And in a Crucifixion he did in 1943, drops of blood, in the same distinctive red shapes, fall through the night sky like candle flames.

Pippin, with his crippled arm, could not make the quick sketch when something appealed to him. He was forced to work slowly and to be patient. He worked much as Milton, in his blindness, must have composed his poetry, or Beethoven, in his deafness, must have heard his music. Working from memory, first he painted the picture over and over in his mind, adding lines here, subtracting a line there, changing another, imagining each color and each detail until he finally had it right. Only then did he put brush to canvas, his left hand inching his right along, stroke by stroke, until he had covered the canvas with what was in his mind's eye. To paint at all was Pippin's victory; but to paint as Pippin did is nothing else but a human triumph.

*Barracks*, 1945, American. Oil on canvas. 64.1 × 76.2 cm. Courtesy of The Phillips Collection, Washington, DC.

continued from p 166

## GEORGE CALEB BINGHAM

war had been fought, an army had surrendered, and a president had been assassinated. The population had more than doubled from its twenty-three million of 1850, and a newly completed trans-continental railroad was carrying many Americans west. Businessmen in New York could telegraph businessmen in San Francisco, the telephone had just been patented, and the incandescent light bulb was imminent. Somewhere during that time the fiddle stopped, the tambourine was silenced, and the dancing ended. The raftsmen were forgotten by a people caught up in commerce, just as "the brown god was almost forgotten/By the dwellers in cities." But because of painters like Bingham and writers like Mark Twain, their vanished way of life can be recreated. Meanwhile, Eliot's river flows on, implacable as time.

*The Jolly Flatboatmen*, 1877/1878, American. Oil on canvas. 66.0 × 92.1 cm. Courtesy of the Terra Museum of American Art, Chicago, Illinois; Terra Foundation for the Arts, Daniel J. Terra Collection; photograph courtesy of the Terra Museum of American Art.

continued from p 170

## JEAN BAPTISTE GREUZE

the intricate machinations of the Salon, and his own personal difficulties. But even cold meteors, after they have fallen to earth, have tales to tell. From a perspective of two hundred years, interest in Greuze is being rekindled.

*The Laundress (La Blanchisseuse)*, 1761, French. Oil on canvas. 40.6 × 31.7 cm. Courtesy of the J. Paul Getty Museum, Los Angeles, California.

continued from p 172

## JEAN FRANÇOIS MILLET

for what she was: harsh, brutal, and unforgiving. Coming from her, as a womb, man will return to her, as a tomb; in between he will live in an uneasy symbiosis and unremitting toil. But even in her rocky ground are springs of water, which, channeled by man's labor, make green and fertile fields.

Millet's successes continued throughout the 1860s. Not only did he win a Medal First Class at the Salon, in 1868 he was awarded the French Legion of Honor. But, in 1874, just as a new style called Impressionism was bearing it first buds, Millet's health began to fail. He died early the following year, aged sixty-one. Among today's critics he has been considered to be "one of the finest talents of the 19th century" and an important transition to the work of Pissarro, van Gogh, Seurat, and Rivera. As Thoré predicted, the sturdy country doctor had indeed persuaded art to apply his "solid recipe."

*Man With a Hoe*, 1860-1862, French. Oil on canvas. 80 × 99 cm. Courtesy of the J. Paul Getty Museum, Los Angeles, California.

continued from p 174

## ROBERT SPEAR DUNNING

perhaps, is what Dunning himself brings. It is nothing less than the same quality of attention—of looking and listening—that is demanded of a physician attending a patient. Both art and medicine demand a willingness and a readiness by the painter or by the physician to be still before the subject so that one may allow oneself to be penetrated by the truth of what one sees. Often, by paying attention, by attending, one can, as did Blake, indeed see "a World in a grain of sand," or in a crust of bread, a basket of cherries—or in the story told by the patient.

*Harvest of Cherries*, 1866, American. Oil on canvas. 49.5 × 66.0 cm. Courtesy of the Terra Museum of American Art, Chicago, Illinois; Terra Foundation for the Arts, Daniel J. Terra Collection; photograph courtesy of the Terra Museum of American Art.

continued from p 178

## EDWARD HICKS

grave" and that "*truth* is infinitely—infinitely superior to everything of this world." Hicks, whose constant message in his *Peaceable Kingdoms* had been the peaceful coexistence of opposites, had, at last, in the Indian summer of his life, found the opposites reconciled in himself. He had learned, as had the ancient Greeks before him, that life, like art, deals in contrasts, in "pied beauty" as Gerard Manley Hopkins calls it, and that one is not had without the other. It is in their reconciliation that one finds at last not only truth and beauty, but that they, too, as Keats reminds us, are one: "—that is all/Ye know on earth, and all ye need to know."

Edward Hicks died on August 23, 1849, happy and peaceful. From 3,000 to 4,000 people came to mourn "the preacher." Mourning the "worthless insignificant painter" would come only a century later. Today, Hicks lies in Newtown, Bucks County, beneath a sycamore tree, his patient Sarah beside him, children and grandchildren all around him, one of America's most beloved artists.

*The Cornell Farm*, 1848, American. Oil on canvas. 93.3 × 124.4 cm. Courtesy of the National Gallery of Art, Washington, DC; gift of Edgar William and Bernice Chrysler Garbisch.

continued from p 186

## ARSHILE GORKY

1946 his studio in Connecticut burned. Twenty-seven paintings were destroyed. Less than a month later carcinoma of the bowel was discovered and he had a colostomy. Over the next two years, however, he did his most creative and productive work, completing 292 drawings in a single summer. Then, in June 1948, he suffered a serious neck injury in an automobile crash, and less than four weeks later, believing his painting arm to be permanently paralyzed, he hanged himself.

In recreating his history, Gorky was as little concerned with facts as he was concerned with putting recognizable images on the canvas. But he was concerned with the reality of feelings, and it is these that he tried to communicate as truthfully as possible. Only historians may be able to reconstruct the life of Gorky, but for the viewer he is already there. He remains only to be discovered.

*Organization*, 1933-1936, American. Oil on canvas. 126.4 × 152.4 cm. Courtesy of the National Gallery of Art, Washington, DC; Ailsa Mellon Bruce Fund.

*continued from p 192*

## JOHN SLOAN

footnote to it. Late in his career, as he was nearing his eighties, Sloan was asked to do an etching of *The Wake of the Ferry*. Angered that he should be asked to repeat himself, he drew a corpse on the back of a ferry and surrounded it with a raucous group of drinkers. With his characteristic wit he entitled it *The Wake on the Ferry*.

Nearly one hundred years after "The Eight" revolted against the confections of the Establishment, the debate over what is and is not art and what subjects are or are not appropriate for portrayal by the artist continues. Perhaps Sloan's remark that the American artist is "the unwanted cockroach in the kitchen of a frontier society" was only half-joking after all.

*The Wake of the Ferry II*, 1907, American. Oil on canvas. 66.0 × 81.3 cm. Courtesy of The Phillips Collection, Washington, DC.

*continued from p 194*

## BENJAMIN MESSICK

County Museum of Art's catalogue, adds a tinge of pink to the walls: the future promises, underneath it all, to be rosy. One can always find, says Messick, something to be thankful for.

Messick died on December 31, 1981, in Apple Valley, California. Meanwhile, *Main Street Café Society #5* had been completed more than fifty years before, when he was in his thirties. But so compelling is the painting that the figures still move and talk and noisily eat soup as though they were alive. Indeed, if one were to walk down Main Street, USA, today one might be tempted to stop and talk to one or another of them, just now coming out of the café, if only to inquire how things were going. "Can't complain" would be answer enough.

*Main Street Card Society #5*, 1938, American. Oil on canvas. 76.5 × 61.5 cm. Courtesy of the Los Angeles County Museum of Art, Los Angeles, California; gift of Velma Hay-Messick.

*continued from p 200*

## ANNA MARY ROBERTSON (GRANDMA) MOSES

In her autobiography she said, "I look back on my life like a good day's work, it was over and I feel satisfied with it. I was happy and contented, I knew nothing better and made the best out of what life offered. And life is what we make it, always has been, always will be." (Moses, 1980)

*The Daughter's Homecoming*, 1947, American. Oil on Masonite. 30.5 × 35.6 cm. Courtesy of the Lauren Rogers Museum of Art, Laurel, Mississippi; © 1972 Grandma Moses Properties Co, New York, New York.

*continued from p 202*

## JEHAN GEORGES VIBERT

stove, which is then capped by the cardinal's hat with its tiers of tassels; the necessary detail of the fire glowing in the opening on the stove from which the saucepan has been taken; the repetition of the magnificent scrollwork supporting the hood of the stove in the generously marbled cut of meat on the table and in the basket handle just beneath it. One could, in fact, go on choosing items indefinitely, just as at a sumptuous banquet. On the other hand, the secret of pleasure is not to glut oneself, but to savor small amounts, especially the sauces. When that is done, Vibert's painting becomes exactly that: *The Marvelous Sauce*. Indeed, the cardinal's marvelous sauce falls short of being called *The Miraculous Sauce* in only one respect: it probably has lots of cholesterol and lots of calories. But as a painting Vibert's *The Marvelous Sauce* is fat-free, yet still tasty enough to make us lick our fingers and to whet our appetites for more.

*The Marvelous Sauce*, c 1890, French. Oil on canvas. 63.5 × 81.3 cm. Courtesy of the Albright Knox Art Gallery, Buffalo, New York; bequest of Elisabeth H. Gates.

# BIBLIOGRAPHY

Arnheim R: *The power of the center: a study of composition in the visual arts,* Berkeley, Calif, 1982, University of California Press.

Baigell M: *A concise history of American painting and sculpture,* New York, 1984, Harper & Row.

Baigell M: *Dictionary of American art,* New York, 1982, Harper & Row.

Baudelaire C: *Art in Paris, 1845-1862: salons and other exhibitions reviewed by Charles Baudelaire,* ed 2, Oxford, England, 1981, Phaidon Press (translated by Mayne J).

Berenson B: *The Italian painters of the Renaissance,* Ithaca, NY, 1980, Cornell University Press.

Boyle RJ: *American impressionism,* Boston, 1974, New York Graphic Society.

Brettell RR, McCullagh SF: *Degas in The Art Institute of Chicago,* New York, 1984, Harry N Abrams.

Cachin F, Moffett CS, Bareau JW: *Manet 1832-1833,* exhibition catalogue, New York, 1983, Harry N Abrams.

Canaday J: *The lives of the painters, I: Late Gothic to High Renaissance; II: Baroque painters; III: neoclassic to post-impressionist painters,* New York, 1972, WW Norton.

Carmean EA: *Mondrian, the diamond compositions,* Washington, DC, 1979, National Gallery of Art.

Castiglioni A: *A history of medicine,* New York, 1958, Knopf.

Clark K: *Landscape into art,* New York, 1979, Harper & Row.

Clark K: *The nude: a study in ideal form,* AW Mellon Lectures in the Fine Arts, National Gallery of Art, Washington, DC: 2; Bollingen Series XXXV:2, Garden City, NY, 1956, Doubleday Anchor Books.

Cohen JM, Cohen MJ: *The Penguin dictionary of quotations,* 1976, Penguin Books.

Corn WM: *Grant Wood, the regionalist vision,* New Haven, 1983, Yale University Press.

de Beauvoir S: *The second sex,* New York, 1970, Bantam Books (translated by Parshley HM).

Delacroix E; Wellington H, ed: *The journal of Eugène Delacroix,* Ithaca, NY, 1980, Cornell University Press (translated by Norton L).

Edgerton SY Jr: *The Renaissance rediscovery of linear perspective,* New York, 1976, Harper & Row.

Eggum A: *Edvard Munch: paintings, sketches, and studies,* New York, 1984, Clarkson N Potter (translated by Christophersen R).

Eitner L: *Neoclassicism and romanticism, 1750-1850, I: enlightenment/revolution; II, restoration/twilight of humanism* (sources and documents in the history of art series, Janson HW, ed), Englewood Cliffs, NJ, 1970, Prentice-Hall.

Eliot TS: *Four quartets,* London, 1949, Faber and Faber.

Enggass R, Brown J: *Italy and Spain, 1600-1750* (sources and documents in the history of art series, Janson HW, ed), Englewood Cliffs, NJ, 1970, Prentice-Hall.

Ferguson G: *Signs & symbols in Christian art,* London, 1982, Oxford University Press.

Freedberg SJ: *Painting in Italy: 1500-1600,* ed 2, Penguin Books.

Friedländer MJ, Rosenberg J: *The paintings of Lucas Cranach,* Ithaca, NY, 1978, Cornell University Press (translated by Norden H, Taylor R).

Fromentin E; Gerson H, ed: *The masters of past time: Dutch and Flemish painting from Van Eyck to Rembrandt,* Ithaca, NY, 1981, Cornell University Press.

Fry R: *Cézanne, a study of his development,* London, 1927, L & V Woolfe.

Gablik S: *Magritte,* New York, 1970, Thames and Hudson.

Gardner H; de la Croix H, Tansey RG, eds: *Gardner's art through the ages,* ed 6, New York, 1975, Harcourt Brace Jovanovich.

Garrison FH: *An introduction to the history of medicine,* Philadelphia, 1929, WB Saunders.

Garver TH: *George Tooker,* New York, 1985, CH Potter.

Gedo JE: *Portraits of the artist: psychoanalysis of creativity and its vicissitudes,* New York, 1983, The Guilford Press.

Gerdts WH: *American impressionism,* Seattle, 1980, The Henry Art Gallery; University of Washington.

Gerdts WH: *The art of healing: medicine and science in American art,* Birmingham, Ala, 1981, The Birmingham Museum of Art.

Gilbert CE: *Italian art, 1400-1500* (sources and documents in the history of art series, Janson HW, ed), Englewood Cliffs, NJ, 1970, Prentice-Hall.

Goldwater R, Treves M, eds: *Artists on art: from the XIV to the XX century,* New York, 1972, Pantheon Books.

Gombrich EH: *Art and illusion: a study in the psychology of pictorial representation,* AW Mellon Lectures in the Fine Arts, National Gallery of Art, Washington, DC: 5, Bollingen Series XXXV:5, Princeton, NJ, 1972, Princeton University Press.

Goodrich L: *Thomas Eakins*, 2 vols, Cambridge, Mass, 1982, Harvard University Press.

Grun B: *The timetables of history: a horizontal linkage of people and events.* Based on Werner Stein's Kuturfahrplan, New York, 1975, Simon and Schuster.

Haesaerts P: *James Ensor,* New York, 1959, Harry N Abrams.

Hall J: *Dictionary of subjects & symbols in art,* ed 2, New York, 1979, Harper & Row.

Hambidge J: *The elements of dynamic symmetry,* New York, 1967, Dover.

Hamilton GH: *Painting and sculpture in Europe: 1880-1940,* ed 3, 1984, Penguin Books.

Harris AS, Nochlin L: Women artists: 1550 1950, exhibition catalogue, New York, 1981, Alfred A Knopf.

Hauser A: *The social history of art, I: Prehistoric, Ancient-Oriental, Greece and Rome, Middle Ages; II: Renaissance, Mannerism, Baroque; III: Rococo, Classicism, Romanticism; IV: Naturalism, Impressionism, the Film Age,* New York, 1951, Vintage Books (translated by Godman S).

Henri R: *The art spirit,* Philadelphia, 1960, JB Lippincott.

Hirsh SL: *Ferdinand Hodler,* New York, 1982, Braziller.

Hodin JP: *Edvard Munch,* New York, 1972, Oxford University Press.

Holt EG, ed: *A documentary history of art, I: the Middle Ages and the Renaissance,* 1957; *II: Michelangelo and the mannerists; the baroque and the eighteenth century,* 1958; *III: from the classicists to the impressionists: art and architecture in the 19th century,* Garden City, NY, 1966, Doubleday Anchor Books.

Hoopes DF: *The American impressionists,* New York, 1977, Watson-Guptill.

Hughes R: *The shock of the new,* New York, 1982, Alfred A Knopf.

Hulsker J: *The complete van Gogh: paintings, drawings, sketches,* New York, 1980, Harry N Abrams.

Janson HW, Janson DJ: *History of art, a survey of the major visual arts from the dawn of history to the present day,* ed 2, New York, 1980, Harry N Abrams.

Jung CG et al: *Man and his symbols,* Garden City, NY, 1983, Doubleday.

Kahr MM: *Dutch painting in the seventeenth century,* New York, 1982, Harper & Row.

Kandinsky W: *Concerning the spiritual in art,* New York, 1977, Dover (translated by Sadler MTH).

Kinder H, Hilgemann W: *The Anchor atlas of world history, I: from the Stone Age to the eve of the French Revolution, 1974; II: from the French Revolution to the American bicentennial,* Garden City, NY, 1978, Anchor Press/Doubleday (translated by Menze EA).

*Larousse dictionary of painters,* New York, 1981, Larousse.

Letheve J: *Daily life of French artists in the nineteenth century,* New York, 1972, Praeger (translated by Paddon HE).

Levey M: *A concise history of painting: from Giotto to Cézanne,* New York, 1968, Oxford University Press.

Levey M: *A history of Western art,* New York, 1968, Oxford University Press.

Loran E: *Cézanne's composition: analysis of his form with diagrams and photographs of his motifs,* ed 3, Berkeley, Calif, 1963, University of California Press.

McCoubrey JW: *American art, 1700-1960* (sources and documents in the history of art series, Janson HW, ed), Englewood Cliffs, NJ, 1965, Prentice-Hall.

McNamara W: *The art of being human,* Garden City, NY, 1967, Echo Books.

Maritain J: *Creative intuition in art and poetry,* AW Mellon Lectures in the Fine Arts, National Gallery of Art, Washington, DC:1, Bollingen Series XXXV:1, Princeton, NJ, 1977, Princeton University Press.

Maxon J: *The Art Institute of Chicago,* New York, 1970, Harry N Abrams.

Morgan CH: *George Bellows, painter of America,* New York, 1965, Reynal.

Moses AM: *Grandma Moses: my life's history,* New York, 1952, Harper (edited by Kallir O).

Murray P, Murray L: *A dictionary of art and artists,* ed 4, 1977, Penguin Books.

Nochlin L: *Impressionism and post-impressionism, 1874-1904* (sources and documents in the history of art series, Janson HW, cd), Englewood Cliffs, NJ, 1966, Prentice-Hall.

Nochlin L: *Realism,* 1978, Penguin Books.

Nochlin L: *Realism and tradition in art, 1848-1900* (sources and documents in the history of art series, Janson HW, ed), 1966, Prentice-Hall.

Norwich JJ: *A history of Venice,* New York, 1982, Knopf.

Panofsky E: *Early Netherlandish painting: its origins and character; I, text; II, plates,* Charles Eliot Norton Lectures: 1947-1948, New York, 1971, Harper & Row.

Panofsky E: *The life and art of Albrecht Dürer,* ed 4, Princeton, NJ, 1971, Princeton University Press.

Pater WH: *The Renaissance: studies in art and poetry,* Chicago, 1977, Academy Press.

Pool P: *Impressionism,* New York, 1967, Oxford University Press.

Rand H: *Arshile Gorky: the implications of symbols,* Montclair, NJ, 1978, Allanheld & Schram.

Rand H: *Manet's Contemplation at the Gare Saint-Lazare,* Berkeley, Calif, 1987, University of California Press.

Read H: *A concise history of modern painting,* ed 2, New York, 1974, Oxford University Press.

Rewald J: *The history of impressionism,* ed 4, New York, 1973, The Museum of Modern Art.

Rewald J: *Post-Impressionism: from van Gogh to Gauguin,* ed 3, New York, 1978, The Museum of Modern Art.

Richardson EP: *A short history of painting in America: the story of 450 years,* New York, 1963, Thomas Y Crowell.

Rosenberg J, Slive S, ter Kuile EH: *Dutch art and architecture, 1600-1800,* 1966, Penguin Books.

Rosenblum R, Janson HW: *19th-century art,* New York, 1984, Harry N Abrams.

Ruskin J; Evans J, ed: *The lamp of beauty: writings on art by John Ruskin,* Ithaca, NY, 1980, Cornell University Press.

Schade W: *Cranach, a family of master painters,* New York, 1980, Putnam (translated by Sebba H).

Schama S: *The embarrassment of riches: an interpretation of Dutch culture in the Golden Age,* New York, 1987, Knopf.

Schneider L, ed: *Giotto in perspective,* Englewood Cliffs, NJ, 1974, Prentice-Hall.

Shikes RE, Harper P: *Pissarro: his life and work,* New York, 1980, Horizon Press.

Sloan J: *Gist of art,* New York, 1977, Dover.

Soyer R: *Diary of an artist,* Washington, DC, 1977, New Republic Books.

Trevor-Roper P: *The world through blunted sight,* New York, 1988, Viking.

van Gogh V: *The complete letters of Vincent van Gogh: with reproductions of all the drawings in the correspondence,* 3 vols, ed 2, Boston, 1978, New York Graphic Society.

Varnedoe K: *The lives of the artists,* 1965, Penguin Books (translated and edited by Bull G).

Varnedoe K: *Northern light: realism and symbolism in Scandinavian painting, 1880-1910,* ed 2, Brooklyn, NY, 1982, The Brooklyn Museum.

Venturi L: *History of art criticism,* rev ed, New York, 1964, EP Dutton (translated by Marriott C).

Vigée-Lebrun L: *Memoirs of Madame Vigée Lebrun,* New York, 1989, G Braziller (translated by Strachey L).

Vollard A: *Cézanne,* New York, 1984, Dover (translated by Van Doren HL).

Vollard A: *Degas: an intimate portrait,* New York, 1986, Dover (translated by Weaver RT).

Weil S: *Waiting for God,* New York, 1973, Harper & Row (translated by Craufurd E).

White BE, ed: *Impressionism in perspective,* Englewood Cliffs, NJ, 1978, Prentice-Hall.

Wise S, ed: *European portraits, 1600-1900.* In The Art Institute of Chicago, exhibition catalogue, Chicago, 1978, The Art Institute of Chicago.

Wittkower R, Wittkower M: *Born under Saturn: the character and conduct of artists: a documented history from antiquity to the French Revolution,* New York, 1969, WW Norton.

Wölfflin H: *Principles of art history: the problem of the development of style in later art,* New York, 1950, Dover (translated by Hottinger MD).

# INDEX